BLACKNESS AND THE DREAMING SOUL

COMMENDATIONS

Since your own experience has been a confrontation of the emerging 'third world' - or 'one world' - your book bears living witness to what nevertheless concerns us all. It opens fields of discussion and opportunities for a new vision, and gives voice to situations as yet unformulated. The terms in which you set forth the problems and solutions of a new multinational society emerging now in many parts of the world - indeed it must be the pattern for the one world of the future - goes beyond politics and anger and looks rather to solutions by which 'problems' may be seen as enrichment, and you indicate what you most deeply believe, which is, that solutions can only be spiritual; that neither, politics nor 'culture exchanges' can in themselves be sufficient answer

- Kathleen Raine

As a participatory observer of the dominant Western way of life, Cy Grant brings a fresh perspective and understanding to the tensions inherent in our prevailing ideologies. He recognises the intrinsic limitations of a world view based on duality, alienation, exploitation, greed and materialism, envisaging the common ground of a harmonious philosophy of non-duality and human interconnectedness with nature. His holistic vision is truly multicultural, implying a new era of mutual respect and the end of a Western monopoly on definitions of reality. As such, it is a truly liberating book.

- David Lorimer, Scientific & Medical Network

Blackness and the dreaming soul

Race, Identity and the Materialistic Paradigm

CY GRANT

Shoving Leopard

Published by
Shoving Leopard
8 Edina Street (2f3)
Edinburgh,
EH2 5PN,
Scotland

http://www.shovingleopard.com

ISBN-10 1-905565-08-9 Paperback

ISBN-13 978-1-905565-08-5 Paperback

The only meaningful life is a life that strives for the individual realization -- absolute and unconditional – of its own particular law....to the extent that a man is untrue to the law of his being... he has failed to realize his life's meaning.

Peter Matthiessen, The Snow Leopard

Acknowledgements

I'd like to acknowledge those people who have supported me through the years, but first my gratitude to my publishers for propelling my particular vision of *nigredo* home to the light.

Next, my thanks to my long-suffering family, for putting up with the many twists and turns of a long and precarious but exciting journey; and especially my son-in-law, Marcus Moxon, for his meticulous formatting of the book.

Special thanks to:

John Moat, poet, novelist, artist and founder of the Arvon Foundation for Creative Writing, who once admonished me not to try my hand at writing but to stick to what I knew best – singing, and acting! (Nonetheless, he required little persuasion to compose the foreword to this book). John was responsible for the remarkable success of Concord in Devon, making what up until then had been 1980s inner-city Multicultural Festivals into a country-wide experience;

Andrew Wood, artist and founder of the Prema Centre, for continuing the country-wide explosion the following year – Concord in Gloucestershire;

Ian Dieffenthaller, my personal editor and author of *The Evolution of West Indian Poetry in Britain*, for reading through several drafts of the entire manuscript, making suggestions that transformed it in so many ways and linking chapters so as to reinforce the wholeness at the heart of the project;

Tania Rose, indefatigable supporter of minority arts groups in the early formative years of the seventies, who as Secretary of the Drum Arts Centre, London (1970s) and Concord Multicultural Festivals (1980s) was a great support to my own work;

the late Kathleen Raine, poet and founder of the Temenos Academy, who made an enthusiastic appraisal of an early version of my book;

Dr. Theodore Hall, founder of the Bio Fractal Evolution Centre and whose work and correspondence was a great inspiration to me;

Dr Bruce Lipton, author of *Biology of Belief*, who read and approved my comments on the Genome Project in Chapter 10 – The Unity of Life;

David Lorimer, Editor of the *Scientific & Medical Network Review*, for reading and recommending my book and for publishing articles of mine in the *Review* and on their website;

Jenny Zobel, with whom I co-edited and presented the narrative anthology *The Tree of Liberty in the Caribbean* at the Purcell Room, London, at the Cheltenham Literary Festival and on other programmes for the World Service of the BBC, for the bi-centennial celebrations of the French Revolution;

Cynthia Kee, for inviting me to be a regular contributor to the BBC TV Tonight programme in the late fifties;

Jane Spiro of Oxford Brookes University, who read and was receptive to early drafts of the book, as was

Stewart Brown of Birmingham University;

Terence Braithwaite of Coventry University for reading the book, providing me with hard copies of my manuscript for review and inviting me to lecture;

Kimani Nehusi of the University of East London for his encouragement and support;

New Renaissance Magazine for publishing some of my articles and reviews;

and a long list of dear friends for keeping the faith –

Anne Baring, retired Jungian analyst and author;

Peter Kempadoo for introducing me to the book, *Introduction to African Theology*,

Arthur Torrington, O.B.E., secretary of the Equiano Society,

and many others too numerous to mention.

Contents

Preface

A Sense of Belonging
Multiculturalism & the Western Paradigm

Visionaries of a new holistic and ecological paradigm are themselves deemed to be neurotic. They have moved out of the society that would have protected them, and into the dark forest, into the world of fire, of original experience. Original experience has not been interpreted for you, and so you have got to work out your life for yourself. Either you can take it or you can't. You don't have to go far off the interpreted path to find yourself in very difficult situations. The courage to face the trials and to bring a whole new body of possibilities into the field of interpreted experience for other people to experience – that is the hero's deed.

Joseph Campbell: *The Power of Myth*

I should say first of all that I am not a visionary; many writers have influenced my thinking. Among these are two undoubted visionaries: the ancient Chinese Master, Lao Tzu, author of the *Tao Te Ching* and the French Caribbean writer, Aimé Césaire who wrote *Cahier D'un Retour Au Pays Natal* [Return to My Native Land]. I discovered the *Tao* in 1976, and the *Cahier* a year later. Both, in completely different ways, were pivotal in helping me confront the crisis of identity which had up until then dogged my life. One forced me to make a statement about who I was, the other lay in the background waiting until I was ready to receive it.

As a West Indian who has lived in Britain for over sixty years, I have had ample time to reflect on my lack of any real sense of identity and belonging; a disillusionment not unconnected to the barrenness of a predominantly secular, materialist landscape – the degraded age in which we find ourselves. Trapped as I am within a white culture, I believe that I write from that liminal space of 'insider, perceived as perpetual outsider', and I invite us all to look at what I believe to be wrong with the prevailing paradigm or dominant world culture: the inherently catastrophic construct of Western materialist dialectics.

It has not been easy to make this statement, even though I have experienced a measure of success within Western culture. Perhaps the difficulty inherent in going against one's family and culture requires the eye of someone on the threshold, able to see beyond the culture trap and seek a wider constituency of truth and meaning. I have been both part of this culture by birth and education, and an outsider because of the colour of my skin. But, above all, I believe that our personal experience of being of sound mind, to use (or extend) our minds to the full, is intrinsically linked to what we consider good for all mankind. Western culture has failed to bring that *whole new body of possibilities* into existence. It has failed to achieve a fair and just experience for human society. It has imposed its values and historiography on the rest of the world; leading to globalisation, racism and the current ecological and spiritual crisis threatening our very survival. The ensuing paralysis renders us unable to deal with cultural issues; having lost the ability to cope that would have been second nature to other, more ancient societies. Our culture is essentially in a state of denial on important subjects. It is alienated from its natural sustaining environment; caught up in the terminal dualism of the prevailing paradigm that maintains that science and spirituality are irreconcilable. Even when we see the need for the integration of science and spirituality, we still seem able to disavow other cultures, failing to acknowledge their contribution to human knowledge.

What is needed is a radical transformation of consciousness – open enquiry about the nature of existence, which in my opinion far exceeds the lifestyle our world has embraced, manifest as it is in the resourcefulness of humanity throughout the ages and across all cultures. I think we need to acknowledge our indebtedness to those cultures which viewed their world as sacred – a sanctity beyond man-made concepts of science, spirituality or religion. The world view of these cultures, typified by Hindu Vendanta, Chinese Taoism and African Modimo, was one of non-duality, founded on the harmonious relationship of indigenous peoples with nature.

To recover the ancient world view, I believe we will have to acknowledge that a truly civilised, enlightened society can only be based on the broad foundation that custom and culture, wisdom, justice and decency are not the sole possession of any one culture, and that another world view, another reality, can be experienced now. This will entail an honest reappraisal of, among other things, our historiography – the subjective versions of history that deny our involvement in the exploitation of and total disregard for other peoples purely for our own self-aggrandisement. Nurtured for centuries by belief in a spurious superiority, Western culture is still psychologically locked in self denial, unable to confront the endemic racism on which it was suckled and conditioned and which has been institutionalised into everyday life. This is understandable, for it is very difficult to go against the generally accepted beliefs of the culture into which one is born or lives. We inherit from our peers their beliefs, their taboos, their attitudes towards other religions, and ethnic groups. As Carolyn Myss states:

Our tribes 'activate' our thinking processes. It is extremely difficult to be at variance with one's tribe. Being part of a culture is extraordinarily empowering. As long as we make choices consonant with the culture of which we are part, we are protected. It is very painful to hold views that others reject outright. An individual who questions the status quo, becomes an outsider and can be shunned or ridiculed by society. He may even be considered insane, a heretic or rebel. In extreme cases, he may be even be imprisoned.

Anatomy of The Spirit, Bantam Press 1997

Nevertheless, we must confront our demons and I have come to believe that even this situation is not irretrievable. Many of the principles espoused by the ancients and by other cultures can be adapted for guidance even in today's technological and secular society. We live in a multicultural world, whose diversity constitutes the very basis of human evolution and existence. Implicit in this is the need to take into account how other peoples in the world interpret their realities. Multiculturalism should be about cultural plurality – learning and benefiting from diversity, eschewing separation and entertaining respect and a deepening awareness of Unity in Diversity – a wholeness within an implicate order of interconnectedness. Viewed from space our planet is a beautiful and majestic symbol of the Oneness of Nature – not one of division into states or nations.

x

Foreword

It was sometime in the early eighties that my trek through the woods wandered into the fast lane: I met Cy Grant and learned for the first time something about his operation called Concord. For Cy, action and conviction were two words whose meaning overlapped. The conviction on which Concord was based had been hammered hot from long front-line experience of how genuine integration within a multi-ethnic society (community, nation or world) can be achieved only through the realisation of "unity in diversity". And of how any such unity is constantly undermined by a common human disposition, a kind of endemic, lost-in-the-blood virus of racism. To discover, and then sustain itself, such unity must mean equal opportunity for essential self-expression – it must be free, open to the imagination and life-affirming.

By 1985 Concord had run 20 multi-cultural festivals in fifteen major cities. The country was still shaken by so-called race riots in Brixton, Birmingham and Toxteth earlier in the decade. Like many others, I was disturbed by what appeared to be the reaction of government and society in general; that the riots amounted merely to an issue of law and order. Wondering how a more constructive nationwide approach could be demonstrated I naturally thought of Cy Grant. On impulse I rang him and suggested extending the range of Concord out from the inner cities to rural communities – to my patch, Devon, for a start.

Cy has never been given to hanging about. A week and he'd come to stay; half an hour's talking and we'd agreed to give it a go, Concord in Devon; six months, with the harnessed, unbridled energy of a young Devonshire woman, Shirley Thomas (who knew the county and had experience of programming) and a four month multi-cultural festival of more than seventy events was under way; a year to the day and Concord in Devon was brought to a close with an inter-faith vigil in Exeter Cathedral in support of the United Nations' Year of Peace.

All of that is its own and largely another story. But there's a reason for mentioning it. Working with Cy on Concord in Devon I began to realise something of the energies, gifts, sensibilities and occasional contradictions of his fiery or sometimes just smouldering character. He was then 65, but he appeared in a kind of ageless prime. When he entered a room with this energy on him (even when there wasn't a young woman in his path) his presence would invade it with a luminosity that disarmed even the men. There was the element of celebrity too, but that was something which, though he might use it to advance a project, he himself wasn't fooled by, and even disdained. And he could ditch that charm in an instant: bureaucratic evasion, political condescension, professional incompetence, let alone the merest and least conscious inference of a racist disposition and the anger in the bank of a lifetime would suddenly be there – a full account.

I learned also of his extraordinary power as a performer – as part of the festival he gave one reading of Césaire's *Return to my Native Land* – I knew at once that, had he followed celebrity's lead, this performance would have had the iconic mileage of say Olivier's *Henry V* or Burton's *Under Milkwood* [he worked with both these actors].

But it was from conversation – evenings at home, or during endless driving through the lanes to meetings – that I was able to piece together the outline of a life so loaded with experience, and with such experience, that it had become a one-off allegory for the journey of consciousness in the 20th century. Childhood as a minister's son in British Guyana; one of the first commissioned black men in the British air force, shot down over Holland, two years a POW in Germany; barrister (black, hence not employed), and so to actor with Olivier's company, film-star, singer, guitarist, black arts convenor, activist, writer….

Yes, but although the book is in touch with all this, the events themselves remain somehow on the surface – it is the story beneath, the underwritten story, that makes the book important.

It becomes clear to the reader that whatever Cy Grant has lived, and however deeply that life has been etched into him, its meaning has been real only in so far as what it has allowed him to make of himself. For instance, even the time when his life was driven by anger finds its place in a wider allegorical dimension. Put another way, the reader shares the sense that this behind-the-scenes exploration has been a not altogether random matter, but imposed unremittingly by "the pilgrim soul in him". Some pilgrim, some story! The story he gives us goes beyond himself – which is why its relevance is beyond him.

In recent years Cy Grant seems to have picked up speed. His interest in the *Tao te Ching*, which had rooted in him years before and become increasingly his way of being, flowered into interest in… well, just about everything, quantum theory, radical anthropology, Pythagorean mathematics and the harmonics of the steel band, Chinese medicine and Tibetan Buddhism, the ethereal ascent of Roger Federer, the lamentable decline of West Indian cricket, and teaching guitar to his grandchildren ('They play much better than I do'). To make space for all this he has become, relatively, a recluse, and to service the energies of a recluse, has trained in and become an IT adept/ aficionado. But the core to all this interest, and maybe in part the panning of all that has been lived before, is this book.

Blackness and the Dreaming Soul is Cy Grant's personal testament; even his analysis of the all destructive dualism that, as he sees it, infects the core tenets of Western civilisation. It is a record of his own experience unfolding. The power of the book, and what makes it relevant to all of us, is the temper of reality reflecting the life of someone whose background and search for his own truth has had him open to some of the sharpest issues currently shaping human consciousness.

John Moat, February 2006

Part 1

The culture trap

Chapter 1 – El Dorado

Tell me what a man dreams and I'll tell you what he is.

Arab proverb

I was born in the little village of Beterverwagting in Demerara in British Guyana, now Guyana, an independent and impoverished Republic on the North East coast of South America and part of the British Commonwealth. Its history is inextricably bound up with that of the West Indies and with the European expansion and domination which started when Christopher Columbus thought he had 'discovered' the Indies.

I grew up in the sleepy village for the first eleven years of my life and then in New Amsterdam, the Capital of Berbice. Dutch place names are everywhere and the flat coastal strip with its canals looks much like a tropical version of Holland without the windmills. Even as a boy I had been aware of class structures and white privilege, but I too had been privileged in a country divided by race and class and the colonial system. I had inherited all the middle class values of British society; my father was a Moravian minister and we lived in a huge manse with servants, next to the impressive wooden edifice of a church with an imposing steeple. The sound of church bells, choir practice and of sermons blend in my memory with the song of Kiskadees (*Qu'est ce qui dit?*) and the tapping of woodpeckers on the tall coconut palm that swayed between the church and the manse, the distant drumming, African and Indian, and the screams of my brothers and sisters; these suddenly ceasing at the approach of my father, a kindly but austere man.

We were brought up in a strictly Victorian manner – respect for our elders, correct behaviour, home work, piano lessons, Sunday School, morning service and outings to Georgetown to the Bourda cricket ground to watch the West Indies against Wally Hammond's England eleven. We were clean and respectful and proud. Like most of our 'class' we had household servants but my mother always insisted that we kept our own rooms tidy and generally helped with the housework. My sisters sewed their own clothes, baked cakes and studied the piano. The household ran smoothly and life was very ordered indeed. Twice a week the house was filled with the delicious smell of baking bread and a healthy atmosphere prevailed. These are among my earliest memories.

Beterverwagting's two main roads ran north/ south, parallel to each other. A canal ran alongside the road to the west separating it from the land on which the church and manse lay and it was crossed by about six or seven bridges. You could walk, drive or cycle along the road, or row along the canal northward towards the railway station connecting all the coastal villages between Georgetown, the Capital and Rosignol. There you could take a ferry across the mile-wide mouth of the Berbice River to New Amsterdam.

As a small boy, together with other boys and girls, I would go swimming in a nearby creek, or visit a sugar plantation in the area called 'La Bonne Intention', dating from the time when Guyana had been French. We would set out on day excursions in small boats along the canal system that led to the sugar refinery, negotiating the big iron punts laden with sugar cane lining the final approaches to the factory, the heat and noise and smell of molasses pervading our senses. We were allowed to sample the molasses and chew the sugar cane by the black foremen in charge, returning home when it was beginning to get dark with tales of the dangers that lurked in the interior – the small bands of escaped slaves, who so many years after emancipation still chose to live apart from the village as the Amerindians did. Whether there were still small bands of 'wild men' we were not to know as I never saw any. But such bands of escaped slaves, men and women and their children, certainly did exist during the days of slavery and after; their memory still lived on in people's minds when I was a boy.

Occasionally, we would catch sight of an Amerindian, or Buck Indian, as they were derisively called. These were the true owners of the country, who had been decimated by contact with the civilisation of the white man. Their 'simple' life styles were scorned, their beliefs considered no more than superstitions. Yet, like all the many and varied native peoples of the South American continent, they knew how to live in harmony with their environment, possessing a vast knowledge of indigenous plant and animal life; information the West is only now beginning to recognise and to respect. But then we did not know a great deal about these peoples, nor for that matter did we know a great deal about ourselves, our origins, and who we were. My childhood had been sheltered, we assimilated the education with which we were provided and our morals and our values were shaped by our upbringing - little did we know about our own parents' histories.

Fifty years after his death, my memories of my father are still strong and the quality of his life continues to challenge my own outlook and, indeed, my life experience. His strong character certainly influenced mine. I may not have realised just how much until recently, while visiting my sister, Valerie, when I started asking questions about him and my mother. It seemed I knew little about their lives before their marriage. I had of course been aware that my father's father had come to the country from the island of Barbados and that my father had been a teacher before deciding to go into the ministry. He had met my mother whilst at the Moravian Theological Seminary at Buxton Grove on the island of Antigua in the West Indies.

As if to remind me that the only significant truth about my father was not to be found in his antecedents but rather in his own life, my sister produced the bible which she had somehow inherited and which had been my father's for most of his life; from the time he began his studies for the ministry until his death some forty years later. On the fly leaf was his signature - it had remained exactly the same throughout his life - and the date, 1901.

To hold this book was like holding a sacred icon. It had been my father's daily companion, the pages discoloured and the edges frayed. It bulged slightly and the covers were in danger of coming apart. It had obviously been rebound to accommodate a vast number of additional pages, swelling its size by at least one fifth, and on which my father had made notes, cross references and marked reflections. My sister explained that my father had studied book binding at some point, hence the neatness and care commensurate with the reverence he had for it. I had always held my father in some sort of awe, but holding this book so many years after his death forcibly brought home to me just what an extraordinary person he had been. Now, so many years on, I believe that this book deserves to be preserved and revered. It would provide valuable evidence for a thesis on religion and colonialism. It had been the corner stone of my father's faith and ministry, his testament to a life of dedication and integrity.

With colonialism had come Christianity. It is ironic that those who brought it to the colonies no longer attend church, whilst forms of Christianity flourish among the black community in England and also in 'darkest' Africa. Christian principles were the basis for all morality for my father; service to the community and value within society the very principles that formed the core of Moravian belief. The Moravians had been ruthlessly persecuted by the Church of Rome, and the leader of the movement[1] for reform of the Roman Church, John Huss, had himself been burned at the stake.

A Short History of the Moravian Church in the Eastern West Indies Province is a book in my sister's possession which had been my mother's. It bears her signature in bold clear characters. In it are listed the subjects that students at the seminary had to study over a five year period, including Latin, History, Logic, Elocution, Rhetoric, Physiology, Greek, English Literature, Ethics, Church History to the Reformation, Systematic Theology, Pastoral Theology, Homiletics, Liturgics, Physics, Composition and Music. No wonder the extreme erudition of the notes attached to my father's most impressive personal bible.

My father's study had been crammed on every wall from ceiling to floor with books on every subject and he hardly ever left it except to visit his parishioners or to take a service. I believe my love of books comes from the hours I spent as a boy browsing in this library whenever my father was out. As well as the classics of English literature and scholarship it contained many books about black heroes and black achievement, material which had not been easy to come by in his lifetime. There was the poetry of Langston Hughes, whom I was to meet later in life in London, and of James Weldon Johnson and the writings of W.E. Du Bois. I also learned that the great Russian writer, Alexander Pushkin, and the Frenchman Alexander Dumas were black, facts which are still not generally known today.

It was my father who introduced me to the exploits of the legendary Toussaint L'Ouverture, the great Haitian leader. One day he called me into his study, showed me a print of Toussaint and asked me to enlarge it. I fancied myself as an artist in those days and it was an honour to be asked by my father to do something for him.

Not only did his scholarship, his imposing presence for a shortish man, and his immaculate dress, hold me in awe, but it had been whispered that my father had been born with a strange light birth mark in the shape of a cross on the dark skin in the centre of his chest which faded as he grew older. I had never been able to verify this. As a very young child I had often watched him shaving, building up a big foam with his shaving brush before scraping at his face with a 'cut-throat' razor. I remember the consternation I caused when I cut myself trying to emulate him after he had left the wash basin in the bedroom to go and have his shower. I was discovered shortly afterwards in tears, one side of my face covered in foam and blood. I bore the mark of that nick on my cheek for most of my life.

When I was older I never dared watch his ablutions nor asked him to show me his bare chest! In fact we never did ask enough questions of our parents about his father and grandfather. What memories they might still have had dating back to the days of slavery! Perhaps we did not want to know - as if shame attached to the slaves for having been made slaves.

My mother was a great beauty and obviously well brought up as would befit the daughter of a privileged upper-middle class family on a small West Indian island. Her father had been a Scotsman, a sergeant in charge of prisons near English Harbour where, a century before, Nelson's fleet had been fitted out. She played the piano and indeed taught it to about grade four of the British School of Music. Most of us children were made to study the piano, but only the eldest, Ruby, attained any great proficiency, up to grade eight I believe. My mother was also a competent painter in oils and water colour and did exquisite embroidery and crochet-work.

Despite the closeness of our family we somehow never got around to ask our mother about her childhood, or about her parents or how it came to be that she had Indian (from India) blood. We also never asked about our ancestry on the European side. We identified so much with the 'coloured' middle class that we had little curiosity about our ancestry on either side of our family tree.

My father was revered by all. A powerful orator, his sermons were masterpieces. He was also deeply concerned for the welfare of his local community: in the drainage and irrigation problems, for instance, of our village, subject to frequent flooding. He helped run a Farmers' Co-operative from an office under the manse, and supported the political campaigns of local men against the stranglehold of the plantocracy, to gain seats in the Legislative Council of the Colony.

He was fanatical about cricket. He had a stack of ball-by-ball score-books from all the major matches he had attended. He formed a cricket club in Beterverwagting with a good pitch and pavilion and many inter-village matches were played there. One of the rules of the club was that cricket must not be played on Sunday. One of my most vivid memories of him was when some people tried to break that rule. A very prestigious match was arranged between some members of a visiting West Indian cricket team and a team from Guyana. When word got to my father that this was taking place, he set off, after his sermon, for the ground armed only with his umbrella. He placed himself between the wickets and stood there all day in the boiling sun. There was no cricket on that Lord's Day, that Sunday in Guyana. It was headline news in the papers the following day.

When I was about eleven years old the family moved to New Amsterdam, in Berbice, where my father was sent as minister for four churches, two on either side of the Berbice River. This move entailed considerable changes in our lives. Before it, my elder brother and sisters had travelled to Georgetown from B.V (as Beterverwagting was known) for their secondary education. New Amsterdam was over sixty miles away and travel by the local railway, always a great adventure, was out of the question. Other arrangements had had to be made. Also my father's work load increased dramatically, and I was later made to accompany him on his frequent visits to his congregations in those remote outposts.

New Amsterdam, although a small town, was very beautiful. Our new home was another huge wooden two-storied house, in Coburg Street. The street was red-brick and shady, and the colour of the flowering trees, bougainvillea, and hibiscus and the wide range of fruit trees imbued a picturesque elegance to our new surroundings - despite the fact that our house was opposite the police station and the fire brigade. I remember making friends with the sergeant in charge of the fire brigade. He was quite a musician, playing the guitar in the typical Guyanese fashion with strong African influences. He also played the saxophone.

I had been getting bored with my piano lessons, the sounds of the guitar and saxophone were seducing me away from the piano. But my father would not hear of me taking lessons on either. I could, however, learn the flute if I wanted, and the sergeant was quite qualified to teach me. This seemed a good idea, as I was a bit young to start on the saxophone. It would also be a good introduction to playing a wind-instrument. But I found playing the flute extremely difficult, and when I realised that my father was expecting me to play in church as soon as I was able to squeak out the simplest tune, I decided to call it a day. I did manage, however, to learn a few chords and some bass riffs on the guitar from the sergeant in between my futile attempts to 'lip' the flute.

One weekend, my younger brother and I and a few friends went swimming in the estuary of the Berbice River. Now this river is at least one mile across, and the currents around the Stelling quite strong at times. The end of the Stelling, where the twice-daily river-boat docked, protruded about a hundred yards from the bank. We rowed out from the side in a small boat towards the mouth of the river and dived off. Soon I found myself on my own and caught up in a strong current. I made for the supporting posts of the Stelling. To my horror they were covered with barnacles, gleaming like broken glass, dark and green, and I knew I would cut myself to bits just trying to hold on against the whirlpool swirling round each post. There was nothing else to do but try to find a way out of the current and head for the boat a hundred yards away. I managed to pull away from the current, but found my strength failing; and panic was making it difficult to breathe. My brother and the others were some way off and I shouted for help. They seemed to think I was clowning!

I was unexpectedly and dramatically fighting for my life. Engulfed in the surge of my effort and my flailing arms, I felt it slipping from me, murky water everywhere, in my mouth, stifling my grunts, in my eyes and nose. The river was claiming me fast, my short life a blur before my eyes, as in a bad dream. Then, the merciful relief one feels on waking - a firm hand was under my chin supporting me as I was about to go down for the third and final time. I knew instinctively that it was my brother's. He had heard my shouts and had kept an eye on me just in case. Were it not for him I would not be telling this story. Unfortunately, over all the long years, I have seen very little of my brother. Our ways were to part shortly after our school days. We were both to become self-imposed exiles living away from the country of our birth, he in Scandinavia and I in England.

We attended Berbice High School in New Amsterdam, passing the Junior Cambridge and Senior Cambridge examinations, the same ones that were set for secondary school children in England. Sitting next to a boy of pure African descent, or of Chinese, Indian or Portuguese descent, the education we received implied that everything black was inferior. The only language we spoke confirmed this. History lessons told us nothing about ourselves or tried to explain the great diversity of our population. Slavery, the slave trade and the true nature of conquest and colonialism were never significantly dealt with. We learned about English kings and queens, the Wars of the Roses and the Napoleonic war. We learnt about English conquests, Nelson and the armada and about the Magna Carta and Queen Victoria. We sang Rule Britannia every year on 24th May (Victoria's birthday celebration day) and England was our 'Mother Country'. We were never told about the civilisations in the New World that were destroyed by the Europeans. Columbus and Raleigh were heroes. We were made to think of some of our forebears as savages.

In Geography we learned about London, Newcastle (that one would not take coal there), of the Pennines (not of the mountain peaks of Guyana and its magnificent Kaieteur Falls) and of Liverpool and Bristol (but not of the vital roles they played in the days of the slave trade). In English, we learned about Shakespeare and of Stratford on Avon, *The Merchant of Venice* (the disgusting Jew), and *The Tempest* (of Prospero and Caliban) of Oxford and Cambridge (to which we all aspired – the literacy level in Guyana was once (alas, not so today) one of the highest in the world!). In Biology we learned nothing of our own flora and fauna - but the different parts of the daffodil replaced those of the hibiscus).

Guyana was idealised in the dream of Sir Walter Raleigh, the English adventurer who had dreamed of discovering the City of Gold, El Dorado. It was not until many years later that I began to reappraise our history and my relationship to it. Raleigh had been released in 1592 from the Tower of London, where he was being held for treason, to go on an expedition to find the mythical city. In his book *The Discovery of the Empire of Guyana* (1596) he described this expedition, claiming that the mythical city, supposed to be Manoa in the Guyanas, had 'more abundance of gold than any part of Peru and as many or even more great cities'. He was to lead two other unsuccessful expeditions between 1595 and 1616 but his dream was not fulfilled and in 1618 he was beheaded.

European expansion had started in 1492, when Christopher Columbus set sail in the Santa Maria, accompanied by the Pinta and the Nina, in search of gold and glory in the name of God and country. He was embarking on an outward journey into darkness that was to set in motion the destruction of cultures, civilisations and races and peoples on an unprecedented scale, setting the pattern for the eventual world domination by the European powers.

Over the ensuing years the conquest of the Aztecs and Incas took place - the greed and brutality of the Spanish conquistadores has been well documented. Many other civilisations perished: the Olmec on the Gulf coast of Mexico and the Maya in Central America. What the Spanish had started was soon eagerly taken up by the Portuguese, the British, French and Dutch. The scramble for new territories to conquer was to last for centuries.

Guyana had not appealed to the Spanish. It was not as immediately attractive to them as their earlier conquests. Columbus had sailed along the low unattractive coastline on his third journey to the 'New' World in 1499, but did not make a landing. And although the Spanish landed a year later and occupied the region now known as Venezuela, it was the Dutch who first settled and colonised the eastern region. Even though it is situated on the South American mainland, Guyana is considered part of the West Indies. The history of these islands is similar – the result of Columbus' voyages of 'discovery' and the ensuing European scramble for possessions which rapidly changed hands. Politically, culturally and economically their destinies are irrevocably intertwined. Their histories are chequered by conquests.

The Dutch settled the eastern territory known as Guyana for a period of over one hundred and fifty years. Their first settlement, in 1616, was on an island some forty miles up the Essequibo river which they called Kykoveral (Look over all) near the Cuyuni and Mazaruni rivers. Later the settlement spread north towards the flat coastal strip.

Guyana has many river systems and it derived its name from this fact – Guyana means 'land of many waters'. With their intimate knowledge of low-lying lands at home in the Netherlands, the Dutch were responsible for the irrigation and protection from an encroaching sea of the low lying coastal strip. The clearing of and protection of agricultural land was hard work and the introduction of slaves from Africa began with a Charter given to the Dutch West India Company in 1621. The indigenous inhabitants, the Carib, Arawak and Warrau, usually referred to as Amerindians, were not considered suitable as they died like flies on contact with the settlers. It is no wonder that they were inclined to disappear into the forested interior.

All the European powers indulged in the despicable slave trade. The most barbaric atrocities were perpetrated and not surprisingly the slaves constantly revolted. The most famous slave rebellion in history took place in Haiti, then St Domingue, in the late eighteenth century. It led to the establishment of the first black republic in the New World. My father had introduced me to the leader of that rebellion, Toussaint L'Ouverture, when he had asked me to enlarge his portrait.

My father's interest in black history and culture was to influence me greatly. In a period rich in remarkable men, Toussaint was one of the most remarkable. C.L.R. James, the great West Indian historian and man of letters, had this to say about him: 'With the one exception of Bonaparte himself no single figure appeared on the historical stage more greatly gifted than this black man, a slave till he was forty-five.' But what is perhaps more significant is that there had been a slave rebellion in our own colony, Guyana, in Berbice, which preceded the famous one in Haiti by nearly 30 years, in 1763. It was led by Cuffy and the slaves gained and kept complete control of the colony for nearly a year before it was finally suppressed.

Slavery was to continue for almost two centuries. The trade itself was abolished in 1807 and the institution of slavery in 1833, not as is often suggested, for humanitarian reasons. Economic considerations were manifesting themselves more and more. But in order to fill the gap in labour which resulted after emancipation, a system of indentured labour was introduced initially from China, and from the Portuguese island of Madeira and later from India. So the population of Guyana comprises peoples from England, Holland[2], Portugal, Africa, India, China, a strange and exotic admixture of all these peoples and the indigenous Amerindian. It calls itself the 'Land of Six Peoples', which is not quite accurate. It is a land of great racial and cultural diversity.

Slavery had shaped every aspect of life, the social structure and the very psyche of West Indians. The mixing of tribes during slavery had disrupted families, social values and the communalism of traditional African cultures. The slaves were mere chattels, brutalised and forced to work in the most appalling conditions, punished with the greatest bestiality, the women raped, the men disempowered. The effects of slavery on the West Indian black population was quite simply traumatic – the men betraying an ambivalence amongst themselves and towards white people who had suppressed and mentally castrated them – distrusting the white man and yet not showing it, distrusting those they did not know including other West Indians.

They were defined by patterns alien to their very being, dividing them further, making them contemptuous of others and of themselves, jealous of those who oppressed them. As Frantz Fanon put it *'Every colonised people – in other words, every people in whose soul an inferiority complex has been created by the death and burial of its local cultural originality – finds itself face to face with the language of the civilising nation; that is, with the culture of the mother culture. The colonised is elevated above his jungle status in proportion to his adoption of the mother country's cultural standards. He becomes whiter as he renounces his blackness, his jungle'.*

I myself am only four generations removed from slavery and a mixture of three racial groups, African, Asian and British. We were colonised in body as well as in mind and a strange darkness pervaded our souls. We divided ourselves into classes, as the British did, but based on shades of colour – the mixed races, the coloured, below the white English and Portuguese, but above the blacks and the Indians who were 'coolies' (we actually used the terms our masters used!). The policy of 'divide and rule' was one of the most effective ploys developed by colonial powers.

Deliberate attempts had been made to stamp out the African heritage. Africa was the continent of darkness and of 'brute beasts'; a country without a history of its own. Africa had contributed nothing to human knowledge, there were no civilisations there – Egypt, like Greece, was part of Europe! The African gods had been worshipped only in secret and in 'primitive' incomprehension. Slavery obliterated the past. The early slaves had been split up into different language groups so they could not communicate. They eventually lost their language and their religious rituals were prohibited; the drum, central in so many of the world's cultures, was only permitted to be played on certain days. Boxing Day, with its masquerades, drumming and feasting had more significance to the African slaves than Christmas Day.

But Africa was not suppressed. It went underground and lived in the heart beat of the black population. To their credit, black West Indians, like their African forebears, have retained a vestige of their lost values. But the loss of communality has resulted in an inability to organise effectively as a community. Individualism - going it alone - became a trait of the West Indian personality. Only in moments of extreme crisis did the need arise for coming together for the common good. But even here individual ambitions frustrated the attainment of desired goals. Economically disenfranchised, the black population was to gain political power much later, creating even more racial tension.

The Indians (from India) had come as indentured labourers. They too had their festivals, pujahs, or tajahs as we called them, with the elaborate, glittering towers that were carried through the streets to the sound of drumming, only to be thrown into the river at the end of the festivities. They were industrious, working in the cane fields as the blacks before them, but setting up shops and other enterprises. They still had their languages and their religious beliefs. Mosques mushroomed on the horizon, alongside Hindu temples and Christian churches where the worshippers were mostly black.

Black and Asian people were not homogenous and so inadvertently served the interests of the white ruling class. The colonial legacy had encouraged division, and created confusion politically as well as economically. The hierarchical structure, even after the Europeans had finally been ousted, left its own value system as the cultural norm. Despite their many cultures, Guyanese were educated to value only the culture of England, and so lost their true identity, as much as Sir Walter Raleigh, the would-be discoverer of Guyana, had lost his head.

In such a climate I grew up, able to appreciate Bach and Beethoven and to recite Keats and Shelley. At the tender age of ten or eleven I was made to recite *Ode to A Grecian Urn* by Keats at Speech Day in front of the whole school; children, parents and teachers. I remember how apprehensive I'd been. I hardly understood the words:

Thou still unravished bride of quietness
Thou foster-child of silence and slow time,
Sylvan historian, who can't thus express
A flowery tale more sweetly than our rhyme……
What leaf-fringed legend haunts about thy shape
Of deities or mortals, or of both,
In Tempe or the dales of Arcady?
What men or gods are these?...

I hardly understood the words: *Sylvan historian, Tempe, Arcady…* obviously referring to an urn made in Greece. Little did I know at that age that the Greece Keats celebrated was linked in so many ways to ancient Egypt. That the Greeks, Diadoros, Danaos and Herodotus, the father of history himself, had recorded these links. But it was the last two lines of the final stanza that have stayed with me:
Beauty is truth, truth beauty, that is all –
Ye know on earth and all you need to know.

Little did I then realise how those words would form the very basis for my search for meaning and become the root spur to me writing this book. Who accurately records our histories? For there are obviously many histories. What is truth and how do we perceive it? What is termed 'the truth' may be shaped by language, culture and national bias. I was to discover that perception is not only a faculty of the objective mind, but of a deeper participatory involvement in everything that exists. I went for long walks in the Botanical Gardens and mused... beauty and truth. I even had a poem, dedicated to 'Poesy', published in the Sunday Chronicle. My father read it aloud to the entire family, my mother, my two brothers and four sisters, before Sunday lunch after he had said grace. My embarrassment was palpable.

I was to discover Aimé Césaire and blackness much later. My true education only began when I came to England and found out that I was black and that England was not my mother country, when I experienced such initial shock and later the deep revelatory and healing potential of that discovery.

Today Guyana is still bedevilled by its past. Privilege and racial conflict have festered beneath the surface of political life. It is little wonder that as a young man I dreamed of going overseas to widen my horizons. I did not have any strong feeling of *querencia*, of belonging. The coastal strip is flat and uninspiring and I never experienced the numinous quality of the interior. My only visit into the heart of the country of my birth was a day trip to the Kaieteur Falls, years after I had finally left. I have always envied Wilson Harris and his ability to create a meaningful mythology with his evocation of Colombian myths and of redemption in the collision of cultures; the brilliant tortured landscapes in the novels of Edgar Mittelholzer, my next door neighbour, who had been barred from visiting our home by my father for his frank anti-puritanical views; A.J. Seymour's long poem 'The Legend of Kaieteur' glorifying a dubious history; and all those who strove so hard to blend a distinct and unique Guyanese consciousness. I could not turn my back on the classical music that had filtered through the house as a child nor the distant drumming, African and Indian, the banned Cumfa dances and the Indian tajah, and the Spanish music over the airwaves, all of which resonated in my soul; as did the sound at night of a lone guitarist accompanying a doleful African melody *"Martha, sweet Martha, Martha, sweet Martha, tell me where you get that money from?"*.

What was distinct about our culture was its diversity but at that period of my life I did not appreciate the symbolic significance of this. The social, political and economic realities overshadowed any awareness of possible cultural synthesis or any real sense of belonging. To my young mind, the unbroken flatness of the physical landscape along with a pervading sense of colonial stagnation seemed to impose limits on my future innermost horizons.

Chapter 2 – Mother Country

As a young man growing up in British Guyana I had dreamed of escaping the narrow confines that life in the colony seemed to prescribe for me. After High School I had worked as a clerk in the office of a stipendiary magistrate and was beginning to acquire a taste for the law. I travelled extensively around the county with the magistrate and learned about court procedure but any prospect of going to England to study law was out of the question because we would not have been able to afford it.

In the last year of his life, my father had been extremely ill and bed ridden. It was tragic seeing such a dynamic person confined thus. Whenever I visited him he seemed to be aware that I was not happy about my prospects. Without expressing it in so many words I believed he understood that I too thought I had something to contribute, though what that could be neither of us would have dared speculate. He hinted at the possibility of my following in his footsteps – it might not be too difficult for me to gain a scholarship to a Theological College in Amsterdam, in Holland. This was a tempting idea as it offered me an escape route and the chance to get the equivalent of a university education; anything would have been attractive to me. But deep in my heart I knew that I was not cut out for the ministry.

I shall never forget the unreal atmosphere that descended on our home when my father finally passed away. There was a great sense of relief that his suffering had at last ceased. My mother was calm as she accepted the condolences of friends who moved about the house like ghosts the following night in a muted vigil. Lying on his bed, my father looked youthful and at peace. The following day, Horace, my elder brother, and I accompanied the body on the long journey, by ferry and by road, to Beterverwagting where he was to be buried in the forecourt of his old church. Along the route, as we passed through the villages where he had had two of his four churches, the hearse was often held up by hundreds of parishioners who had heard the news of his death, uninhibitedly wailing and wanting to have a last look at their pastor. It was a very hot and humid day and we still had a long way to go. It was important that we were not unnecessarily delayed. Horace, as he was the elder, remonstrated with those mourners wanting to take the lid off the coffin.

I knew at the time of the funeral that a phase in my life had come to an end. And then, shortly afterwards, two years after the outbreak of war in Europe, the opportunity to leave presented itself. The Royal Air Force had changed its mind about the recruitment of 'men of colour" into its privileged ranks and was now even prepared to recruit them as aircrew! A year previously, a friend of mine, Sydney Kennard, the son of an English doctor and a black wife, had applied to join the Royal Air Force but had been refused, even though he had a pilot's licence (obtained in America) and had paid his own fare to England for the purpose of joining up. The Air Force (Constitution) Act of 1917 restricted entry into the Royal Air Force to men of pure European descent. Although sections of the act permitted voluntary enlistment of '*any inhabitant of any British protectorate and any negro or person of colour*' in exceptional circumstances, no such 'aliens' were to be promoted above the rank of Non-Commissioned or Warrant Officer. This, despite the fact that during the First World War, the Jamaican Sgt. Pilot Clarke and the Indian 2nd Lieutenant Indra Lal Roy had distinguished themselves in the Royal Flying Corp.[3]

The RAF changed its policy regarding the admission of non-Europeans as a direct result of the great losses, some 3,000 aircrew, sustained during the Battle of France and the Battle of Britain in 1940. Suddenly the doors were open for young men from the colonies, particularly from the West Indies, to enlist. The glamour of flying with the Royal Air Force as a pilot was irresistible, never mind the supreme irony of the situation – the well documented[4] and historic racist recruitment policies of the British Armed Forces even whilst waging a war against a racist Nazi regime.

Suddenly the cream of West Indian young men was being exhorted to apply to join the distinguished ranks of the Few. I was one of four of the first Guyanese to be selected to serve as aircrew and how proud I was that I had passed A1. My decision to join up had been prompted solely by a desire for adventure and to get away from what I foresaw would be a dull future in a British colony. I would not have been able to afford a university education even if that had been possible during the war.

And so it was that I came to England in 1941 to join the Royal Air Force. I was among the first batch of about 500 West Indians recruited as aircrew as against about 6000 ground personnel. I had hoped to fly as a pilot of a fighter – a Spitfire would do. But things were not to work out exactly as I had expected. Just when I was about to do my first solo flight the new RAF policy to split the old observer trade into navigator and bomb-aimer was adopted. Suddenly for every bomber crew another trade was required. I had excelled at navigation on my initial aircrew training and because of this, I was informed, and the need for specialist navigators (and specialist bomb-aimers), I was required to become a navigator and not a pilot. This happened to many would-be pilots but it was a bitter pill for those of us, like myself, who had volunteered from the colonies and who had been tempted by the sheer glamour of becoming pilots – even though this involved taking a calculated risk with our lives. Despite my strong remonstrations, there was little I thought I could do without creating a great deal of unnecessary fuss. As the Commanding Officer said, 'We're fighting a war, young man, and you volunteered.'

I had accepted the reason given for the change, never suspecting that, in my case, it had been anything but genuine. I still had not been subjected to any form of overt prejudice. A war was on and I was wearing a uniform. People were generally friendly. Outside in the streets I occasionally heard a child say "Look, mummy, a black man!" That always brought me up sharp. Before coming to England I didn't think of myself as black – a quite salutary shock! I was to realize that I had been defined in a certain way 'at home' and another in the 'mother country'.

Coming to terms with either label was to realise that I was an outsider – that white people excluded people of any colour other than their own. Walking into a saloon bar in the country, suddenly there would be a deathly hush. It was as though I had suddenly come from an alien planet. Later, as an officer, there was the mild raising of eyebrows when I first walked into the mess. But this would soon turn to acceptance when I spoke the King's English, albeit with my West Indian accent.

It was not until much later that I learned that a black bomber pilot had experienced great difficulty recruiting white airmen as members of his crew. The reversal of RAF racial policies in the recruitment of non-Europeans obviously owed more to expediency than to any genuine change in the attitudes, which had prevailed for centuries and are still with us today.

And so I had gone on to train as a navigator at No. 2, A.F.U Millom. After clocking up seventy-eight hours and forty minutes flying-time (over thirty five of these by night) and before being posted to No. 31 Operations Training Unit at Hixon, Staffordshire, I was again called in to see a panel of officers and this time told that I was being recommended for a commission. This news was extremely welcome and in some way compensated for my disappointment in not continuing my training to be a pilot. The Commanding Officer, no doubt aware of the RAF's previous policies about recruiting 'men of colour', said he was taking an unprecedented step in making the recommendation but that it was fully deserved. He would take full responsibility for the decision and, should I encounter any difficulties in the future, I should not hesitate to get in touch with him.

At my O.T.U I teamed up with my captain, Flying Officer Alton Langille, a French Canadian who chose me to be his navigator as he was to choose all the other crew members – because we were the best at our respective trades amongst the new batch of air crew. The others were four Englishmen, two officers, two sergeants and one more Canadian officer.

My last flight at this unit, where we trained on Wellingtons, ended in a crash landing on Greenham Common in the early hours of the morning of 5th May 1943 after a training flight across the English Channel to drop leaflets on Nantes. No one was hurt. Our crew then went on to training on Lancasters at a conversion unit before joining 103 Squadron, based at Elsham Wolds in Lincolnshire. This was the time of the massive bomber raids on Germany, particularly on the Ruhr. After just one six and a half hour cross-country flight by night on 19th June, we went on our first bombing raid on Mulheim - 22nd June 1943. During my training I had completed a total of one hundred and sixty three hours flying time, half of which were by night. We were destined to complete only one other flight.

On the night of Friday, 25th June 1943, one of the shortest nights of the summer, 473 bombers from Bomber Command of the RAF (twin and four-engine) attacked, among other places, Bochum and Gelsenkirchen in the Ruhr. The attack was part of the RAF air offensive known as 'The Battle of the Ruhr', that started in March 1943 and lasted till the following July. For the operation over Gelsenkirchen, 24 Lancaster bombers from 103 Squadron were incorporated into the operations. We were based at Elsham Wolds, situated below Hull, on the other side of the Humber in Lincolnshire. The aerodrome had been built on land which had been an old farm, and after which it took its name.

At 22:42 hours, the first plane took off from the airfield. All 24 planes of 103 Squadron took off for rendezvous near Harwich, on the east coast of England. We joined the large stream of bombers, which set out across the North Sea in the direction of the Ruhr. The excitement was intense. I was to learn after the war that four out of the 24 planes from 103 Squadron had to return early to base. The remaining 20 bombers proceeded toward our target – Gelsenkirchen, in the Ruhr.

Our aircraft had been trailing slightly behind the main body of bombers when we arrived over the already blazing target. Even amidst the deafening drone of scores of other aircraft, the muffled explosions below, the glow of the target area, the flak, the sweeping searchlights, and the sudden bumps as the aircraft rode the frenzied skies, I never questioned what I was doing there. I cannot remember feeling particularly frightened. The thought of imminent death did not cross my mind. It was as though we were in another state of consciousness, emotionally turned off but our minds functioning clearly whilst we got on with the things we each had to do. As navigator one is continuously occupied. It may have been completely different for my pilot having to fly the Lanc through all the flak, for the gunners looking out for fighters and for the other members of the crew. For myself, my sense of responsibility for getting us there and back was paramount and that might be why the obvious dangers of the situation did not seem to count.

Arriving over the target we dropped our bombs from a height of between 19 and 20 thousand feet. Shortly after doing so we were hit by flak which penetrated the bomb hold leaving the fuselage on the other side, but without causing any further damage. A minute earlier and we would have had it! We headed for home at an altitude of 21,000 feet and trailing a bit behind the big stream of bombers. Shortly after, over Holland, the tail gunner, Pilot Officer Joe Addison shouted over the intercom that a German fighter was closing in from underneath. The German fired a long volley and a jet of tracer spat out towards us. Addison, from his tail turret, returned fire immediately. During the exchange the fighter climbed a little and veered off to the right. This manoeuvre brought him into the field of fire of the mid-upper gunner, Sergeant Geoffrey Wallis, who immediately opened fire. Everything was happening very fast. All hell had broken loose. Flying Officer Alton Langille, the pilot, had pushed the nose of the heavy plane into a dive, which made the world feel as if it were standing on its head.

In a moment the world was turned upside down. With the sound of the vicious cannon-fire from our attacker and of our two gunners returning his fire, Al took evasive action. Then, surprisingly, as suddenly as it had all begun everything was normal again. The German fighter was nowhere to be seen. Our gunners must have shot it down! 'Great work, guys!' the Canadian accent of the skipper betrayed both the strain we were all under and the relief! He levelled out, the plane behaved normally and no serious damage had been observed. Wallis was missing one of the covers of his ammunition boxes next to him, shot away during the attack. But none of us had been hit.

With our spirits high again we were soon lulled into a sense of security. The pilot checked our position with me. Despite the evasive action, I had a good idea of where we should be. The attack had occurred shortly after we were over Holland on route to our base at Elsham Wolds. We should be somewhere south of Amsterdam, near the small town of Haarlem. In half an hour we would be back.

But once again our peace of mind was to be short lived. This time it was the mid-upper gunner's voice over the intercom that shattered our complacency. "Starboard outer afire, Skipper!" So we'd been hit after all! But the fire was only a small one and we never thought for a moment that we would not make it back to base. We dived steeply in an effort to smother the flames, but when we levelled out the flames had spread to the dingy stored below the starboard wing. We dared not jettison it for fear that the slipstream would take it on to the tail-plane. Then one of the wheels of the undercarriage fell away in a flaming circle!

Now, we were up against it! Without our dingy we could not ditch in the sea in the event of the plane breaking up before we could cross the Channel; and even if she did last that long we'd have to face a crash landing in England, and who knew where we might be forced to set down! The situation was tense and worsening as each moment went by. By the time we reached the coast, we were a flaming comet over the Dutch sky. Both wings were afire now and I gave the shortest course to the English coast. Unfortunately we were flying into a headwind of about 80mph at 20,000 feet.

Undaunted, we had unanimously decided to risk getting across the Channel rather than turn back and bail out over enemy-occupied territory. But it was becoming extremely difficult for Al to control the aircraft and he sensed that we would not make it across. He decided to turn back over land. No sooner had he got her round than he was forced to make another decision: 'Well, guys, this is it, bail out and good luck! Get to it!!' Our nose had gone down again and there was no other option! I moved forward towards the hatch in the bomb-aimer's compartment.

I had never contemplated being in this situation. We had been instructed in the use of parachutes but never had to practise leaving an aeroplane by one. When I went forward I found that the bomb aimer and engineer who should have left in that order, were fighting to free the hatch-door which had stuck cross-wise. I later learned that many crews on Lancasters experienced similar problems with the hatch and this must have cost many lives.

The pilot, seeing me go forward, left his controls and came after me. The four of us were piled one atop the other, but despite our weight the hatch door did not give way. Then suddenly there was an explosion and the right wing of the plane was torn off between numbers 3 and 4 engines. The plane went into a lurching spin and dive, rocking from side to side in an alarming way. We were caught up in the centrifugal force and could not move. The whole plane was now burning furiously. We were going down with the burning wreckage, like rats caught in a blazing cornfield. It seemed an eternity whilst we waited for the end, but unbelievably, I felt no great sense of panic. Suddenly, with a deafening blast, which lit up everything, our craft blew up and disintegrated. I found myself swallowed up by the silent stretches of space.

My chute opened readily and I felt a sudden jerk and the strain of the harness on my shoulders as the wind snatched at the sails, buffeting and tugging at them. I was swaying violently from side to side. Except for the rush of the wind I was now in an unreal world of mists and utter silences. It was quite light up there above the clouds which stretched like a white ethereal sea below. To add to the unreality, it seemed as if I were suspended in the air, for at first I experienced no sensation of falling. The sails of my parachute were spread in a sinister shroud, and I felt as if I were being borne swiftly aloft in the claws of an indistinct gigantic eagle.

I became aware of distant searchlights and a glow of a fire far below me. Our aircraft? It seemed that I was drifting aimlessly, with the only sound, the wind, swelling the silk of the chute above me. Then, the sudden rush of a shadow coming towards me at immense speed. It was the ground reaching up to gather me. Instinctively, I grabbed for the release knob on my harness, turned it and slapped it hard. The next thing I knew was that I was running on firm ground with ghostly billowing folds of silk collapsing all about me. I had made a perfect landing. I wriggled out of the harness.

I had landed in an open field, my heart throbbing loudly. A glance at my watch showed me that it was 2.38 am. This was June 26th, one of the shortest nights of the year. It was quite light and I could see that the countryside was flat, with canals everywhere, reminiscent of the country districts of Guyana. I recalled that Guyana had been a Dutch colony before the British acquired it.

Later that evening I made contact with a farmer whose wife fed me and washed the wound I had sustained on the head. But they were ill at ease and said that the Germans would certainly find out that they had helped me and they had already sent for the local policeman to sort out the matter. Soon the policeman arrived and took me to his home on the pillion of his motorbike. It was still light when the Germans arrived to fetch me. There was a screech of brakes and a big Ford V8 pulled up and two gefreiters entered the house. They were matter of fact and abrupt. They exchanged hardly a word with the policeman. I was frisked over and led out to the car.

Then we were driving along the same country road I had come along behind the policeman, but this time in the opposite direction. We arrived back at the farmhouse from where I had been fetched, and one of the soldiers got out. The farmer and his wife came out as if expecting this and stood before their front door. The soldier unceremoniously pulled out his revolver and started shouting at the two people who had befriended me. I felt terrible. Was he going to shoot them then and there?

The man and his wife started speaking together. They were violently denying something. I did not know a word of Dutch or German but I soon realised they were being questioned about my parachute. The parachute was made of silk and would be very valuable to the Germans I thought. To my relief the soldier put away his gun and soon we were off again. For a brief second my eyes had caught those of the young wife, who had been so concerned for me, and I knew that she would have run the same risk all over again if need be. And thus my captivity began.

I was taken at first to a holding unit in Amsterdam for questioning. There I saw my mid-upper gunner, Geoff Wallis, who rushed to greet me but was roughly restrained. Then, together with hundreds of other prisoners I was sent to the famous Dulag Luft, the interrogation centre near Frankfurt am Mainz. I was led away and locked up in a cell with only one small window with iron bars. I was to stay in solitary confinement for five whole days. Every other day I was taken out briefly to be interrogated. Then one day I was dragged out into the bright sunshine and made to sit on a chair in order to be photographed. On the morning of the sixth day I was taken out of the cell and driven with scores of other prisoners to the main railway station. Two days later (there were frequent long stops) we arrived at our final destination.

Stalag Luft 3, near Sagan on the River Bober in Silesia, was one of the largest German prisoner-of-war camps for aircrew personnel. It was famous for the Wooden Horse Escape, the largest mass escape ever to have taken place. That was before my time, but while I was there, the camp was to gain notoriety for the dastardly shooting of fifty-two Royal Air Force officers after another massive breakout in March 1944.

My arrival at the camp created a stir amongst the Germans: a black officer! The Commanding Officer sent for me. I was ushered into the presence of a very handsome officer in his forties. Not the type of man one would expect to see in charge of a pow camp. He had an intelligent dignified manner and was extremely polite to me. He asked me where I came from and thrust a page of a German newspaper in front of me. There! Fame at last. The picture taken after five days of solitary confinement! There I was, staring scared and suspicious, out of the page over the caption: *Ein Mitglied der Royal Air Force von unbestimmbarer Rasse!* (A member of the Royal Air Force of undetermined race). The name of the paper was the Volkischer Beobachter. I still have the cutting I made from the paper he gave me. There was no point now in not telling him where I came from. His face lit up. Unbelievably he had visited British Guyana. Then I recalled as a young boy that a German Moravian minister had stayed with my family. He had been a most charming man. He told us of the horrors of the trenches in the First World War in which he had served as a soldier. His life had been saved when the bible he always carried in his breast pocket had stopped a piece of shrapnel. I recounted this story to the CO. I do not recall why he had been to Guyana, but whenever we chanced to meet on his rounds around the camp he always saluted.

Some months later all the officers were moved to Belaria, an officers camp, where I was to remain for the next year and a half. The years I spent as a prisoner of war were a period of great reflection for me. Had I not been shot down then, I probably would not be here to tell this story. I was to learn later that the period from 1943 to 1944 marked the most intensive bombing of Germany by the Allies, during which an estimated 19,000 air crew lost their lives; and that there had been only a one in four chance of survival during this period. Bomber crews were either killed or taken prisoner and Bomber Command was to lose 47,268 men killed in action during the war.

It was only then that I began to question how I got to be there. I began to think of my life in Guyana; what made me join up. It certainly had nothing to do with patriotism. And although I had not been subject to racism in any form in the services, I was well aware that racism was part and parcel of colonialism and therefore part of my life experience. I had been born into a system which had prescribed an English education – a Eurocentric version of history; and a language which denied me an authentic identity and made me feel inadequate in so many inexplicable ways. It had cast a shadow over my inner being. Later I would question all the values of this *civilisation* – the notions of justice and fair play on which I had been nurtured. But at that time the centre of the world remained firmly in Europe. It was only later that I learned about other cultures, about the true history of Egypt and Africa as a whole; of the spirituality of the East, of the genius of China; of the similarity of Copernicus' heliocentric system to the Aztec calendar; that Muslim, Chinese and Egyptian astronomers preceded Galileo and Copernicus; that the ancient Dogon of Africa knew about the existence of Sirius B long before the West, and of so much more besides, as we shall see. But even before I was to learn all these things, I had never felt inferior as a human being to any other person. True, I was aware that white people always presumed that they were somehow intrinsically superior but my experience in the colonies and in England never confirmed such a view.

I passed the time by keeping a log, reading, playing the guitar in the band, and playing games – hockey and volleyball. I had played hockey for my county in British Guyana. I also was in great demand to make portraits of girl friends of prisoners – enlargements of photographs. I had always been good at this. My father had recognized this talent when he had me 'blow-up' that picture of Toussaint L'Ouverture for him. I did not realize then that he had been educating me. Little was I to know then what a symbolic figure Toussaint would be for me in later life.

There were no other black officers in the camp. As yet there was no obvious racism directed towards me, and perhaps because I was in a predominantly Canadian ('colonial') mess - as Al, my pilot, was particularly popular and sought after, I basked in that popularity too. There was only one occasion I could remember when an American airman called me a nigger! He was from the Deep South I gathered and he just could not understand that I was an officer in the British Air Force.

I always had it in mind that if I survived the war I would study law. The law seemed the best career for those who had political aspirations. Politics per se did not interest me, but I saw it as a possible weapon against colonialism. As things turned out this was not to be the road for me and as a theory it was not necessarily valid, as Burnham, the late Prime Minister of the newly independent Guyana, was to demonstrate.

During my period of captivity few prisoners escaped. Attempts by small groups were always being made, but most ended in recapture. The most notable breakout took place from the centre compound of my original camp, in 1944. It was a massive break-out of many scores of prisoners. The superb organisation that made such an escape possible probably exemplifies, more than anything else, the patience, determination and undaunted spirit of the majority of prisoners. The tunnel had been perfectly constructed with electric lighting – all this under the very noses of the German guards and their dogs.

We followed the course of the war with mounting excitement throughout the latter part of 1944. We plotted the advances of the British and American forces from the West and that of the Russians from the East but it was chiefly to the East that we looked for our salvation as the Russians were sweeping everything before them in that colossal drive that commenced in January 1945. The first visible signs of the proximity of the war came with the first bedraggled columns of the retreating German army.

On the night of January 27th 1945, we were told that the camp was to be evacuated and we would have to march to a new one somewhere else. How far away and how long the march would be was anyone's guess. It was a hard winter that year. The announcement came as a big blow but notwithstanding the obvious ordeal we were soon to face we drew comfort from the realisation that the Germans were being defeated, that the war was coming to an end and our destinies would be resolved sooner rather than later. The long wait was almost over.

We set out at about 8 am on the morning of Sunday 28th January, having each collected a whole Red Cross food parcel. There started a battle against uncertainty, fear and the elements. We were being moved in the wrong direction. The Russians were only forty-five km (28 miles) away, at Steinau. The weather was below freezing and everything was covered in thick snow. It is quite amazing what human beings can endure. In seven days we had walked some 95 km and later we were taken like cattle by rail to our final destination – Luckenwalde.

Lukenwalde was a huge pow camp, 50km south of Berlin. It contained several compounds, Stalags and Oflags, housing many nationalities, American, Russian, French, Yugoslav, Norwegian, Czech, and British – in all about 25,000 officers and men. We were the only Royal Air Force personnel and our Group Captain the senior British officer. Life here in the closing months of the war was beastly. It was bitterly cold. Despite the bed bugs we clung to our desperate bunks for most of the day. At nights we hardly slept. When we did manage to drop off, fear stalked our dreams. There was little to eat. But worst of all there were no books. I never realised how much I had depended on the library at Belaria.

Then on April 9th, a rumour started spreading in the camp. We were to be moved yet again to a place called Moosburg near Munich! The next day this was officially confirmed! To pass the time I decided to continue with my record. Would I be able to sort out the collection of notes made on scraps of paper and in pencil when it was all over? I felt beleaguered and bombarded by a legion of suppressed desires and unresolved mental conflicts – desire for freedom of action, from crowded confined spaces, to be clean, for decent food, for home-life, and friends and female companionship.

Nearly two years of imprisonment had given me the opportunity to reconsider my life and to re-assess my decision in joining the Royal Air Force. Was I fighting for king and country? Or was my fight to escape the life I inherited by being born on the wrong side of the British colonial system? Was Hitler's thirst for empire any different from that of the Europe of the last three hundred years? Already the super powers were carving up Eastern Europe as they had carved up Africa in the last century.

Rumours had also been reaching us about the gas chamber atrocities perpetrated by the Germans on the Jews of Europe. This barbarism was being carried out by Europeans. In the past, European versions of history had somehow always justified its own barbarities. How would they explain this away? How was this latest barbarism different from that of the Middle Passage and the institution of slavery? What was the difference, if any, between claims of racial superiority as an aesthetic and as justification for exploitation for profit? As yet these questions were still unresolved but they continued to simmer in the back of my consciousness. They were to remain central to my life and to my efforts to reconcile my experience as a black man with an understanding of deeper philosophical realities. I was beginning to be aware of the European spirit of domination of man and of nature.

Three days later we marched from the camp and were packed once again into box cars bound for nowhere. We spent the night crammed together like sardines in a can hardly able to breathe, two rows facing each other with feet interlocked. This seemed a great hardship, until I recalled the purgatory endured by slaves, my forebears, of the Middle Passage, a journey of some six thousand miles. What was one night in the cold compared to weeks drowning in despair and violence, vomit and excreta?

The next day the evacuation was abandoned. The engine never arrived! We marched back to the camp to a thrilling reception by the prisoners who had been left behind. The attitude of the Germans had changed dramatically. They became polite and positively obsequious, some asking for good conduct notes! They were hoping that the British or Americans would get there before the Russians!

That night there was a spectacular air raid on Potsdam. We could see the night sky lit up and hear the bombardment miles away. Then we got the news that the Americans had crossed the Elbe south of Magdeburg and had established a bridgehead about 40 miles away from the camp! Even if an engine had turned up to move us there would have been nowhere to go.

The following day the Russian offensive began in earnest on the East Front, the Oder-Neisse line. By 17th we were looking to the West, to the South and to the East. Four days later we became aware of a strange atmosphere in the camp. At first we could not identify what it was. Then we realised that the sentry boxes were no longer manned. By midday the Germans started gathering just outside the main gates and handed the camp over to the most senior officer they could find, an American, before taking off.

At 10am the same day, four tanks, 29 motorised units with the Russian soldiers crashed through the camp. I was surprised to see so many Mongolian features. So these were fighting soldiers. All the Russians were very flushed and excited with the surprising ease of their onslaught. They were armed to the teeth. We greeted the Russian troops deliriously. At long last we had been liberated! But it was not the end of our ordeal.

We were visited a few days later by one of Koniev's staff, Major General Famin of the Repatriation Board. He informed us that the time and method of our repatriation had not been decided and on being further questioned, said that there was 'no immediate prospect' of an early repatriation, but that it would most likely be to the West, although not ruling out the possibility of going via Odessa. He said that the whole question of repatriation of prisoners was being dealt with through diplomatic channels! He greatly deplored the conditions in which we had to live and said he would be making arrangements to have us moved to better quarters.

On May 4th, we had an official visit from the American forces, the outcome of which was a statement that American, British and Norwegian personnel would be evacuated the following day. A convoy of lorries was on its way. Our excitement was unbounded. But the pattern of events of the past four months was to repeat itself. The following day, May 5th, our hopes were dashed yet again. Only the sick would be moved. The expected lorries were part of an ambulance convoy. And so it was not surprising that hundreds of prisoners began taking things into their own hands and making off. That evening nineteen American lorries, mostly driven by black American soldiers, arrived at the camp. What a joy it was for me personally to see so many brothers! They were greeted even more enthusiastically than had been the mixed Mongolian looking troops who had liberated us two weeks earlier. So much had happened in that time.

The following day, May 6th, we eagerly queued up to register with the Russians and the evacuation began at 4.30pm. After about two thirds of the Americans had been evacuated, the Russians again intervened and suspended operations! There had been some misunderstanding, but no one could offer any explanation of what it had been. This time we were so exasperated and deflated we could have given up there and then! But I for one did not intend to sit around any longer for anyone.

Shortly after this, came the news that we had always prayed for: *der Krieg ist fertig!* The WAR IS OVER! The news spread like wild fire through the camp, which then became torn between an overwhelming sense of relief and one of deep frustration. A subtle form of hysteria prevailed. We were smiling but tense.

Then another rumour started spreading through the camp, that the American lorries were parked some distance away. I decided to check this out. I sneaked out of the camp and ran until I came to where they were in fact waiting - as if just for me. It was as though they were undecided whether they should be returning to base with their trucks empty. But I already knew my course of action. I would have no difficulty passing for a black American and I put it to the drivers that I would like to go along with them when they left. This they were very willing to allow, but they were awaiting orders from their own headquarters. They would not be leaving in any case until the following day, so they suggested that I return early the following morning when every one would be asleep. And that was more or less how it transpired.

Whilst it was still dark I sneaked out of the camp and headed for the lorries. On the way I suddenly felt that I was being followed. I ducked behind some bushes. The footsteps were approaching stealthily. The figure of a man was abreast of me, peering ahead. I recognised a white South African RAF officer from the camp with whom I had never exchanged a single word. He saw me at the same moment. I resented his presence, he certainly could not have had the same idea as me! But I also knew that my chances of getting to the lorries would be better if I took him along.

That day, I was to be more harried than I had thought possible. After what seemed like hours, we reached the Elbe and were stopped by the Russians. There was no interpreter. No-one understood us. We were simply sent packing. We were to spend the best part of twelve hours trying to get a permit to cross over to the American lines. We had tried every known crossing point along the Elbe, but the Russians were most uncooperative and always turned us away. At one point they even tried to decoy and send us to a displaced persons camp. This had been the pattern of the last few months, the plight of the eagles. Our feelings of dejection and frustration were over-powering. We were also, by now, absolutely shattered, physically, mentally and emotionally. It was getting dark and we knew that a curfew would be in force by 6pm. Then suddenly someone remembered the Barby Bridgehead where the two American war correspondents who had visited the camp had crossed.

We turned about and headed for it, our hearts racing and hope born again. It became a race against time. With just a few minutes to go to curfew we caught sight of the pontoon bridge in the distance. As we raced towards it we saw a single Russian sentry at his post guarding it. We drew closer - he shuffled into the centre of the road, peering at us. His expression was not unfriendly but our hearts were really thumping. This was our last chance. Would we be stopped again? Behind the sentry lay the pontoon bridge stretching across the Elbe. We could see movement on the other side as some American soldiers casually looked across the bridge in our direction. We kept heading for the bridge. The sentry moved to one side, came to attention and saluted. This was a dream surely. Any moment now I'd awaken and be back in my louse-ridden sack at Luckenwalde. We drove straight on past him and in a moment were crossing to freedom.

RAF Training diary

1941 St John's Wood – Receiving centre
Syerston Notts – meteorology, navigation, G, astronomy, morse code, simulators
EFTS Anstey, Tiger moths
No.2 AFU Millom, Cumberland 72 hours flying navigational training
Commissioned
No.31 OUT Hixon, Staffs Wellingtons – crewed up
Flight to Nantes – leaflets / crash Greenham Common
Conversion Unit – Lancasters
103 Squadron, Elsham Wolds Wolds 163 flying hours
3 ops. only – June 22 Mulheim, June 14 Wuppertal, June 25 Gelsenkirchen, 1943
[Battle of the Ruhr March 43 – July 44]

> *"The difficulties experienced by our crew with the forward escape hatch were replicated that same night when another 103 Sq crew faced similar problems. Alan Egan's crew were hit by flak near the target. With both port engines on fire the pilot ordered the crew to bale out. The forward hatch proved impossible to open and the Lancaster soon exploded. Alan Egan was rendered unconscious and propelled with considerable force out of the cockpit roof. He came to as he fell through the air and was coherent enough to pull the rip cord on his parachute. He landed safely albeit with head and back injuries. Flight Engineer Sgt J S Johnston RAFVR and Air Bomber F/S W Miller RAFVR also had miraculous escapes when the aircraft blew apart."*

See Editor's Note, 103 Squadron Newsletter, 2005

Special Note

After the war, I was to receive a letter from a Dutchman who was 14 years old on the night that we fell from the skies. He had set himself the formidable task of learning as much as possible about the air battle over Holland that night and the operation that resulted in the crash of a Lancaster from No.103 Squadron based at Elsham Wolds on the night of 25/26 June 1943 in a field not far from his village. He had consulted all the records in Holland and in the Air Ministry, he had written to all my crew members and managed to put together an extraordinary record of the events immediately before and after the crash. I acknowledge that I have drawn on this record for some of the details of the events I recount of that fateful night. I was also to learn that the local people remembered me very well indeed, and about their reaction to my sudden appearance amongst them. The burning wreckage of our plane came down to earth at 03.08 hours on the morning of June 26 on farmland a few miles west of Nieuw-Vennep in the Haarlemmermmeer. One of the engines from our aircraft fell through the roof of a farm house, killing the wife of the farmer. All of the airmen with the exception of Ron Hollywood, the Flight Engineer, managed to open their chutes and survived the crash. Joe Addison, the tail gunner, was badly burned and died later that day in the Wilhelmina Hospital in Amsterdam. He was buried in the Nieuwe Ooster Begraafplaats in Amsterdam. Ron Hollywood was buried on the Algemene Begraafplaats in the Haarlemmermeer. All the other airmen were taken prisoner and spent the rest of the war in German prisoner-of-war camps.

Chapter 3 – The World a Stage

Haply for I am black
And have not those soft parts of conversation
that chamberers have

Othello

It was no dream. The American forces welcomed us with open arms. We had hot showers and were given clean clothes, good food (I was amazed by the bread, uniformly sliced, white and soft as I'd never seen before – so different from the rough German bread I'd acquired a taste for), chocolate, cigarettes and a cinema show. In a couple of days, still unable to believe our good fortune, we were driven along the deserted wide German autobahns across country to British Headquarters in Brussels. There we were deloused, kitted out, and made the most of our new freedom to watch the victory parade and visit the city's bars at night. In a few days we were back in England trying to pick up the pieces.

I was now a Flight Lieutenant. Whilst awaiting my demobilisation I worked as a Liaison Officer for a section set up by the Colonial Office and the Air Ministry. Our job was to deal with the particular problems experienced by the large number of West Indian and other colonial RAF ground staff who had been recruited in the last two years of the war. This fitted in well with my stated intention to study law. I was required not only to sit on the bench at Courts Martial but to undertake the defence of overseas airmen whenever, and this was very frequent, they found themselves in trouble with the military police.

On my demobilisation, I paid a brief visit to see my family in Guyana. The family had moved to Georgetown, the capital and so, although a great fuss was made over me, I missed my old haunts – everything seemed unfamiliar in a city I did not know. I was no closer to having a sense of belonging than I had before leaving to join the RAF four years previously. But whilst there I decided to fulfil an ambition I had as a boy; to visit the magnificent Kaieteur Falls situated in the heart of the country, far from the populated coastal strip. It was an impressive sight – overpowering in its pristine grandeur, brimming with life and strange sounds of birds, rivers, cataracts and forest – the world of nature in the raw, an unfamiliar world I did not know. I realised that I'd been a stranger even in the country of my birth.

At that time in my life I was completely unaware of the ecological issues which underlie our present day dilemmas – our alienation from nature; an insight at the very core of my journey of self-discovery. It is ironic that the country that I seemed to be continually running away from should become the focus of the 1998-2002 Iwokrama Rain Forest Programme, whose mission was *'To promote the conservation and the sustainable use of tropical rain forests in a manner that will lead to lasting ecological, economic and social benefits to the people of Guyana and to the world in general, by undertaking research, training and the development and dissemination of technologies.'*

Shortly after, I set out for England on my second voyage of exploration, in order to obtain the equivalent of the university education that had not been possible at the time of my father's death. I was to study law, admittedly much later in life than is usual. I became a member of the *Middle Temple* in London. The name was impressive and mysterious, reeking of the sanctity of the law and of jurisprudence. I was quite unaware of its historical association with colonialism and slavery. Later, I was also to discover that many well-known British institutions and companies had a similar history, a legacy that still determines and defines our world today.

I studied mostly by correspondence course, as attending the classes (held nearby at the Inner Temple) was unnecessarily time consuming. In 1950, at the age of thirty, I was finally called to the Bar. Not only was I starting out quite late in life, but my marriage of just over a year was proving dodgy to say the least. Nonetheless, I returned to British Guyana ostensibly to make arrangements for finding a home and establishing a practice. In reality I was simply buying time to decide on the right course for me. The shoddy state in which the law was practised in the colony provided only one of the reasons why I decided to return to England. Also, the prospect of an unhappy marriage to a European woman in a socially divided country was not something I was prepared to accept. After a brief stay there, I set out yet again for Britain to get a divorce and hopefully set up in practice as a lawyer. I was fully aware of the implications of this decision. Throughout my incarceration as a prisoner-of-war I had given a lot of thought to what I wanted to do with my life: I saw a career in law at home as a stepping-stone to joining the gathering vanguard against colonialism. Now I was abandoning these plans just like that, my priority at the time to sort out the shambles of my private life. Coincidentally, aboard ship was Wilson Harris, trained as a surveyor in the heartlands of Guyana. His poems and novels drew upon his existence on the margins of society and the spirituality of that vast landscape and its indigenous peoples. We had ample time to compare life stories and, in retrospect, my future seems to have been guided by the principles to which Wilson was already attuned.

The question of finding chambers was out of the question. Even if some friendly barrister had taken me in I would not have had enough to live on to get me through those first vital years. I applied for jobs advertised in the national press – jobs that required legal knowledge. Never one reply. The 'country of birth' specification on every application form saw to that. This was Britain in peacetime and I was no longer useful. I was a second-class citizen even though I had fought in and been a prisoner of war. I had been proud to wear the uniform of an officer in the Royal Air Force. I had grown accustomed to the courtesy and protection it had afforded me.

This disillusionment, I believe, was shared by many West Indian officers but I could not have foreseen the extent of racial discrimination I was still about to encounter. I had been fully aware of institutional racism within the military services before joining up, but naively believed that somehow things had changed, at least towards me. I had never considered the possibility of staying on in the Royal Air Force after the war. But it came as no surprise when I read about the great debate that took place at the Air Ministry: what to do with all the black airmen who had served during the war? They were certainly discouraged from continuing in the service. I have seen the minutes of a meeting held in 1945, which quite frankly contained the most outrageously racist remarks by high-ranking officers.

And so it was that I was forced to embark on another career, in the theatre. In preparation for practising at the Bar I had joined an amateur dramatics' society in order to enhance my diction; this, I believed, would help me as an advocate. I even played the leading role (Thomas Mendip) in Christopher Fry's *The Lady's not for Burning*. As it turned out, making the change from law to the stage had not been difficult. Barristers are after all like actors, and courtroom dramas are played out on a stage.

When the opportunity suddenly presented itself, I joined a third-rate theatre company touring the Moss Empire Circuit playing the lead in a play outlandishly called *13 Death Street, Harlem*. Twice nightly performances and the help of the kindly English actress who played opposite me allowed me to gain further insights into the actor's craft, even in such a dreadful production. This was to lead to a successful audition a year later, with the Laurence Olivier Festival of Britain Company at the St James' Theatre, London and the following year to the Ziegfield Theatre in New York. Even though in a small role *carrying a spear*, I understudied one of the minor parts and was paid more than my fellow spear-carriers - I was considered, so a spokesman for the company told my agent, 'leading man potential'.

Even as a member of such a prestigious theatrical company I was refused 'theatrical digs' at my first attempt when shows were being premiered in Manchester. Years later, as a 'celebrity', I was to find that I was welcome almost anywhere. I remember several times being acutely embarrassed whenever I was introduced by a so-called friend or host, my name being spoken out quite loud so that everyone would know it was quite in order for me to be there. I've even been told that I was 'different', that I was not like the rest of 'them'!

Black people could be entertainers or sportsmen and be knighted. Our prowess in certain fields was all we had going for us. As Aimé Césaire, the great poet and politician said:

'(We) can do the soft-shoe, the Lindy Hop and the tap dance. And for a special treat the muted trumpet of our cries wrapped in wah-wah.' (Cahier d'un Retour au Pays Natal [Return to my Native land - John Berger, Anna Bostock, Penguin Poets])

An incident occurred one night towards the end of the London season, which hinted at the bedrock of racism existing throughout the inner cities and at the very heart of our culture. After a performance at the St. James's Theatre, I went with Eddie Crabbe and Elspeth March, two members of the cast, to have a drink in a nearby pub. On leaving, a few drinks later, we were attacked by two 'Teddy boys', who apparently did not approve of a white woman socialising with two black men. Instead of attacking us, they went for Elspeth, knocking her over in the street. In falling she broke a leg. At the time we did not know this as we had both set off in pursuit of the thugs. When at last we caught up with them, Eddie, who was Mr Muscle himself, gave them a good thumping. Retracing our steps we learnt of Elspeth's condition but by then help was at hand and she was whisked off in a taxi.

This all took place a few weeks before the company was due to go to America. Everyone wanted to go. Poor Elspeth, of course, was out of it. I was surprised that no questions were ever asked either of me or of Eddie as to what happened that night, but shortly afterwards, Larry, as we all called him, sent for me. He thanked me for my 'warm and conscientious' work, but thought it would be better if he did not take me to America with the company because 'I might be exposed to racial prejudice!' I could not believe what I was hearing. I'd always held Olivier in the highest esteem and he was, inadvertently, to play a big role in events that were to shape my future plans. Was he being disingenuous? I told him that I thought that English racism was the more pernicious as no one admitted to it. I did not mention the Teddy boy incident and the loud silence that followed it, but I did say that I would like to experience the American version at first hand. And so it was that I went with the company to America.

After we had been there a few weeks, some of the English actors went to see a court case in which the great American actress, Tallulah Bankhead, was involved – in litigation with, I think, her maid. It was interesting hearing the surprise they expressed in seeing that the presiding judge in the case was black! In New York in 1951-52, the black cultural presence was everywhere – in the world of music, sport, in department stores as well as in the police and on the bench. The black political scientist, Ralph Bunche, was in the State Department.

At that time in America, despite the racial prejudice that existed, black people seemed to have a much better presence in all fields than they did in Britain – including TV presenters, sporting heroes, mayors of major cities, state governors, congressmen and the military. But as we all know today (especially from Michael Moore's books), racism is alive and kicking unless you identify with and are successful in pursuing the American dream – as evinced by the elevation of Secretaries of State Colin Powell and Condoleeza Rice.

Whilst in America, I realised that at the end of the tour I would most likely be out of work for some appreciable time. I had been in work without a break for two years as an actor but this could not be expected to last. It is the same for all in the profession unless you have 'made it'; but for a black actor there were fewer opportunities and greater constraints. Most of the roles on offer were what I would term 'black' roles, that is, roles where race was most likely an issue or reflected the perceived status of, or prejudices towards, black people in society. This presented a black actor with an existential dilemma – the colour of his skin defined him as someone 'other', lacking validity or authority, an extra on the stage as he was in life, his roles exactly mirroring his role within society. He had to reconcile his blackness and his chosen occupation as a means of livelihood – a traumatic relationship, desiring acceptance as an actor as well as an authentic identity as a human being; the very things society was not prepared to grant him.

I decided that I would try, on my return to England, to establish myself as a singer as well as an actor. I had always enjoyed singing and playing the guitar. The American folk singer, Josh White, had made a great impression in England and on me personally. Perhaps this could provide a sort of safety net between parts. It would help me preserve my self-esteem as well as widen my field of work and so tide me over during lean periods. On returning to London I began my career as a singer of folk songs of the world – love songs, songs of protest and songs with a message, all to become very popular in the fifties and sixties. In my very first year I had over 50 broadcasts on the BBC, including repeats on the World Service singing the folk songs of the Caribbean.

The fifties were very good years for me. I had moved effortlessly from qualifying as a barrister to acting (London and New York) and broadcasting. I found lots of work in revues and cabaret. On holiday in Rome in 1955 I found myself singing at Bricktops on the Via Veneto and came back to my own mid-afternoon TV series, *For Members Only,* for Associated Television, with the great Trinidadian guitarist, Fitzroy Coleman, and guests like Josh White, Big Bill Broonsey, Georgia Brown and John Williams. And that was only the start.

Noel Harrison and I became regular singers at the chic Esmeralda's Barn, run by Patsy Debben-Morgan, with murals by Annigoni, the in-painter at the time and the haunt of the young bright things of Chelsea and Pimlico, including people like Tony Armstrong-Jones, an up-and-coming photographer who later married Princess Margaret.

Along with folk songs from around the world which I had added to my repertoire, I sang popular calypsos of the time. It was at Esmeralda's that Cynthia Kee (then Judah) of the team planning the new BBC Tonight programme heard me and invited me to be a regular contributor, singing the news in calypso; alternating first with the McEwan brothers and later with Robin Hall and Jimmy McGregor. Noel Harrison, son of Rex, took over from me for a while whilst I was away on location in the Caribbean on the Italian film *Calypso!* – one could not escape the popularity of the image.

Singing allowed me more control over the roles I would accept. But I was to find out that this had its disadvantages too, for once seen as a singer, especially as a calypso singer, it became increasingly more difficult to be seriously considered as an actor. This tendency for specialisation in the arts as in everything else, is a typically Western phenomenon. For me, it added to the existential dilemma in which I found myself.

A year before *Tonight*, in 1956, I had co-starred in the BBC television drama, *A Man from the Sun*, with Errol John and Nadia Catouse, a play about the difficulties the new immigrants faced in their new country. Later that year I had also co-starred in the film *Sea Wife,* with Richard Burton and Joan Collins. Immediately after the first live *Tonight* I had to dash off to Manchester for the technical rehearsal of the play

Home of the Brave by Arthur Laurents for Granada Television, directed by Silvio Narizzano. The play was to receive rave notices, winning two television awards. But appearing for long periods on *Tonight*, in its first two and a half years, although it made me a household name, certainly did not help my acting career.

Tonight was an innovative and ground-breaking programme, which set the tone for the future of television in the sixties and thereafter. It launched the careers of many broadcasters. It was fun being associated with this much- liked and talked-about programme, which, although dealing with serious subjects, at the same time managed not to be pompous. There was always a feeling of excitement in the studio, and a slight touch of panic and spontaneity, for example, when interviewees were late or did not turn up. Anyone who was anyone came through the studio doors, from politicians to film stars. If something went wrong – as it frequently did – this was all live television; I was expected to sing a song at the drop of a hat, as well as the news in calypso at the start of the programme: nerve-racking but great fun.

Whilst on this programme I sang over 200 folk songs from all over the world to my own guitar accompaniment. Bradbury Wood Music Publishers brought out an album of some of my arrangements about this time, yet I am chiefly remembered for the calypsos. This is fine, as calypso is quintessentially a fusion of the West Indian experience that originated in Trinidad – a culture of resistance – song and drumming. The history of that small island is unique in the British Caribbean – the early Catholic *laissez faire* allowing the preservation of African religious beliefs and identity.

Singing a daily calypso on *Tonight* was a strange position in which to find myself at a time when two great calypsonians from Trinidad were resident in England. *Lord* Kitchener and *Lord* Beginner had arrived on the Empire Windrush in 1948. The latter's *Cricket, Lovely Cricket*, celebrating the historic victory on the West Indies cricket team at Lords in 1950 was one of the most popular songs in the country. Kitchener's brilliant calypsos about life in England dominated the fifties. The lesser known George Brown, (a.k.a. The Young Tiger) was also singing in clubs around the country. We appeared together in Caryl Brahms' and Ned Sherrin's *Cindy Ella,* with Cleo Laine and Elizabeth Welch in the West End, as well as on a BBC TV Christmas Special, a radio show and an LP. There was even a book of the play. George sang his famous Coronation calypso *I Was There* which endeared him to royalty. Lance Percival, an Englishman, was also well known as a 'calypso' singer. He mastered the art of improvising at the drop of a hat, something I never attempted. He was to appear regularly on the BBC TV Show *That Was The Week That Was*, an off shoot of the *Tonight* programme.

Calypso, or what was generally considered calypso, became very popular world wide, firstly with the Andrews' Sisters version of *Rum and Coca Cola* (about the impact of American troops on the local population in Trinidad). This was to spark a complex court case brought by and won by Lionel Belasco, its (rightful) composer. [Belasco was known as Lord Invader. Calypsonians adopted grand titles like The Lord Invader, The Duke of Iron, The Mighty Sparrow, Attila the Hun. These epithets adopted by calypsonians are characteristic of the masquerade traditon, whereby representations of 'power' and 'difference' are adopted by participants. Evidence for this appropriation can be traced to slave dancing societies. In the days when I was appearing in Cababet in the 1960s I sang "The Underground Train", the famous calypso by 'Lord Kitchiner'. After my spot, as I was returning to my dressing room, a young debutante rushed after me, grabbed me by the shoulder and shouted "How dare you say my Great Grand-daddy wrote that awful song!" The American presence was also to spark one of the most remarkable inventions of the twentieth century – the Trinidad steelpan, the transformation of discarded waste material into a musical instrument of great subtlety and healing potential; a subject I explored in my book *Ring of Steel* (Macmillan 1999).

The Andrews Sisters had started a trend soon taken up by many other American artists anxious to jump on such a lucrative band wagon – Nat King Cole (*Calypso Blues*), Maya Angelou (*Miss Calypso* LP), Robert Mitchum, and the folk group The Tarriers. Even that great American humourist, Ogden Nash, wrote a 'calypso' making fun of Ernest Hemmingway's air crash in Africa – *A Bunch of Bananas and a Bottle of Gin*. Soon, other bunches were straining heads and bending backs. Belafonte's album *Calypso*, recorded in 1956 hit the air waves. It included his version of the Jamaican mento *The Banana Boat Song*[5]. Overnight Belafonte broke all records for sales of that recording; and he was to play a great role in decisions I had to make about my own career.

I first met the great man whilst still in America with the Olivier company. His name kept cropping up everywhere I went. I was even mistaken for him in down-town New York. At the time Belafonte was making a name for himself at the Village Vanguard in Greenwich Village and so I decided to see for myself. I was taken to meet him backstage after his show, but Harry was in a great hurry when I introduced myself and always remained so every time we met, for example, at the BBC TV centre whilst I was on *Tonight*, and in Zimbabwe for a UNICEF concert, which I helped to put together in 1989.

Belafonte's spectacular world-wide popularity clouded the issue of *what is calypso,* as in fact my own appearances on *Tonight*. Calypsos are songs of social comment and abuse (picong) and the mark of a true calypsonian was his ability to improvise and entertain, as the Mighty Terror sang in *Calypso Wars:*

> *Yes, rebellion and war, war, war*
> *the Terror wants war, war*
> *now I come to the conclusion to expose the secrets of mock calypsonians*
> *If you are not a Trinidadian you are not a calypsonian here in Great Britain.*

For me, the idea of writing a calypso to be performed live every night had not been something I'd been prepared to take up. It would have meant giving up on an already established career as an actor. Someone else was called in to help with the writing. Bernard Levin, who had given a favourable review to the Granada TV play I had starred in the night after the very first *Tonight*, was the unlikely person chosen. There could have been no better choice. Levin was clever, witty on top of the news and the political situation. Maybe that accounted for the great popularity of the calypso slot in the programme.

Sometimes I would receive his version of a topical *calypso* just an hour or so before I was expected to transform and sing it live on TV. It helped both Levin and myself if I stuck to the traditional 'double tone' calypso format: an eight line stanza with four stressed syllables per line and any number of other syllables in between, thus allowing the form to approximate West Indian speech patterns. I opted for the tune of Raymond Quevedo's (Attila the Hun) *Graf Zeppelin*, a great favourite of mine.

I certainly did not like the label *calypso singer,* and I paid the price for staying too long on the programme. I was being categorised in a way which I considered exotic and superficial. Ironically, it was these appearances that made me a household name, thus interrupting a promising career as an actor, a career visited upon me by circumstances rather than choice. This forced me to focus on the singing side of my career but not to the exclusion of my acting.

In the early days of the programme some members of the great British public could not get used to seeing a black face nightly on their screens. The BBC tried to keep the letters of protest from me but occasionally a few got through along with my genuine fan mail. There was a particularly nasty one from an English branch of the Ku Klux Klan. This of course was at the time of the 1958 race riots in Notting Hill Gate, 'when white mobs attacked the homes of blacks, smashing windows and throwing petrol bombs.'[6] I was also aware that my appearances on *Tonight*, whilst fitting in perfectly with the type of programme we were aiming for, were peripheral, and therefore acceptable. Television, like the press and the police and the courts reflected the prejudices of society in which black people were perceived as marginal. Television in those early years merely reflected that reality.

How dramatically things have changed over the past four decades, noticeably in the theatre and on television. Both media have played a major role in trying to deal with the problem. This was not the case when I set out on my career. Then we had to fight every inch of the way – the BBC, the Arts Council, British Actors Equity and the film industry. Today it is no longer politically correct to admit to being racist, but as the Stephen Lawrence Report was to reveal, institutional racism is still very much with us.

My appearance in the film *Sea Wife* is a case in point. My character, No.4, was one of the four main roles in the film, a purser on board a passenger liner during the war. As an officer in real life in the Royal Air Force, I never recalled going around addressing fellow officers, or anyone for that matter, as "Mr. So-and so", unless of course he was a senior officer. Yet this was what the script required the purser, an officer, to do – to address the other main protagonists, two drifters, nicknamed Biscuit and Bull Dog respectively and a nun, Sea Wife as "Mr. Biscuit," "Mr Bull Dog," and "Miss Sea Wife"! That's how racist attitudes were being perpetuated in the industry.

After the ship had been torpedoed, these characters all depended for their survival on the purser, the black man. The Italian director, Roberto Rossolini, had chosen me for the part. He was to walk out of the film the day before we started shooting in Jamaica because the American distributors, Twentieth Century Fox, objected to the dominant role of No.4. During the filming I never addressed the other characters as Mr or Miss as required by the script. Even in the blatantly racist book, *Sea Wife and Biscuit*, the character No.4 never addressed the other characters in this way. The book of the film, however, certainly confirmed the racial stereotypes that were generally accepted at the time of its publication.

I did not know during the shooting of the film that it was to be post-synched, as the sound quality on location would not have been adequate for a major Twentieth Century Fox movie. What came as a shock when I went to dub my lines in the sound studio back in England after the shooting had been completed, was that the 'misters' for Bulldog and Biscuit were still in the script. I refused to play ball and was not called back to complete the job. A few days later I was told that another black actor, Earl Cameron, the very one I had taken over from in my first acting role, had dubbed my voice. I was very hurt at the time but never asked Earl about it when we met many years later. However, it was gratifying to find that when I went to see the movie, there was only one occasion when No.4 addressed the other characters as 'mister' or 'miss'. At the time there was nothing I could have done about it, except to get British Actors' Equity to void my three-year contract with the production company.

Four years after *Sea Wife*, this attitude was still alive, and it was as well that I had added another string to my bow. I began doing cabaret and folk concerts round and about but in 1965 I was asked to play Othello at the Phoenix Theatre in Leicester. I jumped at the opportunity, even though the rehearsal time was short and the role one of the longest of Shakespeare's. It was going to be a challenge in any event, but even more so as I had already been contracted to play a minor role in a film being shot in Rome and had to take four days off from rehearsals. Also, the director, Clive Perry, seemed to take no real interest in the production, leaving it to a young inexperienced assistant director, (later to his credit, to become director of the National Theatre), which did not help the production. But it was a great role to play, even though I was being continually upstaged by the wily, agile actor who played Iago.

It was not surprising that the critic for The Guardian slated the production and me in particular. He did not like my inflections, a bad imitation of Olivier's! (Ira Aldridge, the black American actor, had been accused of imitating Kean). In any case, this could have been taken as a compliment; I admired Olivier's inflections. The way he spoke Shakespeare surprised and delighted me. But of course, the critic was referring to my West Indian inflections! I wondered what a Moor from Venice would sound like. Maybe like Olivier playing a Moor from Venice. However, the theatre was always full throughout its two week run.

I also did not know what to make of Jonathan Miller's piece in The Sunday Telegraph magazine, criticising Olivier's Othello for swaggering on stage with the stem of a rose clenched between his teeth, 'like Cy Grant or Harry Belafonte!'. I was reminded that a lady journalist for the London Evening Standard once described me as greeting her with a big banana smile! To me Olivier's 'swagger' was insulting, a racist caricature of a black man. Nor can I understand what prompted the great man to wear a rose beneath his nose. And is it true that he painstakingly blacked up his entire body before every performance – from head to little toe?

Productions of Othello have often given rise to controversy. Shakespeare took the story from the *Hecatommithi* of Giraldo Cinthio (1565). The play is full of paradox. It is the black man who is the symbol of integrity and honour. Othello was the upholder of law; he was not to be considered an outsider. Although Shakespeare points out the prejudices, the play does not support them. Othello's blackness depicts a moral challenge that an apparently civilised world (Venice and England?) believes it has overcome. Morality and barbarity confront each other symbolically. In the play racism is not the overriding issue, but morality.

The role is a difficult one to maintain. Iago is the scoundrel and the true 'hero' who manipulates his moral superior. Perhaps Shakespeare had insights that are not acknowledged. All we know is that many English writers and critics hated the idea of Othello being black or being played by a black actor. Shakespeare could have hardly envisaged that one day a black actor would play the role. For Charles Lamb and for Coleridge, the idea was quite revolting even before any black actor had played the role. The thought of beautiful, virtuous, white Desdemona in the clutches of a black man would have been sacrilege.

The earliest black actor to play the role was the American, Ira Aldridge, at the Theatre Royal, Covent Garden, in 1833. The Times was dismissive, even though it admitted that the performance was 'extremely well received'. The Athenaeum did not pull any punches - it was quite vicious. But Aldridge's performance was hailed in European and in other British cities. When he returned to London twenty-five years later, the Athenaeum grudgingly reversed its opinion, 'We may claim this black, thick lipped player as one proof among many that the negro intellect is human, and demands respect as such'.

Paul Robeson, another American, played the role at the Savoy Theatre in 1930, to great critical acclaim, thus making it at last acceptable for Othello to be played by a black actor. But the problem of Othello is not just in the casting, it is within the character. Shakespeare himself (or was it in the original?), is ambivalent about his main character. It seems that the noble Moor does not quite know himself. The paradox of his blackness is not resolved. He is honourable and resolute, yet gullible to an unbelievable degree. The great general who commands his men unequivocally even apologises for his blackness 'Haply, for I am black...' at the same time calling Desdemona, whom he unjustly distrusts, 'O thou black weed...'

To say that I did not like Olivier's portrayal of Othello would be an understatement. If Orson Welles at the St James' a decade earlier made him into a gorilla, Olivier's was a white man's ignoble caricature of a Moor. How could such a great actor and warm human being be so misguided? I had watched the production from the gods at the Old Vic. It was the only seat I could get. I dread to think what my reaction would have been if I had been sitting in the stalls to observe it in close up! I was, of course, to have all my fears confirmed when I later saw the screen version. Although I had been invited to go back stage, when I eventually caught up with the production that ended up as completely out of the question.

It seems that for black actors in England there are few opportunities to play the role. Errol John was given a chance at the Old Vic and so was the great Jamaican opera singer, Willard White, in Trevor Nunn's 1990 production. But it was the Iago of Ian McKellen that sticks in the memory. And I know that Sam Wanamaker fancied his Iago, opposed to Robeson's Othello in the Stratford-upon-Avon production in the sixties. Black actors in those days rarely got the chance to play good parts. At every level the strands of the tapestry of their lives are intertwined with the reality of their situation, their very profession a charade; their stage littered with decomposing ambitions and failures – a mirage of distorted dreams.

Olivier's Othello took place in 1968 against a notable political backdrop. This was the year the Conservative MP, Enoch Powell, had made his notorious racist immigration speech in Birmingham. Although he was dismissed from Edward Heath's shadow cabinet, the era ushered in by Powell simmered on for many years. It brought into the open the full extent of British racism. The dockers marched in support of him. Racism was no longer covert. Even a Labour government was to pass legislation restricting the numbers of black immigrants into the country.

And so for me the stage was set for yet another reappraisal. What was I doing acting out a role like some phantom at someone else's opera? The dilemma had to be faced so I tried my hand at poetry.

Turning a corner on the way to myself I collided with myself. There I was, standing on the stage of my life, aware of myself observing me the actor doing purely mechanical things… the business, spouting someone else's lines, trying to get within a character – a play actor, playing some one other than himself, striving to convince, striving for a lifelike portrayal; getting under the skin of the character; then suddenly, colliding with my self, no longer acting…

Surely I could be doing something worthwhile. I decided that it was probably not too late to go back to the Bar. In 1972, I found myself in very distinguished chambers. A friend of mine from Trinidad had been a member. He was now a respected judge in Jamaica; it also helped that I had been a TV personality. So it was that I spent six months at the Middle Temple whilst I mulled over the idea of taking up practice at long last. But although my prospects this time seemed very good, my brief encounter with the stuffy atmosphere in the robing room and the interminable hours spent listening to the sordid reiteration of evidence in criminal litigation, finally made me realise that the law was not, after all, for me. As a young man I had studied law for sound political reasons – to fight the system of colonialism. I really had no desire for power. Change for me was not joining the system but trying to resist it. I was satisfied that I had given the profession a good hard look before finally bowing out for good. I had to resume my career, such as it was.

The following year I did a concert at the Royal Festival Hall. The postal strike was on and bookings were slow at the box office, but as it transpired I needn't have worried. The house was practically full. I was now writing poetry daily. One of my poems had been published in an anthology of Caribbean poetry, edited by John Figueroa. Now James Berry included a few in his anthology *Blue Foot Traveller*. I did readings of my poems *Black & Blue* (unpublished) at Aston University, Birmingham and on the Edinburgh Fringe.

In 1973 the oil crisis was upon us and as a result, art centres throughout the country were closing. There was less and less work on the concert/ recital circuit. At the same time I was becoming completely politicised. Over the preceding ten years, I had read all the powerful black literature coming out of America - from James Baldwin to Eldridge Cleaver. This conjunction of events was making me look very closely at the society in which I had lived and of which I had been part. Instead of a nation drowning in rivers of blood, the flow of black oil was drying up. I wrote a letter to the editor of *The Times*:

> *A black time we'll have of it*
> *Christmas on us, no hosannas*
> *snuffed dreams*
> *of stuffed turkey and booze*
> *only the blues.*
> *thy will be done*
> *goodwill to all men white*
> *Christmas. A black time*
> *without black coal and Arab oil*
> *black-collar workers*
> *inert energy men in some black comedy*
> *even the mercy men hold us to ransom*
> *thy kingdom come*
> *raw deals to thaw the black snow covered scene*
> *black deeds with black oilmen dealing cards*
> *cold comfort now*
> *without black coal, black oil*
> *and striking black collar workers.*

It was politely sent back – they had someone else who wrote that sort of satirical thing. The press it seemed could and can be just as sensitive about the use of the word black when used by black people. A year later I was to test this theory again. I had been watching a discussion by Frank Bough and Leo Abse on the BBC's

Nationwide on the so-called 'black' market in children for adoption. Black children were referred to as being somehow blemished and imperfect and I took great exception to this. I should have complained to the BBC, no doubt, but the damage had already been done. I thought it would be best to write a letter to The Guardian registering my resentment. The reply I received was 'since many of our readers may not have seen the programme... it would seem rather strange for it to be carried in our column'. An opportunity missed, it seems to me, to take a stand - but why should the paper have reacted in this way? It would be out of character; just as the silence of football commentators was the norm in the days when black players of the stature of John Barnes were being jeered by English 'supporters' of the game.

I decided that I would try to take some positive action. At the time, the question of asserting my black identity was paramount. How could I begin to address this issue? It had repeatedly been claimed that black actors had no experience and as a result a chicken-and-egg situation had resulted. The idea of setting up a black arts centre had already been germinating in my mind when one night on TV I watched a tribute to Sir Laurence Olivier. He came over as very warm, a man with great humanity. He had always been very warm to me personally. And although I hated his portrayal of the Shakespeare's 'Noble Moor', I had always admired his bravura style of acting. His technique was staggering, his delivery and control of breath and movement the envy of every actor. Somehow I thought he would be the perfect patron for the Workshop Centre I wanted to set up. I wrote to him and explained my idea.

His reply was courteous and friendly, but it contained a bomb. I do not really believe that it was intended. 'My dear Cy, you are being separatist...' – that was the gist of it; 'you really have to be like us, old boy'. The penny had finally dropped. Now I really knew where I was – the road ahead was clear despite the fog of presumption. This was England and part of Europe, which had been brought up on its own myths, its own presumptions. Only European arts, values and culture are valid. The rest of the world can learn from Europe – must learn from Europe! Anything non-European was marginal. To me this was the greatest heresy. It was the result of five centuries of European domination and of colonialism, both of which have defined, delineated and prescribed the prevailing world view – that imposed its values, its culture, its versions of history on the rest of the world.

Although I could not have articulated it at the time, I have come to see that our entire systems of education, economics and law and order were designed to exclude the rest of the world. It is as if the rest were meant to serve the interests of Europe only – despite the ecological damage threatening our very existence, the deprivation, poverty and the cost in human life and dignity. It insulted my innermost sensibilities and humanity. But I was to discover that there were other corners yet to turn.

Black Words

As image collides with reality,
bounces back,
so **words** mirror the culture..
the limitations that trap
dehumanise repress enslave alienate
Words? We are trapped by them
defined, betrayed

words presume prescribe
words, deed, words lead
wound bleed
stance circumstance
circumscribe circumcise, schism
ostracism.
words that mould our worlds
shibboleths concepts categories
classes religions; eroticism
miscegenation xenophobia..
our future horizons
spheres of fear
an apocalyptic collapse
a one-way membrane,
a white dwarf
inevitably sucked in by our suspended nothingness
into a perpetual vacuum
a BLACK HOLE in space.
Red white blue
brown black yellow
colour is not just colour
but 'coloured'
a different hue,
you even put a different slant
on the word immigrant
you take a coloured view
The new enlightenment
confers on immigrant
wherever born
an ingenious fabrication
the lie
as in alien.

words that mirror culture
through the glass darkly
refracting splintered spectra
a new coinage
for the old hue and cry
And so at Blackpool
you made me the fool
on this English sea-front
the affront is greater than you think
a national affront.
And your Clubs
for members only, Private Clubs
will club you near to death
come Monday
Tuesday even
Friday's outlook will be black.
I think of Blackpool, Wolverhampton
out-post of Empire
and a privy-Councillor.
given power, Powell's facts
can fool
he may yet be viceroy
at Blackpool
Since Enoch's rivers of blood,
the unstemmable flood
rising tides of hysteria
the foam-white spray
engulfing the media
lashing the prows of the Nation
drafting a raft of repatriation
to ride the storm,
erecting a dam of legislation
to stem the flood
to tie the tides by 'ties of blood'
Prophetic dictum.
for racial, read 'patrial',
by Widgery's omniscient
sanction,
the ruling orbiter is now
established precedent.

Note

For an early history of television and Black people, see John Twitchin's definitive programmes *The Black & White Media Show* for BBC 1. Here the whole question of racism is laid painfully bare. His book *The Black & White Media Book* is a handbook for the study of racism and television, dealing with the effects of TV on adults and children, cultural racism, and the role of TV in re-enforcing negative stereotypical images of black people; how to recognise it and what should be done to counter this both in the class room and by programme makers.

Chapter 4 – In The Black

What to my mind makes this indignation priceless, is that it transcends at every moment the anguish felt by a black man because of the fate of Blacks in modern society and, indistinguishable from that felt by all poets, artists and true thinkers, while furnishing Césaire with a special fund of verbal genius, embraces the more generally determined condition of man today, in all its intolerable… aspects

Andre Breton on Aimé Césaire's *Cahier d'un Retour au Pays Natal*

DRUM

Olivier never replied to my letter in response to his. That, I suppose, was only to be expected. In the grand theatre of life, I was peripheral to the main action, a nobody. How dare I question the natural order of things? But my letter was to form the basis for a paper I wrote: The Case For A Black Theatre Workshop, which became the 'articles' for the Drum Arts Centre set up by myself and John Mapondera in 1974. It was to open doors leading to workshops at the National Theatre and productions at the National itself and eventually, an acknowledgement that black people are as good actors as anyone else.

What we were in fact challenging was the deep-rooted hubris of the prevailing culture, the integrationist ethic – an ethic that always turned out to mean accommodation to white institutions and values. Invariably it was we who must integrate with them; we who must adapt and fit in. But as long as we were extras on the stage of life we would be regarded as outsiders. It was clear to me that in a world in which racial, national and class distinctions are overlaid with discriminatory judgements, it is disingenuous to call black selfhood separatist. It was time black people took over the definition of themselves. As Thomas Szasz put it, *'In the animal kingdom, the rule is eat or be eaten; in the human kingdom, define or be defined.'* (From *The Second Sin* Anchor/ Doubleday New York.)

The case for a black theatre workshop rested on whether or not it was separatist to argue for a black consciousness. In an ideal world, concepts like race, nationality and class would be unimportant. To argue for an English cultural tradition as distinct from a French or American tradition would hardly be considered separatist: neither the National Theatre nor the Welsh Eisteddfod is seen as separatist or chauvinistic.

Black consciousness is an existential reality that has been foisted on black people by patterns of European dominance which have existed for centuries. It is in direct opposition to a system of values in which racism is an integral part; an explicit assertion of identity and pride in being black, as well as a call for a return to authenticity and value. Racial harmony will only exist when all groups within society are free to express their culture openly. As Philip Mason pointed out in his book *Patterns of Dominance*:

'We are far more likely to achieve a society in which resentment is kept within bounds if society is thought of not as a homogenous mass but as a system of overlapping circles. This has really two components; in a society which is to be reasonably harmonious, there will have to be full opportunity for the expression of a diversity for which the Welch language, the Sikh turban, may serve as symbols. But there must also be overlapping of groups, so that no one category has overriding priority and people can win esteem in a variety of ways'.

(Patterns of Dominance published by Oxford University Press, London 1970)

About this time, I had come across John Berger's translation of Aimé Césaire's *Cahier d'un Retour au Pays Natal* (Notebook of a Return to my Native Land, published by Penguin 1969). Sections of the Notebook had been included in the Anthology of black poetry to which an essay by Sartre, *Black Orpheus*, had formed the introduction. That book had the profoundest effect on me. The language was poetic and lyrical and obviously the work of a major black poet. It was also surreal and very difficult; huge torrents of words that rushed over me, leaving a sense of stumbling upon something that was not only revelatory but immensely relevant. I would have to work hard to unravel the meaning. I decided to read it into a tape recorder, just sight-read the whole thing. It filled both sides of a 90 minute cassette. I played it back to myself from time to time, each time new meaning breaking through the dense fabric of the text.

It described the whole process of colonisation and its effect on the colonised. Extolling negritude (blackness), it was also a call for new values and for the emergence of a new man. I began memorising great chunks of it, and hoped I would have an opportunity to read it as a performance piece one day. It confirmed my belief that black people must be free to act out their black experience, giving it free artistic rein, and discover unashamedly for themselves a new selfhood in which race is irrelevant. By asserting their identity and making their blackness more explicit they were creating the possibility for it to evolve into a more meaningful, less separatist identity. Jean-Paul Sartre put it succinctly when he wrote *'The ultimate unity which will draw together all the oppressed in the same combat must be preceded by that which I shall name the moment of separation or of negativity. This anti-racist racism is the sole road which can lead to the abolition of the differences of races.'*

"Orphée Noir" (Black Orpheus), introduction to *Anthologie de la nouvelle poésie nègre et malgache.* edited by Léopold Sédar Senghor, 1948.

The next three years were to prove a most difficult period in my life. There was a kind of shocked response of complete incomprehension at my plans to set up a black theatre workshop in London. The very idea was met with open hostility; I was accused of being recalcitrant by the chairman of the Race Relations Board. Our meetings at the Arts Council were embarrassing confrontations. We were met by polite incomprehension by Sir Roy Shaw and his officers. Ironically, racist South Africa had a black theatre in Natal, and their production of *Umabatha* for the World Theatre Season in 1972/73 in London was an outstanding success. At the Royal Court Theatre *Siswi Bansi is Dead* was playing to packed houses.

At times, racist ideology can be so subtle that even the most liberal of people can be unaware just how much it determines their thoughts and actions. We seemed, then, to be locked in separate worlds leading to confrontation and it was inevitable that this kind of situation might occur when least expected. It was like running into an invisible wall of incomprehension. For me, these events seem to confirm how deeply entrenched certain beliefs are – that they are culturally acquired or inherited. This not only causes a great deal of pain, but is an extremely sad situation, showing as it does just how wide the gulf is in our perceptions. I, for one, have always been left with a numbing sense of hopelessness and despair. The inevitable encounter can take place on the most unlikely of occasions; at a dinner party amongst friends whom one has known for many years; in the course of a normal conversation; that Freudian slip of the tongue; that embarrassed confrontation – the person making the remark would be quite unaware of the covert racism revealed and if challenged would most likely deny any such suggestion. Lurking at every corner of the road at that time was that unexpected collision; if not blatant racism, then condescension and paternalism.

During the 1970s the Arts Council and the Regional Arts Associations (RAAS), both constituting the main source of public funding for the arts, took the position that they would only subsidise the work of professional artists, i.e. people whose livelihood was devoted to and secured by the practice of one or other art form. Few artists from ethnic minorities then resident in Britain, working in any medium, were at that time able to qualify, under those conditions, for any kind of public support. Only a very few RAAS took a less restrictive view than 105 Piccadilly, for whom 'ethnic' arts equalled 'folk' arts, equalled 'amateurs.'

When, much later, this policy became less rigidly interpreted, the prevailing Western separation of the arts into different and distinct art forms created even more distress. Artists from these 'other' cultures were forced to apply to different panels for funding, even though their arts were incompatible with such artificial fragmentation. At the time Drum was being set up, we also received no support from the leading black actors. This was a great pity. We viewed each other with suspicion, aware of our common disinheritance but somehow unable to work together to change our situation: it was as though if it had not been their initiative, they did not want to know and there was resistance to, and general suspicion of anyone who had, in their view, 'made it' on the assumption that they had somehow 'sold out'. But we were getting support from various other quarters. There was a great need for a centre such as we envisaged. The Gulbenkian Foundation came through with funds for a specific project. Brynmor John, at the Home Office, had promised further funds towards the conversion costs of a building which the Greater London Council was offering us within the new Covent Garden Development plan.

Workshops were set up at Morley College for six weeks during the summer of 1975 with Steve Carter, a playwright and theatre director from the Negro Ensemble Theatre in New York. This led to a play by Mustapha Matura, *Bread*, being presented at the Young Vic. This in turn led to workshops with the National Theatre the same year and these were repeated, at their request, the following year. In 1977 Ola Rotimi from the drama department of the University of Nigeria came over to produce his African adaptation of Sophocles' play Oedipus Rex, *The Gods are not to Blame*. Wole Soyinka's *The Swamp Dwellers* was produced at the Commonwealth Institute Theatre. The first ever exhibitions of black art were mounted at the Commonwealth Institute and a West End gallery in 1978.

It was all heady stuff. John Mapondera was an imaginative and tenacious project coordinator but he was making unilateral decisions that began to threaten our relationship. Unfortunately, we did not have enough funding for me to be involved in the day to day administration, so I remained as chairman whilst continuing my theatre and concert work – including a short stint with the Royal Shakespeare Company at their London theatre in a production of *The Iceman Cometh* by Eugene O'Neil. As time went by, and despite John Mapondera's extraordinary input, my disenchantment with some of his methods was beginning to worry me. He was at times quite ruthless and was alienating many who had given generously of their time and support. I had expected him to be different from the other purely self-seeking black activists who still abound and who, it seemed, were all competing for a slice of the cake: if one person got a slice he was as good as stealing it from someone else. What struck me most vividly was that none of them seemed to realise that they were all caught up in what I have termed 'the black trap' – asserting a black identity, thus increasing division between themselves and other cultural groups, whilst demanding the fruits of Western materialism. I understood that this behaviour was one of the legacies of slavery and colonialism but I expected them to see this for themselves and surmount it. My relations with John eventually became untenable and after great soul searching I decided to resign from Drum. Césaire's poem had convinced me that blackness transcended the mere assertion of a black identity. It was about new values, the rediscovery of the values that Europe had turned its back on and which Césaire believed were still part of an ancient African system of values. An <u>art</u> centre should be making this explicit; in Africa traditional art and life are not separate.

Drum had been a dream and I had worked extremely hard to set it up. The process had been very painful; lobbying the establishment, politicians, the Arts Council, the Race Relations Board, and the GLC. There had been in-fighting among the committee members as well as a degree of non-cooperation from sections of the black community. The strain had been intolerable at times, but it had been worth it. We had been successful in starting the process for black performance that this country badly needed. We had gone beyond tokenism, beyond the call for a recognition of 'the arts that Britain ignores'[7].

Letting go of Drum was not easy. In order to fill the vacuum that yawned, but without deserting my convictions, I asked the National Theatre if I could do a one-man performance of Césaire's poem as a platform performance. I had come to the end of yet another road and was about to turn a corner on another. The reading at the National led to a two-week production at the Theatre Upstairs at the Royal Court Theatre; a few months later and I was to begin a tour of the piece around the country that lasted for two years. That was a very long tour in anyone's book, but a most important time for me.

My performances of Aimé Césaire's masterpiece had a mixed reception. Predictably, the right wing section of the press did not like them but, all in all, the reviews were very good. The product of the negritude movement in Paris in the 1930s, the poem traces the personal journey of Aimé Césaire. Born in 1913, Césaire grew up in Martinique, one of the Windward Islands and a French colony. Educated at the École Normale in Paris he was to become Mayor of Fort de France, a Deputy to the French National Assembly for 37 years and the author of many books of poetry and several plays. Césaire had been greatly influenced by the French surrealist movement but also by the French poet Lautreamont (Isidore Ducasse), a forerunner of that movement. Together with the black French intellectuals Leopold Senghor and Leon Damas, from Senegal and French Guyana respectively, he developed the theory of negritude. He had also been aware of the writings of German anthropologist Leo Frobenius, whose *History of African Civilisation* was published in 1936. Frobenius considered black culture the cradle of and model for all others.

On its first publication, the Cahier had been acclaimed by Andre Breton, the leading surrealist poet, as '*nothing less than the greatest lyrical monument of this time*'. Césaire was a black man who embodied '*not simply the black race but all mankind, its queries and anxieties, its hopes and ecstasies and who will remain for me the symbol of dignity.*' (From the preface to the Presence Africaine edition of 1971). Sartre said of it '(this) *poem of Césaire... bursts and turns on itself as a fuse, as bursting suns which turn and explode in new suns, in a perpetual surpassing*' (from *Black Orpheus*, trans. S.W.Allen, Presence Africaine 1971). The African writer, Ezekiel Mphahlele, thought it '*...the greatest synthesis of the individual vision and the public voice, of the lyrical and dramatic tones. Its emotional and intellectual range has no parallel*". (From *The African Image*, Faber & Faber 1974).

The English version that I chose to perform had been translated by John Berger and Anna Bostock and was published by Penguin in 1969. The poem was an attack on colonialism and European values. Negritude was about a system of values which transcended race, and the issues that Césaire addressed in the thirties seemed to me to be still relevant. They related directly to my own experience of racism within contemporary British society and that is why it was so important for me to do it. Whilst it had seemed noteworthy when I first came across it, on leaving Drum I knew I wanted to perform it so as to make a public statement: now everyone would know exactly where I stood. I had already lost many of my white 'friends' and work was becoming much harder to find. It had been difficult enough whilst setting up Drum.

You do not perform a piece of this intensity for two and a half years without it becoming part and parcel of your thoughts and outlook on life; this explains my dwelling at some length on the way in which the work has shaped my views. The poem is not only about asserting one's negritude; it is a statement of a staging post on one's journey of self-exploration. It is an impassioned plea for the deconstruction of colonialism and for a new man with new values; a true humanity which can teach society how to love, how to rediscover its real identity, and how to employ technology for the benefit of all. Negritude was to become a system of values necessary for *all* mankind and not limited to the narrow issues of blackness incorporated within the term's current meaning.

Césaire's orphic journey has not been in vain, challenging the West's view of his proper place in the world. In an ideal world, black people would not need to extol their blackness, but in a racist, exploitative European world, there needs to be a first step. As an African who knew who he was, Wole Soyinka famously remarked that '*a tiger does not proclaim its tigritude.*' This may well make sense, but for many of us, Africans included, who have lost or are in danger of losing our own traditional values, negritude is that necessary first step. For Césaire, surrealism was a logical instrument with which to smash the restrictive forms of language which 'sanctified' rationalised bourgeois values. The breaking up of language patterns coincided with his own desire to bring down colonialism and all such oppressive forms and also his wish to return to nature – to his true spiritual home:

> As frenetic blood rolls on the slow current of the eye, I want to roll words like maddened horses like new children like clotted milk like curfew like traces of a temple like precious stones buried deep enough to daunt all miners. The man who couldn't understand me couldn't understand the roaring of a tiger.

I felt the anger was justified – it was not the anger at being rejected by society but rather at society's purely materialistic values. For me it was also about having the courage to stand up and speak those words, to shout from the roof tops: 'Accommodate yourself to me, I will not accommodate myself to you'. I recall that after one performance in London, my daughter who had come down from Cambridge with some of her friends to see the show, told me how uncomfortable it felt for her seeing how confrontational my performance had been. That was a very salutary observation for I realised that I could temper my anger: the truth spoken quietly is irresistible. The power of the spoken word is enormous and works at the subconscious level. And Césaire's words were powerful; they captured the horrors of this system of the domination of man…

I identified completely with Césaire's attack on colonialism and his call, as Fanon put it, to leave this Europe '*that was forever talking about man yet murdered man where ever they found him*'. I did not fully realise at the time that the poem was not merely an indictment of colonialism and of Europe, or just another statement of black identity. It went much deeper than that. It was a call for a return to just those values I had hoped to engender in Drum and specifically a return to nature, to that which is natural.

Most of the critics of the poem, black or white, and there are many, have failed to comment on Césaire's connectedness with Nature – that the poem conveys a state of total participation with Nature – the state of total belonging. Césaire had no desire to harness nature but to be a part of it like a tree: '...*finding nourishment and growth in the invulnerable sap. To a dispersed race the tree offered the advantage of being rooted in telluric solidity and security while reaching for the sky. It had both the openness to the Cosmos that constituted the special gift of the blacks and the strength necessary for survival and regeneration. It partook of the Orphic quest and the Apollonian triumph, or death and joyful life':* (Aimé Césaire, *The Collected Poetry*: Eshleman & Smith. California, 1983)

> *my negritude is neither tower or cathedral*
> *it plunges into the blazing flesh of the sky*
> *my negritude riddles with holes*
> *the dense affliction of its worthy patience*
> *Heia for the royal Kailcedrate...*
> *Heia for those who give themselves up to the essence of all things*
> *ignorant of surfaces but struck by the movement of all things*
> *free of the desire to tame but familiar with the play of the world*
> *truly the eldest sons of the world open to all the breaths of the world*
> *fraternal territory of all breaths*

Return to My Native Land

Césaire goes back to the 'invulnerable sap', to Nature and to Africa. Basic to ancient African culture, as in other traditional cultures, is a close relationship between man, 'Muntu', and nature, a topic I shall be exploring in a later chapter, (An Ecology of Being); a relationship that I had not been aware of, educated as I had been, in the Western tradition.

As I toured the show around the country, I began slowly to identify with this ideology. The tour also gave me the opportunity to openly express my innermost feelings about the experience of colonialism and of racism. As previously stated, to be on the receiving end of racism is deeply humiliating and people do not find it easy to talk about because it is so painful for them to accept in themselves. People are ashamed to own something for which they themselves were not responsible – something inherited by history, the legacy of Empire; the 'psychic shame' addressed in the novels of George Lamming, a fellow 'exile' of mine. Also, I was to find very few people willing to admit harbouring feelings of inherent superiority.

Until racism is owned, until it is recognised for what it is and the untold damage it has caused acknowledged, society will never change. It is at the very root of a society manifestly fragmented, mechanistic and materialistic. Its pervasiveness affects every aspect of a black person's life. It is naked and tangible and immoral to the utmost degree. For black people living in Britain, and who were encouraged to come to this country as British citizens, this open expression of racism causes great distress. Racial discrimination and abuse is bad enough to bear but being considered a social outcast was traumatic.

When, in 1968, Enoch Powell made his notorious speeches inciting people to racial hatred, he was never indicted. Instead his speeches were reproduced in every newspaper. He became a national hero. If he had been indicted, well you would have had to indict the entire nation – he was only saying what the vast majority believed to be true. Government immigration legislation in the sixties and seventies was blatantly racist. Was this the England of justice, fair play and morality that I had been made to believe at school in Guyana? In many respects life in England is better than it would have been in the British colony where I was born. The voluntary exile of so many West Indian writers and creative people is proof of that. I was incensed by the utterances of Powell and the National Front, and I hoped that things would change; but government policies and the ineffectiveness of bodies like the Commission for Racial Equality did not augur well. All my forebodings were now confirmed. And this explained why, even privileged as I obviously was, I never felt completely at home in England.

At the time, I thought, racism is a legacy of history and part of the culture. It floats in the air, is breathed in at the cradle, is nurtured by language and tribal pride. Henceforth my task must be to learn about this Europe, to study the relationship between Europe and the rest of the world, Africa and Asia; the history of colonialism and slavery, the role of language and of religion and philosophy. I must try my best to understand the prevailing human condition.

Drum did not, unfortunately, survive much longer. Soon after I had embarked upon my new task, Zimbabwe was to win its independence and John Mapondera left for *his* native land and the opportunities there for an ambitious young man who had established good credentials for himself in England. What we achieved together in providing a focus for the arts of black people all those years ago has certainly paved the way for today's considerable black presence in theatre and film.

PLAY MAS

I was to experience yet more of the division within the black community whilst still Chairman of Drum, when I was asked by Selwyn Baptiste, an organiser of one of the two Notting Hill Carnival factions to join his Committee. I attended one meeting only. I was made to feel a complete outsider. Drum's work was not in any way opposed to Carnival but complementary to it. In fact one of our earliest ventures was a 'Mas' fortnight of exhibitions, plays, music and poetry at the Institute of Contemporary Arts as part of the 1975 Carnival. These were organised by Leslie Palmer, a mas-man if ever there was one (even though he was not a Trinidadian). Drum was about setting up a black arts centre, specifically for the arts of black people in the centre of London and not confined to the ghettos – an entirely new venture to serve the black community wherever they lived. It did not see itself as elitist, unrelated to the grass roots. Like Carnival it was about identity and excellence. But what seemed to concern certain members of the Carnival committee was that I was not a Trinidadian: what could I possibly know about organising Carnival? The two Carnival Committees, it seemed to me, were at each others' throats. Why is it that

West Indians found it so hard to work together? This seemed to go against the very spirit of Carnival; something that has dogged successive Carnival committees to this day. I thought that my input might have helped bring them together. But of course we were never given a chance; I was also aware that there had been infighting within my own Drum committee.

By some strange irony I found myself, almost 20 years later, Chairman of the short-lived Carnival Committee based at Roehampton University (then Institute) in London. The Institute had recently appointed the Trinidadian Carnival scholar, Patricia Alleyne-Dettmers, as a Fellow. Her research was into Carnival in Britain and, with the support of the Arts Council, her brief was to set up a database of Mas bands throughout the country. The Committee comprised members of leading Carnivalists who were there to support the initiative and so give Carnival a higher national profile. Carnival arts were already been taught in the University, and I secretly entertained hopes that one day Roehampton would host an international conference on Carnival, not just the West Indian version, in order to understand the phenomenon of Carnival world-wide. The drum was of great significance in the birth of the Trinidad Carnival and thus of major importance to my own Drum and my journeys subsequent to touring the Cahier.

Carnival takes place in many Roman Catholic countries in the last days of the pre-Lenten season. The term 'carnival' probably comes from the mediaeval Latin, *carnem levare* or *carvele varium,* meaning to take away food. It is the last feast before the long forty day fast of Lent, during which Catholics abstain from eating meat. Its origin is probably in festivals which marked the advent of the New Year and the rebirth of nature. The start of the festivities varies according to national or local tradition. Carnival and similar festivals occur throughout the world; in Europe, in Italy, Spain, France, Belgium (the Gilles), Poland, Greece, Germany and Austria (Fasching), and Switzerland (Fasnach[8]). They flourish mostly in the predominantly Catholic Mediterranean countries, where their ritual could have being linked to the Dionysiac or Saturnalian festivals of ancient Greece and Rome. The ancient Egyptians also celebrated a spring festival in honour of the god of fertility. Festivals from other parts of Africa were transported into the New World as a result of the slave trade and these were incorporated into and then transformed the European originals.

Similar festivals also take place in India, China, Japan, USA (the most famous being the New Orleans Mardi Gras), Mexico (Fiesta); in South America (for instance, Rio Carnival in Brazil), in the Caribbean – the Santiago de Cuba, Puerto Rico – and in Canada (Caribana – an off-shoot, as in Notting Hill, of the Trinidad Carnival).

The Trinidad Carnival began with the arrival, in the then Spanish colony, of French speaking immigrants and their slaves in the late 18th century. A Catholic festival, it had itself evolved from a mainly pagan festival and retained much of these elements. But it was soon to become *'no longer a European inspired nature festival, but a deeply meaningful anniversary of deliverance with a ritualistic significance rooted in the very experience of slavery'.* (Errol Hill[9]). The procession of torches was replaced by drumming and singing; then African 'canboulay'[10] elements were incorporated; later the tambour-bamboo bands evolved and, since the second world war, the steel band. In the last century, the British attempted to control Carnival in Trinidad by banning the drum. This act was as cruel as destroying the indigenous languages had been. It led, however, to the evolution of the tambour bamboo bands in which bamboo 'reeds' were cut to varying lengths and music made by striking them on the ground or with sticks. In the twentieth century, during World War Two, when Carnival itself was banned, the steel band evolved – appropriately from the tambour bamboo bands.

Throughout the Caribbean, but most significantly in Trinidad, Carnival, or Mas as we know it, grew out of a search for identity. Each island has its own version. It was always seen as subversive by governments. As Eduardo Galeano observed in *Faces and Masks*, *'The fiestas of those at the top are displays of obligatory celebration, but the fiestas of those at the bottom provoke suspicion and punishment. Dark skins conceal threats of witchcraft and dangers of rebellion. The songs and music of the poor are a sin. The mulatto who likes to laugh risks prison or banishment, and on a Sunday of merriment a black slave can lose his head.'*

But as Ronald Segal noted in *The Black Diaspora*, *'Play mas (the Trinidad Carnival) is an exhortation which others in the Black Diaspora and beyond would do well to heed, so as to discover, through the liberation of the mask, what the face of humanity should be.'*

The right to *play mas* is deeply rooted in the archetypal human and Dionysian need for a sense of meaning and validation. Dionysus was not the god of drunkenness but the god of 'ecstatic vision' and we each need our ecstasy. If we do not get it legitimately, we will get it in an illegitimate way. Carnival, or Mas, is not only an ongoing re-enactment of historical reality but a psychic process, integrating the dark and the light, the masculine and the feminine, eventually leading to individuation.

It is as if the West's reluctance to acknowledge the cultures and values of Asia and Africa is symptomatic of its reluctance to confront the shadow. Jung felt that loss of connection with that part of us (relevant if it is true that Africa is the birth-place of human kind) most intimate with nature and instinct is part of the collective tragedy of the Western world. Jung travelled to Africa *'to find a psychic observation-post outside the sphere of the European'*. He realised how inadequate life is when myth and nature are lost and life experienced only through the intellect.

Since the ruling aspect in most societies involves order, law and discipline, Carnival reflects the energy repressed or forcibly suppressed by society. In Europe it seems largely to express the assertion of animal instincts against a cold, moralistic religious order. In countries where the core culture reflects the feminine, the magical and the intuitive (Latin America and the Caribbean for instance), Carnival can be more uninhibitedly joyous because it *is* the core expression of the culture. At the same time it can quite naturally become the vehicle of protest and mockery of a dominant order and repressive church. It is therefore not surprising that it is associated with the Mardi Gras – the last outcry before the time of total abstinence.

Seen in this essentially subversive guise, it can easily be understood why the authorities have felt jumpy. They sense revolution. To the unimaginative eye of the dominant culture, Carnival appears trivial, or at best is there to haunt the dominant culture with all that is alive and abiding, joyful and ultimately creative in ordinary man. The very paradox of the dark (evil to Apollo, glorious to Dionysus) is flaunted in the face of the dominant culture. Perhaps this is why Carnival is of such potent significance and relevance just now. It is the type of essential life-giving ritual, the redemptive dance in the barren cities of rationalism and materialism.

Carnival, then, is a 'mas' celebration of collective identity that in West Indian culture, as in most other traditional cultures of the world, exhibits an explicit desire to affirm that life and art are not separate, and that merely to be a passive recipient of artistic activity is alien to the life and creativity of these communities. Joyous participation is not only essential, but symbolic in the extreme. Carnival, or Mas, is total theatre, out front, on the streets – music and dance, costume and masquerade. And underlying all this are the parallels with the historical reality that it enacts and expresses. For the people of Trinidad for example, Carnival is also a highly creative expression of the political life of the ordinary man and woman. It is not so much an 'art' form, but a total participatory celebration which at the same time provides a powerful collective critique of traditional social institutions. As such it has great significance for black people in this country.

Any study of Carnival necessitates the study of issues of authority, domination, popular initiative and resistance, relevant to all societies including our own. Has contemporary British society, for instance, lost its appetite for popular celebration or has this spirit of joyful self-expression been eroded by institutional intervention? The fear of anarchy, a hang-over from the puritanism fostered in order to get people to work, can clearly be seen in the overkill methods adopted until very recently by the police towards hippies (also social 'Others') at the Summer Solstice celebrations at Stonehenge. And it seems that this same puritanism has put out the spark that once kindled the wood of celebration. It is as if, in England, the wood is somehow always damp.

I suspect that police attitudes towards the Notting Hill Carnival are but an extension of the suppression of popular festivals which began in the 17th century. Only official celebrations such as the Queen's Jubilee celebrations, were historically sanctioned in this country. The police saw the West Indian version of Carnival, or Mas, as a threat against law and order and a breeding ground for criminal activity. Hence their massive attempts to outlaw it. The British press endorsed this view, calling for it to be banned. But despite all this Carnival was unstoppable. 'The road make to march on Carnival day', as calypsonian Lord Kitchener once put it.

Play Mas has traditionally appropriated the licence that, for two days a year, permits anything to happen behind the mask. The puritanical attitude towards pleasure which leads to its repression coincides with the beginnings of colonialism, and the fear of rebellion and anarchy. The first recorded carnival in Trinidad took place in 1834, and was an expression of freedom after slavery had been abolished.

It became an ongoing act of defiance and a means of cultural survival. On one level Carnival is a fusion of music, street theatre and politics; at another, deeper level it is a universal declaration of the need to go beyond the masquerade. The right to play 'mas' is the perspective which recognises a peoples' innate vision of themselves, a vision that lies at a deep unconscious level of their being, empowering them to discard the persona mask they are forced to adopt, and allowing their true identity to emerge. This vision underlies the universal quest of the human spirit to know and manifest itself. It is a vision of survival and of catharsis leading to liberation.

For centuries Western countries have viewed the world from a Eurocentric standpoint. Other cultures were seen as less developed or enlightened, their arts, at best, 'primitive' or exotic artefacts to be viewed in museums, or written up in books on anthropology. With the advent of global communications and the increasing awareness of the inter-dependence of all countries, it is now possible, and indeed of the utmost importance, to go beyond this limited vision to reassess our understanding of other cultures in which art and life are not separate. Such a reassessment is necessary, particularly in the field of education, for it would equip a new generation to deal with the problems that affect our ever-shrinking world.

An understanding of the global nature of the phenomenon of Carnival necessitates laying bare the historical and psychic processes that have shaped it – the metamorphic processes which perennially recreate mas. The unconscious expresses itself through playing mas and without the play of fantasy and the imagination no true creativity is possible. Play, as Jung points out, is the forge of the imagination and creativity. He speculated that "It is just in the imagination that a man's highest values may lie." Understanding these processes would have helped to allay the suspicions and misconceptions of the authorities and the media; for when the code is deciphered we can all begin to share in a celebration of who we really are and deepen our relationships with ourselves and to each other. Such an understanding acknowledges that cultural diversity is an enrichment of life – that the Trinidadian adage *'all ah we is one'* aptly expresses the concept of unity in diversity.

By learning about the history of Carnival and its manifestations across the globe (not only in the Black Diaspora), we can learn about aspects of ourselves and our history; aspects of which we are normally not aware. We will also become aware of our interconnectedness from a global, more humanitarian perspective, encompassing all the peoples and cultures of the world. Carnival is multi-media and interdisciplinary. It is about participation – its arts are not separate from life. It is also about identity, communality and celebration. Understood historically, it would not have been perceived as such a threat to the authorities who have always sought to ban it. Any attempt to ban or to impose undue restrictions on the Notting Hill Carnival would most likely have led to rioting and violence in direct proportion to the violence daily visited upon black people.

To sum up, I would say that, deriving in part from a form of European festival, Carnival's present manifestations in the New World are now returning to Europe, going beyond the Western paradigm, in order to embrace all art forms - costume, design, music, poetry (calypso), live performance, dance and kinetic movement - in one theatrical event. A living art form, forever recreating itself, it is about total participation and an expression of a people's traditional, oral, social and contemporary experience. As an art form it is not separate from life but an ongoing dialogue and celebration of life. As street theatre, it is an annual ritual of survival and identity, of creativity and community, of unity and diversity. Finally it is about joy and freedom, an invitation to transcend the limitations of a mundane existence. It takes courage for some to play mas, to jump up, abandon themselves, bare themselves to public view. Centuries of cultural pressure have imposed such behavioural conventions upon Northern Europeans, that they have almost lost the capacity to put aside their inhibitions in public. They have largely lost the courage to move their bodies except according to some predetermined formula. Letting one's self go, confronting the shadow, one's hopes and fears, is an alchemical process going beyond the ritual shout, the unknown territory behind the mask.

Carnival gives voice and opportunity to both the conscious and the unconscious self. However, unless this is understood it becomes mere spectacle: it reduces to passive entertainment what could be and should be a creative liberation of all the levels of being. According to Wilson Harris:

> 'the greatest danger of cultural hubris is that it can conceal the latent seeds of fascism that lie hidden in so many societies in the late 20th Century... In this light the complex ramifications of carnival possess a practical bearing on the politics of our age and on what we tend to call 'human rights' or the values of freedom'.

[Carnival, the Carnival trilogy, London 1993 Faber & Faber]

The first West Indian 'Carnival' in Britain was organised by Claudia Jones, one of the outstanding leaders of the black community at the time. It was an indoor affair, in which all cultures participated, and was held at the St Pancras Town Hall in 1959. I had taken part as one of the judges of the costumes. It had been organised as a response to the race riots in Notting Hill the previous year, just as the Concord multicultural festivals I was to present in the eighties had been a response to the race riots of a later period. Moving outdoors for the first time in Britain in 1965, in the wake of a lone steel band, the Notting Hill Carnival has now evolved in its own unique way, incorporating along the 'road made to march', cultural groups from around the world – from over-loud sound systems, reggae and soca music, to African, Asian and some European groups; each new generation rediscovering and reinterpreting the symbolic ritual of self-expression and freedom. It became no longer just relevant to the Trinidadian carnival cognoscenti, but also to both black and white youth culture of the inner cities. It has been recreating itself each year, a continual process of regeneration and evolution.

Although not against authority, Carnival as conceived by Jones and her successors, was to be opposed to indiscriminate authoritarianism, obeying its own inner convictions and collective knowledge, perpetuating its own life and its own indomitable spirit, asserting pride, identity as a community or a sub-culture and incorporating the need, no the right, to express oneself – an understanding that could have led to acceptance and joyful participation from the beginning. The dilemma the early organisers of the yearly Carnival faced was its dependence solely on funding from agencies like the Arts Council, the Royal Borough of Kensington, the G.L.A.A and the C.R.E, some of whom sought to impose conditions on how it should be organised and routed, whereas the very nature of mas is that such controls should be minimal.

Today the present commercial exploitation of Carnival without respect for the true spirit of mas, has further undermined the whole process. Vast corporate sponsorship of the event has defused what was an act of defiance and the right to march into mere exoticism. Big business sponsoring multiculturalism is a travesty of what it should be. Multiculturalism is not about exoticism and skin-deep integration but an intertwining of, and respect for, all cultural groups within society.

It is quite ironic that the Notting Hill Carnival has recently received its highest accolade, leading the way at the official Royal procession during the Queen's Golden Jubilee Celebrations.

> 'Notting Hill Carnival's journey from a response to race attacks in 1958 to pride of place on the Mall in 2002, passing revelry, riot and resistance on route, is both powerful and painful. It is the tale of how a marginalised community built, protected and promoted what is now the largest street party in western Europe, using the radical cultural politics of the Caribbean to confront Britain's racist political culture.'

[Gary Younge: The Guardian, Saturday August 17th 2002]

Once a ritual where black people sought to celebrate their identity and creativity and where anyone could join in, play mas is now mere spectacle rather than creative liberation, providing the uninhibited street party ambiance – steel pan music, pulsing sound systems, elaborate costumes – a jamboree for all and sundry. But this is not a true expression of cultural diversity; nowhere can the drum be heard. In the early 1980s I set out to promote multicultural festivals throughout the country, to reflect and celebrate the true nature of present day British society. It is in this exploration that the drum continues to echo for us all.

> Play mas is not jus' stick fight, 'jump up' an'
> bacchanal;
> play mas is persona mask an' shadow,
> mas man an' mas woman flouncin' dislocation,
> gyratin' the ancestral dance, floutin' the face of repression...

refutin' the monuments of cultural imposition
canboulay an' jouvay,
excess an' exorcism,
baby doll an' dame lorraine, perrot grenade an' midnight robber,
moco jumbie, jab jab, john canoe an' jammet,

ole mas, road march, prancin' warriors..
play mas is butterfly wings of psyche.
You can' ban de mas – ban de drum, tamboo bamboo beat ban;
ban de mas, muse of reed transmute to pan,
soul bread an' Satyr.
panache an' pandemonium, panic an' mas-hysteria
no route to panacea.
'keep you han' off me mas!
steel ban' an' kaiso, reggae, sound system and
soca socialise de System;
myth an' symbol, magic transfiguration;
Lent, reclamation, resentments turnin' Ash,
return an' being,
individuation, self confrontation
LIBERATION

Tania Rose's comments on DRUM & CONCORD

Tania Rose was a member of both the Race Relations Board and the Commission for Racial Equality, as well as Secretary for Drum & Concord.

Cy Grant's opinion of the Race Relations Board and its successor, the Commission for Racial Equality, is typical of the low esteem in which both bodies have been held ever since the first Race Relations Act was passed in 1965. The law has pleased nobody, neither the majority community nor the minority racial groups it was intended to protect. The three original Acts (1965, 1968 and 1976) specify that it is unlawful to treat any person 'on the grounds of colour, race or ethnic or national origin' less favourably, in any situation to which the law applies, than other persons would be treated. The situations to which the law applies were progressively spelled out, as the law was amended to deal with evidence of discrimination in fields not already covered by it. These situations referred overwhelmingly to discrimination in employment, housing, and access to public services or places of public resort.. The 1968 Act also provided that the newly-created Commission might be allowed to give financial assistance 'to any legal organisations appearing to the Commission to be concerned with community relations.' But neither the law nor the body set up to secure compliance with it, were originally seen as funding organisations, let alone arts funding organisations.

The suggestion actually came from a member (at the time) of the staff of the Arts Council, Chris Cooper: that here was an opening which might be exploited by the Commission for Racial Equality for the purpose of securing public funding for organisations concerned with the arts of ethnic minorities. As Cy Grant has pointed out, the first hurdle was to persuade funding bodies that their embedded policy of only funding 'professional' artists, in whatever medium, did in effect discriminate against artists from ethnic minorities. The next objective was to set about putting the latter into touch with local and regional arts funding organisations. The Commission organised a series of meetings throughout the country, between local authorities, regional arts associations, community relations officers and the local artists. This took the better part of a year, but by the time of the formation of Concord, enough contacts had been established to make the organisation and funding of the Concord festivals a feasible proposition.

Drum had been an idea ahead of its time. The importance of establishing and maintaining artistic identities, for all the reasons set out by Cy Grant, was then hardly understood. Indeed the Race Relations Board, under the 1971 Act, was concerned that a complaint might be brought against any organisation which was based on membership of a racial minority. The factor which made the difference was simple: communication.

References

Patterns of Dominance; Philip Mason: Oxford University Press, 1970

Return To My Native Land; Aimé Césaire, trans. John Berger/Anna Bostock: Penguin, 1969

Black Orpheus; Jean Paul Sartre, trans. S.W. Allen: Presence Africaine

Chapter 5 – Concord

The undiscovered vein within us is a living part of the psyche: classical Chinese philosophy named this the interior way "Tao", and likens it to a flow of water that moves irresistibly towards its goal. To rest in Tao fulfilment, wholeness, one's destination reached, one's mission done, the beginning, end, and perfect realisation of the meaning of existence innate in all things.

C.G.Jung:, The Development of Personality Collected Works vol 17
Routledge, Kegan, Paul

Despite the ground-breaking work of Drum, our efforts had been fraught with periods of great frustration and anger. At the time, the need to express my black identity had been paramount. Now I know that it had been a necessary stage of my personal development. How one reacts to racism or to anything for that matter, says a great deal about oneself. Much later I could see that, in a different context, my preoccupation with Drum could have been construed as separatist. Was this what Olivier had implied? Somehow I doubt it.

I am by nature an easy-going person with a great lust for life – music, books, sport, travel, friends, conversation. Suddenly my life had changed. What was all this about black identity, a black arts centre? People I thought to be friends had begun to avoid me, and work became more difficult to find. At the same time my own family were greeting me with knowing smiles when I took up meditation. 'He's at it again' – if it was not the Alexander technique it would be something else. I was more isolated than ever. Yet I was finding greater inner strength. I was moving away from anger. I had resigned from Drum, making my final statement on race and identity by performing the Cahier of Aimé Césaire.

Whilst on tour, the true meaning of the concept of *negritude* was slowly dawning on me. In some mysterious way it had prepared me for another book that I came across at the time, a book that would shape my philosophy on life. It was just as dense and difficult to understand as the Cahier had been. But I stuck with it; I felt as if I had been guided to it. With hindsight, I can see that this is how it has always been with me. I was being guided by something I did not understand, but the unfolding was making sense and giving me purpose in my life.

This new book was a slim volume on ancient Chinese wisdom, the *Tao Te Ching* by Lau Tzu, a contemporary of Confucius. The language was paradoxical and quite inaccessible at first but I could not put it down. I soon realised that the profundity of its philosophy was beyond anything I had known or could conceive – a new way of looking at reality and of making sense of our world. As I understood it, The Way, or wisdom of Nature, is natural law. Could there be links with Césaire's 'state of total belonging', and the Chinese concept of Tao? I was becoming aware of the great difference between the way the West and the ancient Chinese viewed nature; becoming increasingly conscious that the former was responsible for the state of the world today.

I immersed myself in the Tao completely, trying to make sense of the many translations, which differed so greatly from each other. This I understood was because of the inherent difficulties of translating Chinese anyway and the fact that many of the translations were not by Chinese. Chinese writing is ideogramic, that is, it consists of 'hieroglyphs' or pictograms allowing for a certain degree of abstraction and more freedom of interpretation. And therein lay the difficulty; the Tao Te Ching addresses itself to fundamental questions of existence, which all our western philosophies and religions do not seem to answer fully. Also the highly poetic nature of the writing encourages individual interpretation, and it is thus open to different levels of understanding. The very first line states that it is impossible for words to describe the indescribable. *'The Tao that can be spoken is not the eternal Tao'.*

It was a revolutionary approach to how we looked at reality; an alternative philosophy negating everything I thought I understood about the world about me; a way of being and of deep ecological concern. I was reminded of a saying that I had heard some years before when I had taken part in a Service organised by the fledgling Amnesty International on Human Rights Day, December 10th 1962, in the crypt of St. Martin's-in-the-Field. Amnesty had been set up the year before, the brain child of Peter Benenson, with the aim of defending freedom of speech, opinion and religion in all parts of the world and for the release of prisoners of conscience[11]. Benenson, a lawyer, had been inspired by an ancient Chinese saying "It's better to light a candle than to curse the darkness"[12].

It seemed that we were always cursing the darkness. The Tao te Ching seemed to confirm that things are not just what they seem; that duality, the dark and the light, the good and the evil, were only different aspects of each other; and that this understanding was the very nature of reality. Gradually I began to withdraw from confrontation without condoning what disturbed me. Instead of cursing the darkness around me – the constraints of the Western paradigm, its racism, division and dualism – I was beginning to find a new way of relating to the world about me. This idea prompted me to make my own paraphrase of certain chapters by first comparing seven different versions, (notably those of Gia-fu Feng and Arthur Whaley) and by reading as many authorities on Taoism as I could find. I found that all the translations differed widely from each other. Making my own version not only helped me to gain some valuable insights into this mysterious text but it changed my outlook on life. In 1980, I recorded (for the BBC World Service) a series of six short programmes based on 24 of the 81 chapters of the Tao. Having done a workshop with Gia-fu Feng, the great Taoist master, I had received his permission to use his work. The series was so successful it was repeated the following year. African animism and Chinese non-dualism seemed to gel in my consciousness.

When shortly afterward I was asked by a friend, Tania Rose (who had worked for both the Race Relations Board and the Commission for Racial Equality, and also had been secretary of the Drum Arts Centre), to direct a one-off event at the Commonwealth Institute, the opportunity presented itself for me to do something not just for the black community but for all communities in British society. A number of people concerned with community relations had discussed the idea of a performance which would reflect the wide variety of multicultural arts available in Britain within the course of a single generation. Sponsored by the Commission for Racial Equality and the Gulbenkian Foundation, "An Evening of Many Cultures" was presented to an invited audience of MPs from both sides of the House along with representatives from local authorities and regional arts associations.

It was not an easy operation as the Commonwealth Institute's theatre was not equipped for a good theatrical presentation. The stage was not very deep, the lighting was rudimentary, backstage facilities were limited, technical staff were inexperienced and worked to set hours and, to add to my apprehension, technical requirements for each group appearing had not been asked for until I had taken over and there was just a week before it would take place. All of this spelt disaster. I was very nervous.

But despite everything the evening went down pretty well and I immediately had the idea that similar events should be presented throughout the country. My work with Drum had been primarily to give black actors a chance to become more proficient by setting up workshops and to validate their own cultural identity. During the next few years it was becoming clear to me that all minorities in Britain needed to make their cultural identities explicit. I approached Tania Rose and Patrick Gilbert of the SPCK (Society for the Propagation of Christian Knowledge) with the idea of setting up an ad hoc committee to coordinate this kind of activity. Tania Rose had worked harder than anyone else in setting up the Drum Arts Centre. Barclay Price was to join us later. The support of these three people was incalculable in the next six years. We had the blessing of the All-Party Parliamentary Committee chaired by the Conservative MP Patrick Cormack. Originally called The Ethnic Arts Touring Committee, the project's name was changed to *Concord, A Festival Of Britain's Multi-cultural Arts*. The National Westminster Bank commissioned me to do a feasibility study.

My initial research led me to conclude that a number of cities would be interested in staging one-day festivals, although somewhat reluctantly, of artistic events and activities from ethnic minorities within their communities. Seven cities had either committed themselves to holding a festival or were considering one by the time the research ended in the spring of 1981. That same year The Concord Festival Trust was officially set up.

1981 also happened to be the year of a new wave of race riots in many of the inner cities in Britain. The causes for these riots can be traced to racism within society, the uncaring attitude of the government and local authorities, and low expectations of black students by teachers and educational authorities, which in turn resulted in low achievement; deprivation, frustration, unemployment and police harassment. These attitudes were (and still are) kept alive by some sectors of the press and are reflected in the behaviour of the police. They permeated the entire society; the legacy of colonialism and Empire. The findings of the McPherson Report in 1999, revealing the extent of institutional racism at the heart of our culture, would have been vigorously refuted in those days.

The government was later to make half-hearted attempts to deal with the problem. The appointments of Michael Heseltine and Lord Scarman to investigate were quite inadequate and did not address the real problem, which was racism. It was as if we had anticipated the frustrations within the black community, and provided, as it turned out, a timely and positive response to the prevailing 'law and order' measures that were proving consistently counter productive. [See The Scarman Report, 1981]

The new wave of riots taking place confirmed my belief that Concord had a very vital role to play. Race, like party politics and religions, connotes division and fragmentation – probably the root of all our human problems. Our differences should be a cause for celebration. Diversity is the essence of nature. One of the biggest challenges facing our society is not that we are in danger of being over-run by foreigners – St George, let us not forget, was an immigrant from Cappadocia – or that our culture will be swamped; but that we allow our differences to fragment and divide us. *'I rather think of human culture as a unitary whole'* said the German theologian, Alfred Jeremias, *'and its separate cultures but the dialects of one and the same language of the spirit.'*

Most of the people who belong to minorities within our society were British even before they settled here. Their children are British born. It is not only quite possible but quite common to be British even if one has taken no part whatever in the process of colonisation. Britain was by then a microcosm of the world and Concord's philosophy was that if we can live harmoniously together, then maybe we can become world leaders again, but this time by demonstrating a genuine concern for the future of our species, of the entire world, and to put it bluntly, for survival. We surely don't want to dominate like the dinosaurs and then disappear.

During the last two months of my research, I had been appearing at the Derby Playhouse in Tom Stoppard's *Night and Day*. Derby was quite close to Nottingham, where the first Concord Festival was due to take place at the Playhouse Theatre. Wyndham Heycock, Director of Leisure and Recreation for Nottinghamshire County Council had seen to that. He had been a friend of long standing – I had even acted as a reference for him when he had applied for the post at the County Council. He had attended the evening at the Commonwealth Institute and was one of the first members of the Concord Committee. And this, undoubtedly, was an important link in the chain of events that seems now to have been preordained.

That first Festival, held at the Nottingham Playhouse one Sunday in October 1981 was a resounding success. Looking back at the sequence of events that brought me to this point in my life, I can see that it all started on the night in the sixties when

I went to see Olivier's Othello. Leaving the theatre at the same time was the film actress Joan Collins, with whom I had appeared in the film *Sea Wife*. She was with her newly married husband, Anthony Newley, and she introduced us. He immediately asked me to audition for the musical, *The Roar of the Greasepaint, the Smell of the Crowd,* which he had written with Leslie Bricusse. A few days later I auditioned successfully and the show eventually opened at the Royal Opera House in Nottingham.

When years later I began rehearsals for that first Concord, I was a bit concerned at the very short time available for rehearsals - from 10am till 5.30pm with the show starting at 7.30 the same Sunday night. Sundays were the only days available for events outside the theatre's normal programme. That meant going through technical rehearsals (props, microphones, lighting) for a large number of individuals and groups who had never been in a professional theatre before, in a very limited amount of time. But as fate would have it, the theatre's chief technician turned out to be someone who had worked at the Theatre Royal when I was there ten years before. He could see the problem facing both of us – there could be no rearranging the lighting design that was in place for the show that was currently running. Unperturbed he smiled and took me up to the control box and began to bring up all the lighting states that were already plotted – for an American musical – and they were breath-taking. He told me that I could use as many of the states that I thought appropriate, as every one was programmed into a computer and was available at the touch of a button – I simply had to note the state I wanted for each act. As we flicked though the entire lighting design he took notes. He also said I could avail myself of the revolving stage which featured in the show. Needless to say, the result was sensational. Chris Cooper from the Arts Council had travelled up specially to see what we were about. He claimed that the hairs on his body stood on end; he could not imagine that a show of 'ethnic minority arts' could be so brilliantly produced, and in such a short period of time.

The next Concord Festival took place later in the year at the Birmingham Repertory Theatre. The night before I had phoned to find out about ticket sales. There was an embarrassed but reassuring voice at the other end – very few bookings, but not to worry. When I arrived the next morning, I was surprised to see the hive of activity in the foyer and all around me. The Regional Arts Association had been in charge of organising local foyer events and exhibitions. Local artists were turning up on time to set up stalls and exhibitions or in anticipation of technical rehearsals, which were to take place on stage in the Theatre. I worked all day as in Nottingham, putting the show together for the evening performance, and to my delight the Theatre was completely sold out!

BRMB, the local radio station, had given us financial support and their publicity obviously worked. They were so excited by the turn out that they proposed sponsoring another Concord in 1983, this time at the Alexandra Theatre. A local black activist, with no experience of theatre, objected to initiatives coming from London and even threatened to boycott the Festival at the Alexandra. In the event, the boycott never materialised but a huge, mostly black, audience did – another sell out.

There were also outstanding successes in other cities: at the Crucible Theatre in Sheffield, in 1983, 1984 and 1986; twice in Liverpool, at the Playhouse in l983 and for a week as part of the International Garden Festival in 1984! Concord also produced three evenings as part of Sadlers Wells' week long *Summer Arts Festival* in 1982. There were Festivals in Manchester (as part of the Manchester Festival), Coventry (as part of the Coventry Festival), Reading (as part of the Reading Festival), Cardiff, Brighton, Derby, Newcastle, Southampton, Walsall (for the National Federation of Community Festivals) and Leicester (as part of the Leicestershire Schools' Festival).

During its first four years there were twenty inner city Festivals. The programmes consisted in part of the best work available from local artists and groups as well as from artists of national renown. The evening performances were the culmination of a day of multi-cultural events – exhibitions, crafts, workshops, fashion shows, food stalls, Tai Chi, flower arrangement, hair plaiting, hand and face painting, reggae, steel bands, Bhangra dancing, poetry readings, African drumming, and what-have-you. They varied from city to city, each having its own unique flavour and relevance to their initiating communities.

Each Festival was organised by Concord in conjunction with local committees, the relevant Regional Arts Associations, Community Relations Officers, and the Local Authorities. Some times there was involvement by local Radio, as with BRMB in Birmingham. The idea was to produce well-staged, well-lit artistic events which showcased the culture of all minorities. Instead of being relegated to the margins and to the ghettos, these arts were to be seen and appreciated by all who cared to come along. The venues were the best theatres in each city.

With very few exceptions, all these Festivals attracted large audiences who were surprised and delighted. One of the problems I encountered in dealing with local arts organisations was that they tended to be bunkered away from the front, and out of touch with the communities they should have served. They tended not to interact effectively, or to collaborate, even when they commanded resources which, with concerted effort, could have maximised services to the community. Another problem is the questionable criteria used for funding minority arts. In the absence of adequate information about the arts of other cultures, there is often counter-productive 'tokenist' funding which tends to open the doors to the assertive but not necessarily the most talented, and causes rivalry induced by stress and grievance, even between different minority groups active in the arts.

By 1985, Concord had run out of funds. The Gulbenkian had funded us for the first three years. We had finally taken part in the Leicestershire Schools' Festival. The shows were brilliant, but audiences small. It was a mistake to have taken part in a Schools' Festival which ran for two whole weeks, as parents only went to see their own offspring, and Concord was not targeted at the general public. What did not help was that Concord's input took place on the last two days of the fortnight when everyone (it seemed) was rushing off to Skegness for the holidays! There was a strong feeling of disappointment, and I was beginning to think that Concord's innovative role was over. Without central funding the going had been pretty rough but our track record had been outstanding.

A month after the Leicester festival, I was invited by John Moat (the novelist, painter and poet who had set up the Arvon Centre for writing), to come to Devon to explore the possibility of doing a Concord in that County. He had come across a Concord brochure and had also been concerned at society's apparent conclusion that the issues behind in the race riots were purely those of law and order. Now, Devon was lily white, well more or less so – there was a small Chinese community in Plymouth – but the fact that racial minorities mostly gathered in inner cities did not mean they were any less citizens of the United Kingdom, any more than rural Devon was any less a part of multicultural Britain. Both John and I felt that culture was a reflection of every aspect of society's life, as much, as John put it, *'as in its methods of farming and health care as in its shops' signs and slaughter-houses, its religious beliefs, its music, theatre, dance and poetry'.*

We began to draft a blueprint for a week long festival to take place the following summer, and by the end of the meeting we realised that there was no way that the sort of festival we were planning could be contained within a week. We had no idea where the money would come from. John generated so much enthusiasm that we were both caught up in making it happen. We realised that if we appeared tentative we would convince no one, so for a month we would act as if it were all going to happen, and then assess what responses this conviction had achieved. We simply went for it.

Our first sounding was at the Beaford Centre. There we met Shirley Thomas who was in her last weeks as Programme Manager for the Centre. Not only did she have exceptional knowledge of the arts network in Devon, she was herself a Devonian who knew the County. She was becoming as excited as we were about the concept. She believed that the idea would only work if it could engage active response not just from the towns but from Devon's rural and village communities. In the absence of core funding it might be possible to finance such a festival by coordinating existing resources, harnessing existing energies, and by inviting organisers to write events into existing programmes.

This was a completely new way of working for me. But it was exciting and made a lot of sense. All we would need was to raise enough to pay someone to co-ordinate and make it all happen. Shirley? We dared not hope. But she was hooked by the magnitude of the challenge and by the 'disestablished' quality of our approach. John Moat promised that he would give the next six months of his time to the project. I knew I would be doing this for love. Both John and Shirley were inspirational people and in any case I loved Devon. Quite a few of the people I most respect live there.

We went to see Anthony Everitt, the Director of ACGB, but he was no help. I remember being interviewed by him at the Derby Playhouse (where I was appearing on stage) before he took up his first post as an arts administrator - he was to become the Director of East Midlands Arts. This was during my feasibility study for the Nat West. He had asked me then what guarantee did I have that my idea for setting up multicultural festivals would be successful! I had replied that I did not need guarantees – it was work that was urgently needed if we were to foster respect for the arts (and thereby for the people) of other cultures in Great Britain. He did not see that Concord could have been centrally funded. It was not a central initiative, after all. We should apply to the Regional Arts Associations for financial support for festivals in their areas.

Help was forthcoming though. The responses locally, almost without exception, were enthusiastic. In several significant fields, notably the arts and educational and religious organisations, it was as if the idea for a Concord in Devon provided an opportunity people were already looking for. By the end of the month we had secured enough funds to employ Shirley to act as co-ordinator and had secured indications from arts and educational funding bodies that they would be able to float a programme of performances, workshops and educational residences. We had been given reason by numerous contacts to suppose that virtually every subdivision of the blueprint had a chance of being realised.

By the end of March 1986, our programme was published. The festival was to last four months. The programme included not only the arts from other cultures but authentic, unrecognised local arts. As well as Art Centres, and local festivals (for example, the Dalton and Dowland Festival), the entire county was involved, from Dartington and the Exeter Museum to community organisations, schools, colleges, and churches. Exeter Cathedral held an inter-faith vigil 'The Quiet Flame' with Buddhist, Jewish, Jain, Christian, Islamic, Hindu, Taoist and Baha'i elements. The Theatre Royal events were the highlight and the theatre continued to include Concord Festival for some years after. What an accolade.

We seem to have involved all sections of the community, including people on the fringes of society: the young, the old, the unemployed. Tours were undertaken by local, national and international artists and these included a group of school children from the Tagore Santiniketan School in West Bengal, visiting England for the celebrations commemorating Tagore's birth (their school had links with Dartington); Joshikazu Iwamoto, Shakuhachi (based at Dartington); Youssou N'Dour et Les Super Etoiles De Dakar (courtesy of WOMAD); The Guo Brothers; Nahid Siddiqui, Kathak dancer, the Academy of Indian Dance; the Czuplak Ukranian Dance Company; Union Dance; The Taishen Chinese Theatre and Rumillajta. (The Ghana Dance Ensemble pulled out of the Sidmouth Folk Festival in protest over U.K/South Africa policy).

The extraordinary success of this Festival can be attributed to many things. Maybe the time was ripe for it to happen in Devon. But the main reason was that we had gelled into a unique team. John Moat is someone possessed of the highest imagination and integrity one could find in a person. His generosity and commitment were boundless. Shirley Thomas, was a charismatic and charming dynamo who knew the territory, and was equally as dedicated as John, once she had come aboard. It was a joy working with them. If only people in the arts were a bit more human, our arts would become more human. It was because we saw our roles as enabling that so much was achieved on such a minuscule budget and with so little time. We were a small informal team with considerable freedom of initiative that allowed almost all contacts, even in large bureaucratic organisations, to be explored on a largely personal level. In this way individuals armed with enthusiasm and setting their own conditions and deadlines could short-circuit the formality and built-in inertia of bureaucracy.

Maybe it was the 'disestablished' quality of the Concord approach that gave it its unexpected power and accounted for its success. The power of personal contact is that the response can be both excited and immediate, and both these are essential to the creative nature of the operation. Once these personal contacts have been established in different organisations, or within different departments of the same organisation, individuals can be introduced to one another on the strength of the one imaginative idea. I think that this is what John Moat saw and was able to inspire in both Shirley and myself. In this way an efficient, and in a sense subversive, net of excitement was created where the structure and hierarchy made no provision for contact.

This was a very powerful discovery. Working this way, any agency can uncover almost limitless creative potential simply by cross-fertilising existing energies and resources which would be circumscribed under ordinary conditions. For Concord in Devon this happened between arts and church bodies, social concerns and charities, and within administrative organisations. By the end it was hard to imagine any concern or group which could not have been drawn in some way. The permutations of possible co-operation were countless and included not just the obvious links - between educational and arts projects, for example - but between smaller groups and societies such as bell-ringers and individual schools for disturbed children. We were convinced that there still remained untapped in the community a vast potential for social harmony and integration.

If Concord had been successful it is because we had, I hoped, never sought to tell people what to do, but only to realize what they could do themselves. In theatres that many of them had never been inside, they found out what good production techniques and lighting could do. By providing workshop opportunities we challenged people to raise their standards. Time and again audiences leaving the theatres, the workshops or whatever, seemed not just surprised but delighted, even staggered by what they saw for the first time as part of the life around them

At the same time, I was also painfully aware that despite our success, the real issues - the acceptance of other cultures and the significance of their arts to contemporary society - did not come across or change attitudes. We had merely scratched the surface. It was fun, for a few months, to have all these exotic arts visiting rural Devon – the colour, the movement and the unaccustomed sounds. The deep relevance of what these could be saying about our most elitist and precious art forms was totally missed – that the arts of the minorities are not separate from life; that art can bring meaning and value to all our lives; that we were divorced from our arts, which no longer sustained and nourished our lives.

It was, notwithstanding, a wonderful experience and I could not imagine the logistics of such a festival coming together and working so well somewhere else. True, the formula was a simple one and might be adopted by arts organisations anywhere by maximising existing resources and creating networks, but to my great surprise I found myself involved in yet another county-wide festival the following year. Andrew Wood of the Prema Centre in the village of Uley in Gloucestershire and a friend of John Moat had seen what had been accomplished in Devon and invited me to do the same in his county. He was very persuasive. He himself would be heavily involved in all areas and he ran a brilliant operation at Prema. It is not true that lightning doesn't strike twice! This time it was even bigger, with an exceptional array of artists from all traditions and cultures. There were over one hundred events in the four months of the festival. But it did not quite match the almost magical quality of Devon. Devon had Dartington; the County Education Authority had taken an active interest; there had been involvement with the Museum in Exeter and of course there was the Theatre Royal in Plymouth. We did however manage to be involved in the Cheltenham Music Festival with a few events taking place in the Pittsfield Pump Room.

It was a different team this time around. Andrew and I got on extremely well and he managed to persuade Di Porter, from Bristol, to be our co-ordinator. Like Shirley in Devon, she was a dynamo and knew her patch. I was provided with office space at the Prema Centre (in the beautiful village of Uley in Gloucestershire). This time I was resolved that we would try to keep all the essential ingredients whilst sticking to the same simple formula. There was one change. Both Di and I knew that we had to be paid. The Commission for Racial Equality came up with the funds for the administration. But the time was just as short and everything was just as frantic as the year before. We had committed ourselves even before we knew that all the funds would be available. They were. Gloucester did not have a decent theatre and generally the arts were pretty dead there. The Education Authority was a bit half hearted, so our input into schools was disappointing. One third of the events took place at Prema, thus continuing Andrew Wood's exemplary artistic policy. Prema even hosted a two day conference: *Black Arts, White Institutions.*

After seven years of very hard graft with little remuneration, I decided that Concord had shown what could and should be done. The world is an allegory of creation. It is the one and the many, the paradox of matter and energy, of matter and spirit. Britain, without wishing it, has become an allegory of the world - a multicultural society - and Britain can learn something from the arts of these other cultures, which do not view art as being separate from life itself. They are intrinsically about value.

I was not sure that the message had come across. The media did not give us any meaningful coverage. They seemed to concentrate only on the riots, violence and negative news. But there was a particularly good review in The Listener by Gerald Kaufman (18 November 1982) for the festival held at the Northern College of Music in Manchester, and a brilliant one in Resurgence Magazine by Nick Stimson (No.103 1994). The Birmingham Post and Birmingham Evening Mail (Dec 1981), the Southampton Advertiser (April 1982) the Liverpool Echo (Aug 1983) and dance & ballet columnists of the Daily Telegraph, Sunday Times and the Morning Star (August 1982) also gave favourable reviews. The Gulbenkian Foundation published a full report on Concord in Devon, with photographs by James Ravillious (Stellar Press 1987). But the importance and significance of Concord's work went generally unnoticed by the British media.

Concord had pioneered a new interest in multicultural arts but not the lessons we can learn for the good of our society. A culture based on consumerism, competition and opportunism creates a materialistic and largely hedonistic society – a culture without value. Eclectic and superficial, it appropriates and devalues even those things which in themselves have value. Hence 'multiculturalism', essentially about cultural pluralism and respect for other cultures, is subsumed, trivialised and incorporated into the prevalent fashionable pseudo-culture.

So, too, the prevalent culture devalues as 'fads' any oppositional cultural trends, as for instance those towards holism, ecology, natural healing and reconciliation, ascribing its own superficial face-value image to them. The prevalent computer-designed, global TV culture imposes its own spiritual impoverishment on everything it encounters in an effort to perpetuate itself. The role of the arts has likewise been trivialised, as a consequence, for example, this country has lost its best theatrical director - Peter Brook. His work has been long acknowledged for its quality, yet his production of the *Mahabharata* could not find a home, even in London. His long sojourn in Africa showed an openness to the cultures of that continent and in his book *The Conference of the Birds*, John Heilpern traces Brook's quest for something he could not find in Europe.

Although Brook is hailed as an innovative theatrical genius his work has not changed the Eurocentric mould of the arts establishment. Despite the tame gesturing of the Arts Council (e.g. the 1980s report euphemistically titled *The Glory of the Garden,* purporting to celebrate our cultural diversity), the arts still reflect the overall cultural bias of British society.

On reflection I now see that Concord's work was a natural progression of my journey of self-discovery, which had begun with the setting up Drum in the seventies with John Mapondera. What came as a pleasant surprise was that very shortly after letting go of Concord, John Mapondera, then Head of the Zimbabwe Arts Foundation, contacted me. He wanted me to assist in putting together a festival in his country, organised by UNICEF to coincide with an International Conference on Children in Southern Africa. This could be an opportunity for reconciliation after our falling out over Drum. Somehow a bond was still intact, as were it seemed our objectives for the common good.

This was a major initiative involving many trips to Zimbabwe and one to UNICEF's headquarters in New York. Unfortunately, it turned out to be yet another stressful and only partially successful operation. I learned a lesson that would still haunt me years later. It is always difficult to pick up the pieces when the original organisers are failing to deliver or if the initiative was not your own in the first place. In this instance, not only did we have to deal with committees on either side of the globe, but we first had to persuade the Zimbabwean government to permit us to use the wonderful Chinese-built stadium for the event. It had only ever been used as a sporting venue even though it had every conceivable facility for staging an international event. The whole episode was fraught from the onset with people vying with each other for artistic and other control and I began to think that there must be other ways in which black people could work together to raise funds for starving African children. It should be possible, I thought, to mobilise black millionaires, sportsmen, musicians, entertainers, opera singers etc. throughout the Diaspora, encouraging them to donate a tiny percentage of their earnings to Save the Children in Africa, instead of relying on emotional appeals to the white community as Bob Geldof had done in 1986.

Shortly after that historic concert, I had myself visited Ethiopia in the hope of organising a reverse operation – a visit of Ethiopian artists, musicians and dancers to England to thank the world for its help and also to try to dispel the only image of that country of starving children with bloated bellies and outstretched begging hands. Before setting out I had been told by the Ethiopian Minister of Culture, a mutual friend of Graham Hancock, that Ethiopia had a rich cultural heritage in dance and music. Hancock's book *Under Ethiopian Skies* had made me aware of the country's ancient spiritual heritage both Christian and Muslim. In fact it was through Hancock that the trip was arranged. Despite the poverty I was amazed to see the long queues of ordinary people outside the Ras Theatre waiting to gain entry to the weekly show which comprised spectacular variety productions of music and dance interspersed with dramatic sketches.

This was during the oppressive rule of the Mengistu government, certainly not prepared to acknowledge the aid it received from the West but at the same time grasping the festival as an opportunity to promote tourism. They actually toured a small group of artists abroad a few years later, playing mainly to Ethiopians in exile.

By the end of the 1990s Britain still lagged behind America and Canada in acknowledging the contribution of their ethnic minorities. This was apparent when, in 1988, I attended a BAAA Conference in Washington DC. It was clear that the Arts Foundation in America was actively supporting and promoting the arts of all its cultures. Later that year I was to witness the well-organised (and well attended) 20th anniversary of Toronto's annual international festival. This led me to propose, as a then governor of the Commonwealth Institute in London, a similar programme of events in Britain which might serve to revitalise its flagging relevance. At a time when Britain was no longer a super power, its influence as a moral leader in world affairs could be demonstrated by an ongoing relationship with the former Commonwealth – and not just with Europe. In a letter to the editor which was published in the Independent on Monday 15 November 1993, I pointed out that Britain had always claimed to be guided by a set of values which had put it in the foreground of world affairs; and that this kind of leadership was still needed in a world beset by ethnic, tribal, cultural and religious divisions. Supporting the Commonwealth Institute would demonstrate an awareness of global concerns. Britain owed its past glory to the old commonwealth; and now it seemed to be saying that this was no longer relevant? Besides its role as an educational resource centre, the Institute was a symbol, not only to people in Britain, but to the member countries and the world in general, of Britain's commitment to achieving good relations worldwide. One way to demonstrate this might be to host an annual or bi-annual Festival of Commonwealth Arts, thus strengthening the bond between the two.

All along, I had been aware that the arts by themselves would not change attitudes which have developed over centuries. A radical change in the way we view national and global problems is absolutely necessary and this will only be achieved if there is radical change in our educational system. When, in 1987, the Arts Education for Multicultural Society (AEMS) project was set up, I had great hopes for it. I was invited to be a member of its National Steering Committee. AEMS attempted to bring a multicultural/antiracist approach into the whole area of curriculum development using the arts from other cultures as an entry point. I saw the work of AEMS as an important step forward because education should not be Eurocentric or geared solely to the demands of a materialistic, mono-culture. Multicultural studies, per se, may help change attitudes but they do not in themselves challenge the racism that, sadly, is inherent in European culture. An anti-racist education would be the best possible education, for not only would it confront issues like racism and ecology but could lead to a fundamental reappraisal of our perceptions and attitudes and to a true understanding of our interconnected world. It could reintroduce value into our lives and to a deeper form of knowledge showing the connections between race and ecology.

When, in the run up to the Millennium, proposals were being invited for the celebrations at the ill-fated Dome, John Moat contacted me, suggesting that the Concord formula for providing a focus for the celebrations might be welcomed. I agreed, especially as the theme for one of the areas in the Dome designated for performances and exhibitions had been given the title *Spirit at the Dome*. In due course, in early 1999, I submitted a proposal which drew attention to Concord's successful series of festivals throughout the eighties, as a creative response to the enduring, and generally unacknowledged, racial divisions and prejudice in our society which had found expression in widespread riots of the past and the current disturbing profile of the Stephen Lawrence affair.

Concord's vision would demonstrate how Britain existed already as a country vastly enriched by the cultural wealth of its assimilated ethnic minorities; a richness promoted not as some exotic import, but as a fully realised and integral part of the country's own expanding culture. Celebrating multicultural arts was for me synonymous with my idea of Unity in Diversity, and seemed to be a perfect way to express *Spirit at the Dome.* In this way it was possible to see Britain not pessimistically as a place with an insoluble racial problem, but flowering out of its chequered past as a place of unique and relevant opportunity in the world. Instead of faceting or fragmenting the country's religious/spiritual life by assigning individual shrines or spaces to the various religions, they could be united within the single sanctum or performance space in an unbroken programme of observance and performance: the space would be consecrated by all the contributing faiths, and so signify and enshrine an unfolding or new millennium national identity founded in this emerging consciousness of Unity in Diversity.

My thinking was that it would be relatively easy and economical to devise a programme representing participation by every one of the country's religious communities. A programme of inclusiveness: from cathedral choir to village hand bells, all forms of spiritual expression – music, dance, professionals, amateurs, children, the colours of pageant, appropriate respect for the feast days of any religion, the country's leading performers from every resident culture as well as towering performances from international virtuosi, choirs, groups. This bringing together of religion and the arts would in itself be an act of healing, and would underwrite the resolution of a nation reconciled to all its people, and to the future.

Sad to say the administrators lacked any vision of the magnitude of the proposal. Receipt of the proposal was acknowledged, but that was as far as it got, despite my efforts to meet and discuss it. This is a pattern that repeats itself and was more recently borne out when, in July 2004, I was invited by CRONEM (The Federal Centre for Research on Nationalism, Ethnicity and Multiculturalism) to give a paper at a seminar at the University of Surrey on Youth, Ethnic Identity and the Future of Multiculturalism in Europe. I decided to speak on multiculturalism as I had long experience of how it is interpreted. The title of my paper was *Beyond the Jargon: Redefining Multiculturalism.* I was aware that it would be raising questions beyond a purely academic remit; aimed precisely at a Western ideology that seems to have less and less space for such topics.

CRONEM's policy statement had stipulated that a multi-disciplinary approach would be adopted in its research and I interpreted this to mean that not only would all faculties of the academy be called upon to contribute to the discussions but that global perspectives would also be brought to bear on them. We live in a multicultural world, which constitutes the very basis of human evolution and existence. Implicit in this is the need to take into account how other peoples in the world interpret their realities; in other words, the adoption of a holistic approach would be essential to the discussions.

I have always been concerned about the fragmentation that bedevils all of our systems of learning and epistemology. I am especially so these days with the breaking up of scientific knowledge into its constituent parts, so that what should enhance our perception actually obscures our view of the fundamental interconnectedness of all things. This, as you may have guessed, is the main argument of this book, writing as I do from the liminal space of outsider/insider, recounting my own journey through the minefield, or should I say, the *mind* field, associated with migration, ethnicity and multi-culturalism.

Having been involved in multiculturalism in practice, I felt the need to redefine the notion itself. The term is an increasingly problematic one, both for those on the Clapham omnibus and for theorists in the academy. For many, it is little more than the political expedient of an umbrella over peoples co-existing by limited cultural exchange. For others, its ultimate purpose lies in the true cross-cultural model that can lead to new ways of perceiving ourselves and of learning from other cultures. Too often, the ideas imbedded in the notion of multiculturalism are lost within the jargon surrounding theoretical constructions of ethnicity and hybridity. What we need to explore is the inter-culturality that does not exclude other cultures.

The paper stressed that there is a urgent need not only to define multiculturalism, but also what it is to be British. What was termed 'multiculturalism' is in fact part of an expanding culture flowering out of a chequered history and providing a unique and relevant opportunity to show that it is more than a political expedient, and can be a model based on a spiritual understanding of the universe. We need to cut across all conventional categories and realise the potential for unity in diversity not only in Britain, but throughout the so-called 'civilised' world.

The core concern should be less about integration *per se*, and more to do with a vision/version of community beyond globalisation, in which all things are connected; man and nature, earth and cosmos; a notion curiously confirmed by recent scientific discoveries that human beings, animals and plants all share the same DNA code. An interconnectedness proposed, as we shall see, by the theoretical physicist, David Bohm, in his book *Wholeness and the Implicate Order* – a holographic view of the universe and one of which many scientists are also becoming aware. We, too, need to inculcate this *interconnectedness* in our outlook.

It seems that the West as a whole is driven by a rationality that destroys balance, that the duality inherent in any balanced system is replaced by a dualism that results only in elemental discord. This is a subject I explore more fully in Chapter 11 (The Seven Pillars of the Prevailing Paradigm), and which points toward the need to rediscover and develop ancient societal models which cut across all conventional categories in order to realise the potential for unity in diversity.

Our world view creates our reality – how we perceive things. If we see division we get division. If we see our culture as the only one that matters we do not see the whole picture – that we live in a holistic world. This is what I had tried to challenge with the Concord festivals. In order to realise a world without fragmentation and confrontation, and to ensure the very survival of our planet and all species, we will require radical reconstruction of the way in which we make our reality; to first look out of Europe to ancient cultural practices which may inform our own situation and allow us to view multiculturalism in a new light and so reclaim the ability to go beyond meaningless, debatable categories.

What do we mean by culture? According to the Shorter Oxford Dictionary: '*it is the training and refinement of mind, tastes and manners; the condition of being thus trained and refined; the intellectual side of civilisation* – *acquainting ourselves of the best that is known and said in the* world; i.e. not only in Europe. The Penguin English Dictionary defines it as a '*state of intellectual, artistic and social development of a group, type and degree of civilisation'*.

The fact is that cultures are not static. They change or evolve as everything else in creation does. Similarly, ethnicity, as we know it, is socially produced. We need to challenge the idea that ethnic identity claims are inescapable and unequivocal, i.e. historically determined and irreversible. Just as there are no pure cultures, so there are no pure races biologically. This question is dealt with in the next chapter.

A former head of the Commission for Racial Equality, Sir Herman Ousley, pointed out in a recent article in the Guardian newspaper, that the word *multiculturalism* has been *hijacked* to serve the agendas of the scare-mongering racist media. This was indeed a strong indictment of the situation in which we find ourselves. Nevertheless, I believe that this issue must be discussed within the framework of the existing paradigm here in the West – the endemic racism that is a *de facto* element in the equation involving native and immigrant.

The present incumbent at the CRC, Trevor Phillips, rightly considers that multiculturalism is '*in danger of being a slight of hand in which ethnic minorities are distracted by tokens of recognition, while being excluded from the real business. The smile of recognition has turned into a rictus grin on the face of institutional racism'.* [The Guardian 28 May 2004]

For him the ideal would be one nation, many faces: '*integration only works if it both recognises newcomers' differences and extends complete equality. Celebrating diversity but ignoring inequality inevitably leads to the nightmare of entrenched segregation… the equality of the ghetto is no equality at all.'*

In other words, multiculturalism should not be about integration but about cultural plurality – to learn and benefit from its diversity. It is not about separation but about respect and the deepening awareness of Unity in Diversity. What is required is an *integrative capacity* that can pave the way for a better understanding of the *basic commonality that exists in all multiplicity*, a wholeness within an implicate order of interconnectedness. It is time to move on to confront the real dangers of racism, discrimination and fanaticism.

Any interpretation of multiculturalism is fraught with difficulties. I have pleaded on behalf of diversity, on behalf of the globalisation of spirit above matter, that any concept of multiculturalism worth its salt can only be understood within a holographic, non-dual paradigm. But its implementation will not be easy. It would require a multi-disciplinary, multi-dimensional ethic which may be impossible to achieve. Each culture would maintain its own intrinsic value and at the same time be expected to contribute to the benefit of society as a whole in some way (an extrinsic value). But this does not mean that all cultures can contribute equally to the overall well-being of a predominantly secular state.

Today, we may agree theoretically (politically correctly?) that we all have the same intrinsic rights to certain freedoms, but that does not mean to say that we are all *equal* in all respects. Some of us are better musicians, for instance; or thinkers or whatever. Some of us may aspire to creating a more caring, spiritual dimension in our lives, something that the dominant culture has rejected. My point is that qualitative differences that may contribute to the good of the whole society may be rejected out of hand by the host culture as irrelevant; a clash between different perceptions of reality.

It would appear that the concept of an ideal multicultural society would be almost impossible to achieve, for how can one expect a predominantly secular society to understand a wider holistic concept which would embrace the rights of all individuals making up society, and at the same time take on the responsibilities that those rights demand, for instance, in the case of a culture with an inward looking, separatist religion (a culture with a fundamental qualitative difference). For although it has an intrinsic value, and so intrinsic rights, nevertheless, this religion may not be contributing to the overall benefit of society.

A case in point is the Muslim concept of personal law; how can this be accommodated within the overall common law of the present legal system? It is, as I've already said, a matter not of integration or of accommodation but one of negotiation. But first we need to develop a global perspective – to move from hybridity to heterosis; to a tolerant inclusive ideology that does not preclude a spiritual understanding of the universe; that everything is connected, that balance can resolve what has been seen as the clash of civilisations and the apparent duality of all existence, so leading to unity in diversity.

What is needed is a re-evaluation of how we interpret our diverse multicultural world. Multiculturalism, properly interpreted, can provide a model that can accommodate diversity of all kinds – cultural, philosophical and religious, so that we can create a world without conflict and strife. Britain, because of the lessons of Empire, is ideally placed to assume this role of accommodation and concern for all peoples, for our planet and indeed for our survival.

As with my proposal for a Millennium Concord my paper was received with polite incomprehension. The root of this cultural intransigence will be discussed in the next chapter, *Roots, Genes and Language.*

Part 2

Eurocentrism

Chapter 6 – Roots, Genes & Language

Who are we and what?
Admirable question.

Aimé Césaire

Alex Haley's book, *Roots*, was made into a long television series, shown in the United States in the early 70s during a long and severe winter when the whole country was snow bound. It gripped the imagination of the entire nation, black and white, as it watched the gruesome history of slavery unfold before its very eyes. For the first time Americans were able to understand the true barbarity of slavery – what it had inflicted on blacks and even more, the guilt of whites in the wake of the holocaust. It made it quite clear that racism was responsible for the shameful trade in human beings as slaves and that it was still the *root* cause of the angst and disaffection that had led to the rioting and revolt of the previous decade. It showed that slaves had been mere chattels to be traded - indispensable to producers of crops and raw materials for the triangular trade: manufactured goods were shipped from Europe to Africa in order to buy more slaves, who were then shipped on the *middle passage* as cheap labour to the Caribbean and the Americas, the product of their labour (sugar, cotton, tobacco) being shipped back to Europe thus completing the triangle.

For black people, wherever they were, watching the series was a history lesson that had never before been so powerfully brought home to them. It was easy for them to deduce that the Christian church had condoned this traffic in human souls, pronouncing that slaves were not fully human. Elements of this belief already existed in Christian thought, as evidenced by the holy wars against the infidels and the treatment of the Jews. Applied to the dark races, the descendants of Ham, these elements had taken on a new and all-pervasive dimension. Native peoples were seen as distinctly inferior, put here on earth to serve the white races, at the same time providing millions of heathen souls to be saved for the greater glory of God. Haley had done a symbolic service for all black people interested in their roots. We learned a great deal about Africa, its customs and its culture - traditions from which we could draw pride.

Whilst the early 20th century saw Indigenism in Haiti and Negrismo in Cuba, the first *international* assertion of Black Pride was by a group of black French students and intellectuals in 1920s Paris and their ideas soon spread to America. The movement grew out of the writings of the distinguished black psychiatrist, Franz Fanon from Martinique and was a great influence on Aimé Césaire with whom I was so familiar. But as a young man I never felt any urge to try and trace my ancestry, part in Africa, part in Europe and part in Asia, back to its roots. I never subscribed to any feelings of inferiority; and despite a certain ambivalence about my diverse roots, it would have been well-nigh impossible to trace them back through three continents and as many centuries. Where would one start? In which country or continent? It would be a most complex and soul-searching journey raising fundamental questions about who we all are and whence we came. The difficulty can be exemplified by an encounter I had whilst on a tour of music societies in Scotland. I had been entertained by the Laird of the Grant Clan who graciously treated me as a member of the family, or so it seemed. A beautiful meal was followed by a tour of the great House with its many portraits of famous ancestors. I had asked my host about the origins of the Clan. He said that the name was derived from the 'de Grands' from southern Spain. That was a surprising answer to say the least. I knew that there had always been some controversy about the origins of the Clan, but no one had ever suggested a Spanish connection. There had been consensus, though, that there was a common ancestor by the name of Gregor Mor McGregor; and that the Grants and McGregors were branches of the same Clan. But the middle name of that common ancestor was prompting bizarre speculations. Could there be a connection between the Moors of North Africa and the 'de Grands' of southern Spain, between Scottish Lairds and commoners and emigrants to the Caribbean and back again?

The head of the Clan had mentioned that many Grants had emigrated to the colonies and may have intermarried. He did not seem to know that the slaves on plantations were the property of the slave owner and bore his name, as did the plebs in the ancient homeland. As a recent TV programme, *Motherlands,* has shown through DNA analysis, while many of us still do not appreciate how complex are the genetic journeys of the human tribe, it is clear that over the centuries European and African ancestry have become greatly intertwined. I should make it clear that these speculations have nothing to do with my particular interest in tracing my ancestors, African or European, but they do illustrate how a climate of ignorance and a lack of curiosity underpinned society at that time.

'Roots' was shown in England about the time I was setting up Drum. In the book, Haley tells us, he had very little to go on. He had learned a few stories about his family from his grandmother who had learned them from her mother, who had in turn had learned them from her mother. In his case, the oral tradition inherited from Africa was very strong. How this eventually led to him actually tracing his family in Africa is a remarkable story of persistence and chance. It must be acknowledged though that some of the descriptions of African customs in the book had reminded me of passages from Harold Courlander's *The African,* which I had read a few years earlier. Later, I understand, Haley had been accused of plagiarism. This, however, did not affect the impact it had made on readers of the book and for those who saw it on TV.

As a journalist, Haley had been sent over to England to interview the rising young British film actress Julie Christie. I remember this story well because a few years before, I had found myself 'chained' to the lovely Miss Christie on the inaugural Amnesty International Service in the Crypt of St. Martins-in-the-Field on Human Rights Day, 1962. At the time, the actress was just out of Drama School and completely unknown. As Miss Christie was filming at the time he was only able to interview her whenever she was available, and he found that he had lots of time on his hands. He did what a great many of us would do in similar circumstances. He took himself off to the British Museum. There he saw the Rosetta stone. He had read how Jean Champollion, the French scholar, had matched the unknown with the known characters on the stone and had finally been able to prove that the demotic and the hieroglyphics had the same text as the Greek. On the plane back to America, the idea came to him that maybe the few facts he knew about his family history could be matched with the unknown facts, to trace his ancestry back to Africa. It must have appeared a daunting proposition, but with dogged perseverance and by a chain of chance, circumstance and coincidence, he succeeded in a most spectacular manner.

I have always been fascinated by coincidences or synchronicities (that strange sequence of events that link past and present) that link people and more especially cultures. Very few of us know or care to admit, for instance, that Greek philosophy once traced its roots directly back to Pythagoras and his secret society[13]. The Greek philosopher had studied for twenty-one years in Egypt and has been acclaimed by some as 'the presiding genius of Western culture and the originator of so many of its guiding principles'[14]. There are also many Greek legends about Egyptian colonists under Danaos, occupying parts of Greece. Nevertheless European culture only traces *its* roots back as far as ancient Greece. The English scholar, Martin Bernal, goes even further claiming in his controversial work, *Black Athena*, that the *roots* of classical civilisation are Afro-asiatic – that Athena, the patron saint of Athens, is of Egyptian origin, a point, Richard Poe tells us, that has been corroborated by none other that Plato in his Timaeus. [*Black Spark White Fire*, p121]

Bernal undertook his massive project only after he had stumbled on the fact that as many as twenty to twenty-five percent of Greek words have Egyptian roots; and even more surprising, that only fifty percent of the Greek language was of European origin. Is also quite significant that Herodotus, the Greek historian, known as the father of history, had stated that the Egyptians were black. However you might want to interpret that, it is clear that what he was saying was that the Egyptians were not European. As Bernal points out, for the past two centuries European scholars have had problems with this for obvious reasons: Egypt had somehow to be disassociated from Africa, however disingenuous the claim. Europeans can include people from countries as far apart as Scandinavian and the Mediterranean, but apparently this reasoning does not apply to people born on the continent of Africa.

Richard Poe concurs with the black American bio-anthropologist, Shomarka Keita who rebuts the anti-Afrocentristic claims in Arthur Schlesinger's book, *The Disuniting of America*. '*If Europeans, with all their warring tribes and cultures, could be regarded as a single people sharing a common heritage, then why should Africans not likewise be entitled to a common cultural identity?*' He went on to show '*that large portions of Egyptian culture can be traced back to the heart of Africa, as Diodoros maintained*', for example, the belief that the Pharaohs as well as other

African monarchs were able to control the forces of Nature; the cult of the dead, mummification and ancestral worship; the reverence of animal gods in religious cults; along with similarities in art and sculpture.

The recent discovery of a 5,500 year old mummy of a black child (named Uan Muhuggiag after the rock shelter in the central Sahara where it was found), challenges the idea that the Egyptians were the first to mummify their dead. It has led to further archaeological and other research[15] which has revealed that the first advanced civilisation in Africa was not Egyptian. Black Pharaohs had ruled for long periods of time not only in Egypt but also in Nubia; both countries shared the same royal insignia, such as the serekh, the White Crown, falcons and rosettes. In fact it now seems that black Nubia may well have been the very first country in history to have developed a monarchy, a precursor to the Western model. [Bruce Williams, Archaeology Sept/Oct 1980 & cited in The Incense Burner, Black Spark, White Fire]. Yet even today, the obvious links between Egypt and Nubia are still unacknowledged by scholars reluctant to discard what orthodox versions of history had instilled into them – that Egypt was not part of Africa and that Egyptians are not Africans.

Even more to the point are the linguistic roots of the Hamito-Semitic languages. The linguist Joseph Greenberg was to show, in the middle of the last century, that this language family was quintessentially African, with five distinct branches, four of which were to be found exclusively in Africa. The fifth, Semitic, although found in the Middle East, included others in Africa. He was to rename the language family Afroasiatic, a term retained by Martin Bernal in *Black Athena*.

As we have noted, then, misconceptions abound about nearly everything about Africa, the so-called Dark Continent. It has turned out that ancient Egypt, an African country, was the bringer of culture – music, literature, science, agriculture and ritual; that if we all were able to trace our human ancestral tree far enough back, we would find that our roots and genes are on that continent. Recent research in the field of molecular biology suggests that we are all directly linked through maternal genes to an African great grandmother, a Mitochondrial Eve, who lived 200,000 years ago. Yet, throughout the history of living memory, it seems that human communities have tended to see themselves as different from others, with tribal notions of superiority or uniqueness. Racialism, or prejudiced beliefs and behaviour, is not a modern European invention. The Japanese considered themselves vastly superior to Europeans, and both the Japanese and the Chinese saw themselves as superior to other races. In Africa and in India, tribal and caste distinctions blight the lives of many of their peoples, just as class and colour distinctions had led to violence in the country of my birth.

When an ethos of 'racial' superiority determines the very way a society is organised, this is known as *racism* and it cannot be justified on any grounds. The human suffering resulting from racism through the ages ranges from the atrocities of the slave trade to the genocide of the North American Indians, the Aztecs of Mexico, the Incas of Peru, the Caribs and Arawaks of the Caribbean, the Australian aborigines, the Bushmen of the Kalahari and the Jews at the hands of the Nazis in the last century. This is not an exhaustive list. The abuse, discrimination, social injustice, psychological damage and schizophrenia suffered mostly by non-white people everywhere, is a serious indictment of the West. A victim of racism is humiliated and deprived of his or her basic self-esteem and human dignity, if not their very lives.

The categorisation of human beings into racial species has given substance to racist theories. Despite the efforts of people like the American psychologist, Arthur Jensen, the French Count de Gobineau (*The Inequality of the Human Races*, 1853), the British archaeologist Colin Renfrew, Carleton Putman, Elliot Smith and Adolph Hitler to show biological determinism, there is no scientific evidence to support the racist classification of peoples. The myth of inherent white supremacy, in other words the genetics of race, has now been biologically discredited - all humans derive from a common stock starting in Africa and constituting a genetic continuum. Genetically there are few real differences between human races. It is now the view of most modern geneticists that human beings are a homogeneous species. (Reith Lectures 1991, Dr Steve Jones, BBC Radio 4, 1992). All theories which support differences in ability have now been completely discredited, and when applied to differences in intelligence they appear quite contemptible, deriving from a Eurocentric world view which is fundamentally flawed and, as we shall see, racism and the domination of nature are two sides of the same coin. Although it is no longer politically correct to speak of race as a scientific concept, *'biologically determinant ideas live on – race and racism are virulently alive in cultural and political reality'.* (UNESCO 1950)

As we have seen, this is amply illustrated by the ongoing dispute about Egypt and Africa. Egypt was a melting pot of races, from black to any Mediterranean shade of colouring. In *Black Spark, White Fire*, Richard Poe, exposes 'the myth of the pure race' as proposed by so many champions of this Master Race theory, claiming that it violates not only the evidence of history, but 'one of the core principles of modern genetics' known as *heterosis*, proposed by Luigi Luca Cavalli-Sforza, Professor Emeritus of Human Genetics at Stanford University, California. Cavalli-Sforza has been one of the most important figures in post-war studies of genetic diversity and the evolution of biological (or genetic) and cultural diversity in their most general sense. His theory is that *'when widely different gene pools are crossed – whether among people, plants, or animals – the hybrid offspring often turn out to be healthier, stronger, larger, or otherwise better developed than either parent',* a phenomenon known as 'heterosis', or 'hybrid vigour'. His scientific refutations of racism go back a long way, dismantling the determinist explanations for ethnically-based disparities in IQ scores, and suggesting that racist research should not be publicly funded. He shows that race and racism are destructive fallacies and that what is needed is a multi-disciplinary approach to anthropology; research that is collaborative on questions involving ethics, race, language and culture – in other words, an holistic approach. He believes that *'mixed marriages including those between people of very different origins* (incidentally, like my own and my parents before me and those of my own children), *create a more robust line of descendants'*.

Poe argues convincingly that when adapted to the domain of human psychology, this phenomenon may well have played the crucial role in the *'joining of the peoples of Europe, Africa and Asia in a melting pot of unusual size and richness'* within the Mediterranean basin, where Greece benefited most from Egypt. This African/Egyptian influence on Greece underpinned by the scientific fact that human beings *'need diversity to thrive'* had led directly to the greatness of ancient Hellenic culture from which Europeans naively claim lineage, resulting in intellectual and technological prowess, without acknowledging the Afro-asiatic influence on Greece itself. But he is at pains to point out that it is not just *biological* heterosis, but a kind of heterosis of the mind that accounted for this phenomenon. *'The peoples of the Mediterranean traded cultures, religions and ideas'* - a significant reason why so many civilisations flourished in the area whilst Europe was still uncivilised. He cites Cyrus Gordon's interpretation of the phenomenon as 'international stimulation', which proposes that *'all highly technologically developed civilisations are the result of international stimulation so that all of them are connected by what they have learned from each other.'*

Gordon held that 'cultural flowering' was the result of the melting pot of cultures. He believed that no people were pure racially or linguistically. *'Creative peoples, and the languages they speak, are the results of felicitous combinations.'* It is a theory that can account for the unique vitality and supremacy of ancient Egyptian civilisation. Today few Egyptologists deny that there had been black Pharaohs, yet Egyptians generally do not consider themselves to be 'black' Africans. As someone from the Caribbean, a region of great heterosis, I think I understand why. I myself had never considered myself black when I was growing up in British Guyana. I had to come to Britain to rediscover my blackness. How ignorant and confused we can be when we succumb to the categorisations that the West has imposed on us! I remember when I visited Egypt in 1997, that our official guide, a well educated Egyptian with great charm and in-depth knowledge of the history of Ancient Egypt, had confided in me that he imagined that his father, who died when he was a boy, would look exactly as I did if he were alive today. I was not in the least surprised, as all around me I could see that Egyptians were as mixed as the people of the Caribbean – they come in all shades. Were it not for the camera around my neck, as I strolled around the Cairo Museum, Karnak, the Valley of the Kings, the Sphinx and the Great Pyramid, I might easily have been mistaken for an Egyptian myself.

The psychological phenomenon of 'mental heterosis' or 'international stimulation' supports my championing of the theory of 'unity in diversity', a subject that is central to an understanding of the cross-cultural awareness that is needed in all human affairs. The Caribbean area, like countries neighbouring the Mediterranean Sea, is one where cultures and peoples have collided. It is an area of hybrid vigour of *genetic and cultural stimulation,* the result of the convergence of diverse groups of peoples that migrated there voluntarily or otherwise - a concept explored in his many books by the Guyanese writer Wilson Harris (see, for example, his first and best known novel, *Palace of the Peacock*). This 'collision of cultures' may explain the extraordinary virility of the Caribbean area which has proved such a potent force in European literature (Gabriel Garcia Marquez, Jean Carpentier, Nicolas Guillen, Aimé Césaire, CLR James, Derek Walcott) as well as producing earth-shaking revolutionaries who ushered in the demise of empires (people such as Simon Bolivar, Toussaint L'Ouverture, Frantz Fanon, Jose Marti, Che Guevera, Stokeley Carmichael, and George Padmore).

In tracing his own ancestry, Haley had also been tracing the continuity of African people, fully aware that nothing could assuage what had happened to them throughout the Diaspora. Many black writers and scholars not only from the Caribbean but from Africa, and America, were also writing about their experience, and there is now an impressive array of literature in English by authors from both continents, writers of the stature of Ngugi Wa Thiongo, Chieikh Anta Diop, Chinua Achebe, Wole Soyinka, Leopold Senghor, James Baldwin and Ralph Ellison, as well as translations from the French of the work of black writers. Today their contribution to world literature has been widely acknowledged. Quite a few have received high literary awards – Derek Walcott, the West Indian poet, the Nobel Prize for Literature 1992, Wole Soyinka, the Nigerian writer and playwright, also Nobel laureate of 1987; Leopold Senghor of Senegal was honoured for his services to the French language by being made an honorary member of the French Academy; and Chinua Achebe was invited to give the South Bank lecture in 1990.

Also, a new generation of white historians and scholars was becoming increasingly critical of versions of European history (Christopher Hill, Basil Davidson, Martin Bernal, Richard Poe). Books on other cultures, and civilisations and systems of knowledge were proliferating, amongst them books on the new physics and the nature of reality itself. I immersed myself in trying to put what I had learned in school into some sort of perspective.

In the 1960s I had been a member of CARD (The Campaign against Racial Discrimination) and very aware of the racial tension in Britain since the docking of the Empire Windrush at Tilbury in 1948. At one such meeting at the West Indian Students Centre in Earls Court, Malcolm X had looked in briefly, probably to assess the British black response to racism in Britain. He stood at the back of the crowded room and I do not think many people attending were aware of his presence. But I had read Alex Haley's '*Auto-biography*' and had been vastly impressed. When in 1968 Enoch Powell made his racist remarks, every one of us in the black community felt threatened. When the dockers marched in support of him, I found myself walking in the front row of a counter march organised by CARD to hand in a letter at No.10 Downing Street. Powell's speech was to galvanise me into reassessing my entire life and provided the impetus that eventually led to the writing of this book.

Mine has been an attempt to synchronise what I have learned from many writers and thinkers with my own experiences. It is not a biography in the usual sense of the word, but an account of the salient factors and concepts which have determined how my ideas have developed, shaping my attitude to things and the decisions I have made along the way.

One early conclusion was that the roots of racism are located not only in our history but in our language. Just as racism and exploitation are synonymous, so is language synonymous with culture. The Kenyan writer, Ngugi Wa Thiongo, unequivocally states that: *'Language as culture is the collective memory bank of a people's experience in history. Culture is almost indistinguishable from the language that makes possible its genesis, growth, banking, articulation and indeed its transmission from one generation to the next.'* He showed how the imposition of European languages and 'values' affected the colonised: 'native' languages were forbidden to be spoken in schools throughout the colonies. He recalls the traumas of his school days. *'There was often not the slightest relationship between the child's written world, which was also the language of his schooling, and the world of his immediate environment in the family and the community... Europe was the centre of the Universe'*; the colonial language, the 'carrier of culture' even when this culture dictated that you snitched on your class mate if he spoke in his native Gikuyu during school time! *'We who went through the school system were meant to graduate with a hatred of the people and the culture and the values of the language of our daily humiliation and punishment'.*

This policy was the same meted out by the Americans to the native Americans, and by the Australians to the ancient Aborigines. When a people's language and culture (the collective memory bank of the nation) is destroyed, their very reason for living is destroyed. Hence the drunkenness resorted to by those people who had deep spiritual traditions of their own. Colonialism was a prescription for loss of soul and for genocide. This had also been the case with the Incas in the Andes, a people with a highly developed civilisation of co-operation and caring; a people with a knowledge of agriculture, irrigation and astronomy. Their loss of faith in themselves and their gods explains how they were so easily overcome by a few hundred conquistadors. Their whole internal landscape, their belief system, was destroyed, resulting in a complete loss of power, of spirit and of soul.

As Ngugi implies, identity is closely allied to language for all African writers. What language should the African use, his own or that of the European system of education under which he was brought up? Africa has over one thousand languages and has always had a rich oral tradition providing an accurate and continually updated historical record of the events in its past and of its beliefs. The tradition of the 'griot' was sacred and placed great attention on the transmission of these beliefs. The art of writing itself started in Africa, on the banks of the Nile in Egypt as, according to Herodotus, did geometry, the solar calendar, stone carving, medicine and astronomy.

Ngugi claimed that *'the choice of language... is central to a people's definition of themselves'.* By controlling which language a people use, their very souls are imprisoned. By deliberately denigrating a people's culture, their art, history and way of life, 'the mental universe of the colonised', is dominated. He does not believe that the language of African literature can be divorced from the social forces surrounding it. It is continuously engaged in the struggles against colonial and neo-colonial values, which still exist even in the newly independent African States. Because of colonialism, then, the question of which audience a writer should try to reach is of the utmost importance. He or she has a responsibility towards the masses of his or her people, to educate them and to reinforce their traditional values which colonialism had always attacked. Ngugi himself had established his own considerable reputation as a writer in English. His decision to write in future in Gikuyu was a political act of great significance. For him *the physical violence of the battlefield (had been) followed by the psychological violence of the classroom... (with the object of) making the conquest permanent... language (was used as) the means of spiritual subjugation'*. Unfortunately, the view that African Literature should only be written in an African language has been seen as subversive by the ruling classes, while paradoxically, African writers of English literature have been imprisoned for their political beliefs by African ruling classes.

Chinua Achebe has argued for his right to write in the language in which he was educated without betraying his essential Africanness. He said he had been given the language, English, and he intended to use it accepting *'the fatalistic logic of the unassailable position of English in our literature'*. That language was able *'to carry the weight of his African experience but it will have to be a new English, still in full communion with the ancestral home but altered to suit new African surroundings'*. By choosing to write in English he reaches a wider audience within his own country, Nigeria, where there are over two hundred languages. Ngugi, by choosing to write now in Gikuyu, (and having his books later translated into English) is reaching a wider audience amongst his own people, the Gikuyu. Both writers are highly aware of their African traditions and culture. Both attack colonial and neo-colonial values. The legacy of colonialism, of European languages and literature will continue to be the subject of severe soul searching not only by the colonised but perhaps also by the carriers of the culture.

The situation in the Caribbean for writers of African descent was somewhat different. Unlike Ngugi and Achebe, they had no other language in which to express themselves. They had to write in the language of a culture that had colonised and brutalised them. Yet, the Caribbean, as we have seen, is an area like the Mediterranean, of hybrid vigour and international stimulation. It has produced some of the greatest writers in European languages, who remarkably, were able to transform that language into something which, whilst retaining a quality quintessentially of the language, deals with a physical landscape beyond its collective memory. Derek Walcott's *Omeros* is a case in point, overlaying Classical Greece on the lives of West Indian fishermen. For these writers the issue is not only one of language but also of identity. The Barbadian poet, Edward Kamau Brathwaite, in searching for a language, a *voice,* to describe the Caribbean experience, said that *'the hurricane does not roar in pentameters'.* In his *History of the Voice,* he described how Caribbean writers employ the received language along with modified forms – *Creoles* – which are now viewed as languages in themselves – essentially African syntax with English vocabulary. The writers certainly never identified with the colonizer, except perhaps V S Naipaul who infamously claimed that the West Indies never produced anything of merit – and this statement must itself be unpicked for all the nuances embedded in the Caribbean psyche.

The West Indies is a melting pot of the races of mankind, from the European conquerors to the indigenous peoples and those taken there as slaves or as indentured labourers. As a result the world's gene pool is centered there, from Europe, Africa, Asia and The Levant to those already there. West Indians can be European, African, Indian, Chinese, Lebanese or Amerindian to any admixture of these in any variety of degrees. No two islands, no two territories, have the same racial composition. There exists no cultural allegiance which can lead to nationhood. In a sense it is a cradle of fertility – writers, cricketers, revolutionaries in a volcanic 'collision of cultures'; but politically there is no sense of unity. The possibility does exist, however, for West Indians, because of their unique composition, to transcend the slave mentality and view themselves positively by cultivating the strength that comes from unity in diversity. They must choose the best from all the world's cultures and create that 'new man' Césaire spoke about from all the cultures that have divided them.

I believe that it was Wittgenstein who said *'Our language determines our view of reality.'* If that is so, then not only do we live in a language trap but in a culture trap. Language gives us our linguistic self-awareness as well as our racial awareness and how we define ourselves and other people, excluding some. We are conditioned by our language and language is not innocent or transparent. Our view of reality is coloured by our cultural spectacles which reflect the culture, yes, but also mirror the mind.

Where does this leave someone in Britain who is black and whose only language is English? The letter I had written to The Times in 1973 was only one example of the dilemma I tried to address. Now it seems that my entire life has been a journey of enquiry. First the experience, becoming conscious of that experience, and finally, trying to know who and what I was. I had learned at an early age that the word black denoted everything that was bad. As a black person this was a very black scenario in which to find oneself. Flicking through any dictionary the definitions of blackness were the same: *sinister, wicked, dismal, sullen, portending trouble or difficulty; (of humour) morbid, cynical; (of goods etc.) banned by workers on strike from being handled by other trade-unionists; black magic, involving the invocation of devils; black mark of discredit, black market, illicit trade; black sheep, a discredited character in an otherwise well-behaved group; black propaganda, misinformation generated by our political opponents; and as a verb, to denigrate, as of character, to blacken, to blackball; black list, to reject etc. etc.*

It will not take a great deal of imagination to gauge the extent of the psychological damage which this one word causes to black school children even in present day Britain. Language as a social phenomenon not only affects the role and status of individuals and groups, socially and psychologically, but it reflects the very nature of the culture itself. Not only does it say everything about a culture, but unless understood as being part and parcel of that culture, it is likely to create deep psychological rifts within the culture itself, as deep as the rift it creates when it foists itself on other languages and on other cultures. In confronting the issue of cultural domination, Frantz Fanon, in *Black Skin, White Masks*, described the psychological and philosophical impact of colonialism on black people and how this deforms both black and white. *It forces the people it dominates to ask themselves the question constantly 'In reality, who am I?'* Fanon's book deals with the dilemma faced by blacks in a white culture. It also addresses the process of rediscovery or re-evaluation of the past leading them to confront the system that had exploited and degraded them. His most acclaimed book was *The Wretched of the Earth,* a searing critique of colonialism; it became the bible of the Black Power movement in America in the sixties. What happened on one side of the Atlantic always affects events on the other and the Civil Rights Movement in America certainly acted as a spur to black people in Britain. It challenged the racist diatribe of people like Enoch Powell and was directly responsible for me setting up Drum. It had forced me to look at my situation and the purpose of my life. Educated in the European tradition, I had once been a voracious reader of books mostly written by white authors. In the sixties my diet was to change completely; it became exclusively black, James Baldwin, Eldridge Cleaver, Ralph Elison – the list is unending. This was the time of black consciousness, of Martin Luther King and Malcolm X. Alex Haley's biography of the latter had been an inspiration. Now his *Roots* were reaching and spreading deep below the threshold of consciousness of both blacks and whites.

Martin Luther King's call was for a radically new kind of revolution – a change of heart, and a complete revision of Western values. He was aware that that all life is interconnected, that what we do to others we do to ourselves. He had written that *'In a real sense all life is inter-related. All persons are caught in an inescapable network of mutuality, tied in a single garment of destiny. Whatever affects one directly affects all indirectly. I can never be what I ought to be until you are what you ought to be, and you can never be what you ought to be until I am what I ought to be. This is the inter-related structure of reality.'*

Fanon's motto had been: *Make of me always a man who questions.* Both of these thinkers have inspired me, not least, as the Jamaican poet Mikey Smith said, to beware the cultural smuggler who will misappropriate Fanon's call to arms as a way of reversing and perpetuating cultural supremism.

The offspring of those who came to Britain on the Empire Windrush suffered the same dislocation in British schools as their parents had suffered in the colonies. Yet almost no one seems to seriously take on board where this situation might lead. The cultural deprivation and disenchantment of the youth coupled with the blatant racism and brutality of the police generated the most explosive resentment simmering behind the unconcerned face of British society, just waiting to be ignited in the early 1980s. In the 60s and 70s, John La Rose, the author and political activist, resisted the labelling of Caribbean school children as educationally sub-normal (ESN). Literacy in the Caribbean, at least in Guyana, was higher than in England, proof that it was the prejudice of society that vitiated against Caribbean school children.

When I had left Guyana all those years ago, because of the stultifying atmosphere that pervaded the colony, I had been too young and too close to them to know the extent of the problems facing the Caribbean. Later I had studied law in the hope that one day I would be in a position to make some small contribution. I had been pleased when there had been talk about federation and disgusted when this had failed. As an 'exile' in Britain, I had to explore questions of identity and of race. My love of the English language was natural; it was the only one I knew. But I see now that I had been trapped(?) within it. With time I was to realize that it is not only black people who are trapped by the English language. Everyone living within a culture is trapped by the language, for it reveals the tensions within the culture itself, the inherent ambivalences which undermine its very sanctity or authority. It can do so whilst projecting its values upon those unfortunate enough to be colonized by the carriers of the culture.

The question I am forced to consider is whether the West's apparent need to justify its anxieties about its past made it project them onto other cultures. I am forced to conclude that this is the direct result of racism which is itself the result of the culture. Africa, the Dark Continent, the land of the blacks, of Stygian ignorance, and without a history (Trevor Roper) but at the same time the victim of the most brutal exploitation and the prime source of Europe's wealth and power, is the ideal candidate. As Chinua Achebe notes in *Hopes and Impediments*, *'the West seems to suffer deep anxieties about the precariousness of its civilization and to have a need for constant reassurance by comparison with Africa'*. Be that as it may, I have tried to show how prescriptive and constrictive language can be and just how much it determines a group's view of reality, imposing limitations on its very systems of knowledge and of evaluating itself.

The Western world view may not be what is best for life on earth. European languages divide the observer from the observed, subject from object, creating a dualistic relationship of separation not found in cultures where consciousness is inclusive – a concept which is very difficult for us to grasp. Other cultures view things differently, for instance Chinese pictograms and the Egyptian system of hieroglyphs, which allow for a certain degree of abstraction when dealing with fundamental questions of reality. In South African languages there are no possessive pronouns. For example, the word *ubuntu* implies a person's identity as primarily of his community – *'I am because we are'* – very close to the sacred Hindu mantra *sohum 'I am because You are'*. [Resurgence #221, 2003 p13] and just the opposite to the Descartian dictum that enshrines Western thinking.

These are holistic concepts or *gestalts*, instead of linear systems. This is also the case with Native American languages. According to David Peat, their language was the doorway to their entire reality. *'To speak it is to enter into an alliance with the vibrations of the universe' (Blackfoot Physics)* – a universe imbued with meaning, a web connecting all living things; of co-operation with the spirits, a continuum with the ancestors and with mother nature. Peat was a friend of the English physicist, David Bohm, who believed that European noun-dominated languages lead to the present dominant world view. What was needed was a new language more adapted to his vision of wholeness and an implicate order – that is to *'a reality of enfolding and unfolding matter and thought'.*

Within Native American culture, thoughts are inseparable from language, which goes against Chomsky's claim that deep linguistic structures are embedded in the human brain irrespective of language; that languages are surface structures for expressing what is at a deeper level. According to David Peat, this is not how indigenous people see it; further, there is a striking resemblance between the language of quantum physics and that of the native American peoples. Maybe this explains why the philosophical implications of the New Physics have not changed the way we look at our ordinary reality. Wittgenstein[16] might have suspected something like this when he suggested that *'The sole remaining task for philosophy is the analysis of language!'* But thoughts are inseparable from language. The problem of science and philosophy is that they are both trapped within the boundaries of a limited language system. Philosophers, it seems to me, should not confine their field of inquiry only to an analysis of language but to how our language affects our view of reality.

For the Native Americans, as with most conquered peoples, the arrival of the Europeans brought about cultural disintegration and loss of soul. They were to claim that since the arrival of the Christians to their lands, the old woman who lived at the top of the burning mountain never visited them again to advise how to conduct their lives; echoing an African Elgonyi laibon, *'Since the whites were in Africa no one had dreams any more. Dreams were no longer needed because the English knew everything.'* [qd. C.G.Jung, *Memories, Dreams and Reflections.*] To pursue my dream, it seemed I would need to know more about the machinations of colonialism.

References

Black Spark, White Fire; Richard Poe: Prima Publishing, 1997
Decolonising the Mind; Ngugi Wa Thiongo: Heineman, 1986
The African Trilogy; Chinua Achebe: Picador, 1988
Hopes & Impediments; Chinua Achebe: Doubleday, 1988
Black Skin White Masks; Frantz Fanon: MacGibbon & Kee, 1968
The Wretched of the Earth; Frantz Fanon: Penguin, 1967
Blackfoot Physics; David Peat: Fourth Estate, London, 1996
Memories, Dreams & Reflections; C.G. Jung: Vintage Books, 1989

Chapter 7 – A New World?

Columbus as Icon 1492-1992

Tell them that the greatest crime is this: when you rob a people of its soul, when you want to prevent it to be itself, when you want to shape it into what it is not, then the people have to fight against that, and the breadfruit tastes bitter. Tell them that we love the whole world. That we love what is best, what is true about them. That we know their great works, that we learn from them. But that around here, their faces look ugly. Say that we used to say "over there at the Centre" meaning France; but that first we want to be at peace with ourselves. That our center is right here inside us. Its here that we've looked for it. Its because of that, that we sometimes have this bitterness, this taste for sadness. Yes, because of all that struggle in the deep of the night, with the tom tom that flares up inside us, urging us to go and beat it... it's our knowledge, it belongs to all of us…

Edouard Glissant ['La Lezarde': The Ripening trans. Jenny Zobel]

In early 1989, when the bi-centennial celebrations of the French Revolution were being planned, I was asked by a friend of mine, Jenny Zobel, to join her in putting together and presenting a production as part of the South Bank season of events. We had collaborated before on a programme for the World Service of the BBC, called *Upright now, my Country and I*, based on the life of Aimé Césaire the author of the *Cahier*. In keeping with the theme of celebrations, we decided to make it a narrative anthology which traced the history of black revolution in the Caribbean from the time of the historic slave revolt in Haiti to the overthrow of colonialism. We would read poetry and prose interspersed with songs and slides. We called it *The Tree of Liberty in the Caribbean* and performed it at the Purcell Room and also at the Cheltenham Literature Festival the same year. I was later to do a solo performance for the Open University Third World Studies Summer School.

The French Revolution with its calls for Equality, Liberty and Fraternity had inspired Haitian slave Toussaint L'Ouverture to lead a massive revolt on the island which had led to the defeat of the French and, ironically, the setting up of a black monarchy, modelled on the French Court in the New World. This part of Haiti's history remains generally unknown and the fact that the freed slaves went on to help the colonists in America defeat the British, is another ironic morsel of information that illustrates this. Yet another is that Haiti, on the Western side of Hispaniola, was where Columbus had made his first abortive attempt to set up a colony in 1492, a fact only verified as late as 1958. This was the very year, by some strange synchronicity, that I happened to be in that country. What is also little known is that *Colon* was the name Columbus most used. His voyages were of course to lead directly to the *colon*ization of large sections of the globe by those European nations in search of the pot of gold at the end of the rainbow – the rainbow representing all the various colours of mankind.

When, in the run up to the fifth centenary celebrations of Columbus' 'discovery' of the New World in 1992, Europe and America were making plans to mark the event as a crowning example of European achievement, I was forced to look at the wider implications of Columbus' enterprise. Firstly, Columbus may not have been the first to cross the Atlantic. Some 500 years before the birth of Christ, the ancient Egyptians and Greeks had known that the earth was round[17] but at the time of Columbus, it had still not been circumnavigated. It has been claimed that the Vikings may have got there first; or St Brendan of Ireland, or Prince Madoc of Wales, or the Chinese monk Hui-Shen. Also, according to Norwegian scholar, A W Brogger, there is mounting evidence of a series of pre-Columbian sea-faring epochs at their height in the Late Bronze age. [*Black Spark, White Fire*] This seems to be borne out by a seminal book by the Guyanese linguist and anthropologist, Ivan Van Sertima, in which he examines evidence of a significant black presence in *Ancient America* centuries before Columbus, the result of trade between West Africa and America. [*They Came Before Columbus:* Random House, 1976]

Further, the word 'discovery' is a misnomer to describe the event, for the places Columbus arrived at on this voyages already existed – they were visible and known to their inhabitants; they had their own names and their people had their own ways of life and government. His first land-fall he had called San Salvador, after the Saviour whose light he now brought to the 'darkness.' To the island he first settled, he also gave a Spanish name, *La Isla Espanola* – Hispaniola. Columbus had literally claimed title to land on behalf of a European power thousands of miles away, taking possession of the islands as if they were uninhabited, and establishing dominion over them by renaming them. He had thought he had found a route to the fabulous empire of the Khan and that the island was a part of Japan, but he was still prepared to rename it. The Arawaks, the indigenous people, of course knew it by another name.

The Arawak and Carib Indians on sighting these strange ships had set out in their small craft made from single timbers to greet them. Eduardo Galeano recreates the setting for us: *'These boats without sails, made of the trunk of a ceiba[18] tree, welcomed Christopher Columbus. Out from the islands, paddling canoes, came the men with long black hair and bodies tattooed with vermilion symbols. They approached the caravels, offered fresh water, and exchanged gold for the kind of little tin bells that sell for a copper in Castile.'*

'From that day everything belongs to those remote monarchs: the coral sea, the beaches, the rocks all green with moss, the woods, the parrots, and those laurel-skinned people who don't yet know about clothes, sin, or money and gaze dazedly at the scene.'

It was as if continents and peoples had not existed before the benign intervention of Europe brought them into being – as if the great civilizations in China, India, Africa and the Americas had not preceded those of Western Europe and as if the Great Khan or other Oriental potentates would immediately recognize the superiority of the Europeans and become their subjects. Subsequent history has shown that by and large these assumptions still remain. Columbus, himself, could not have foreseen that very soon all the major European powers would be emulating him. It is as if European domination had been seen as preordained or won without any struggle. Also, our history books have not given us an unbiased appraisal of the events ushered in by the Columbian era. Most do not take into account the disastrous impact it had for millions of peoples in the New World – how it completely destroyed their world and set the pattern for the disruption and exploitation of entire continents. The history we are taught continues to comprise only selective events as interpreted and recorded by European historians. Certainly the history I was taught at school reinforced the presumptions of western thought and scholarship in which everything emanated from a one-sided and predominantly ethnocentric, European world view. This was true not only for history but for everything else.

When in the 3rd Century AD, Sextus Julius Africanus, a Christian historian, synchronized the events of the Jewish and Christian myths with the dates of pagan myth, that act, shrouded in the depth of ancient history, was the very first attempt to provide a model of universal chronology. It was to lead in turn to the now generally accepted system of historiography – the letters BC denoting the period of Antiquity before Christ, and AD the years since the birth of Christ. This model has been extended to all fields of knowledge imposing definitions on the rest of the world regardless of culture or geographical position. Even the time of day worldwide is calculated by reference to the Greenwich meridian and the maps of the world made by European cartographers. They project an image of Europe at the top and at the centre of the world and substantially larger than it actually is. It should be clear to anyone that viewed from space there is no reason why the northern hemisphere could not be seen as the southern hemisphere. Until the Peter's projection in 1967 (itself by a European) Africa was represented as substantially smaller than it is. Africa is in fact larger than China and India put together. The significance of Africa, however, does not lie in its size. It is now common knowledge that East Africa was the cradle of mankind - where human history first began - and Egypt, in North Africa, the temple of the sacred – the mystical reality underlying the material world.

Henceforth, there would be no conflict between the colonists' lust for gold and their faith in a Christian God. These exploits still plague the rest of the world, the so-called 'developing', or 'third' world. Columbus' voyages marked the beginning of an era of expansion, colonization, empire and great wealth and Europeans may well have wanted to commemorate it. But for the majority of the peoples in the world Columbus' achievement was no cause for celebration. For me 1992 was a time to reflect on the links between colonialism and *enterprise*. It was at a time when the legacy of Thatcherite policies still dominated the cultural and economic climate of the country and the Columbus celebrations seemed to be a clear example of the eurocentrism that has been with us for centuries – yet another occasion reinforcing and perpetuating the myth of the primacy of European civilization. I believe strongly in celebration and ritual when they commemorate seasonal change, rites of passage or cultural landmarks. Unfortunately, what is a celebration for one group is not necessarily a cause of celebration for another.

At the end of the period known as the Middle Ages, half a millennium ago, an event took place which was to change the course of history. At the time Europe had been doom-ridden and quite desperate. According to one commentator, Admiral Morrison, in his biography of Columbus of 1942, '*With the practical dissolution of the Empire (Holy Roman) and the Church's loss of moral leadership, Christians had nothing to which they might cling. The great principle of unity represented by emperor and pope was a dream of the past and had not come true...Throughout Western Europe the general feeling was one of profound disillusion, cynical pessimism and black despair*'. Then came news of a discovery that was to give Europe another chance. It was of such significance that I believe the letters BC can just as well denote the period of the history of Europe before Columbus. The 'discovery' of the New World was to affect the lives of everyone on the planet. Henceforth the West acquired '*implicit governance of the world in politics, economics, social and cultural values*' [Wilson Harris: *The Mask of the Beggar*, Faber 2003]

For whatever way you look at it, it was central to the way we now view the world. Not even man's spectacular exploits in space culminating in the moon landing in 1969 can compare in significance. Columbus' journey was much more that one further step for mankind. It was the beginning of a quantum shift for its destiny. At the time, Columbus could not have envisaged just how his belief that great riches lay in the West was to shape the very *raison-d'être* of the West. His journeys paved the way for European expansion and domination and he can be said to be a symbol of what the West stands for. His exploits represent the spirit of Europe, the Western spirit against both man and Nature. It is significant that he called his venture The *Enterprise* of the Indies; a search for profit that is still the over-riding principle of Capitalism as we know it.

Columbus, for many, has become the supreme icon of Western domination. His career had been symbolic from birth. Cristoforo or Cristobal Colombo (there are many variations of his name in different languages – Christopher Dove, in English) was born in Genoa on the Italian coast, son of a weaver. He went to sea at an early age and rose through the ranks to become his own master. He made his way not as a sailor but as a merchant's clerk, later becoming an investor himself. He was keenly interested in navigation and geography and had a flair for seamanship. He was helped by his brother, Bartolome, to become a travelling merchant, something not unusual in those days. Named Cristoforo after the pagan, turned saint, who carried the burden of the Western world on his unwitting shoulders, Columbus was to think of himself as fated to carry the burden of the Christian faith across the unchartered waters of the unknown. He believed that he was chosen by God to discover a western route to the Indies. After his first voyage he often signed his name simply in the Greek, XPO Ferens, a reference to St. Christopher, linking that event to his great achievement. [Kirkpatrick Sale, *The Conquest of Paradise*]

He believed in his destiny as he believed in the Holy Trinity, and destiny played a remarkable role in shaping the course of his career. In 1476 as a member of a Flemish merchant ship which was attacked and sunk by French raiders he drifted clinging to an oar to the port of Lagos on the Portuguese coast. Lagos had been the launching place for Portuguese sorties down the African coast and also south west to the Canaries and beyond into unchartered seas. As early as 1444 the first African slaves had been brought to Europe at Lagos. The disgorgement of the cargo has been vividly recorded by Gomes Eannes de Azurara, and it was there that Columbus had been introduced to the slave trade and received another lesson of his civilization. In 1481 he had taken part in an expedition to the Gold Coast to set up the notorious Cape Coast Castle, a storage place for slaves.

According to John Dyson in his book *The Columbus Conspiracy*, Columbus might have learned of fabulous lands to the west from a pilot who had survived a shipwreck in 1477 and may have managed to acquire the charts made by this man. It is also known that Toscanelli, a Florentine philosopher (branches of learning and science were not as specialized as they are today), had made a map of the world, influenced by Marco Polo's travels, and had tried to persuade King Alphonso of Portugal to undertake an expedition taking a western route. Columbus would have known about this when he himself approached the King of Portugal for backing for him to undertake the expedition. When this was not forthcoming, he switched his allegiance to Spain. We now know that Isabella and Ferdinand of Spain were interested in such a voyage but it took another eight years before the venture got under way. According to the terms of the arrangement Columbus was to receive great financial rewards and a grand title for his services to the Spanish Crown.

There are many conflicting versions of Columbus' story, mostly based on the record of the official log that Columbus himself had kept – one by the Dominican Priest, Las Casas, and the other by Columbus's own son. It is common knowledge that he kept two logs, one to deceive the sailors about the distance actually travelled in case they grew restive. Even his official log, according to some nautical experts, contained misinformation. One can only guess at his motives. Was it made to deceive the Portuguese in case they found him in their waters or not to let on that he was not the first with the idea of a western route to the Indies?

In his book and TV documentary, The Columbus Conspiracy, John Dyson reports on the long and arduous research by the Spanish nautical historian, Dr. Luis Coin, investigating the discrepancies that appear in the daily logs that Columbus kept. Both Dyson and Coin believe that Columbus had not simply sailed due west, as is usually claimed, but that he had first sailed southwest to the Canaries before setting his course due west. The discrepancies did not match the facts as revealed by modern oceanography. And there were other indicators as well, such as Columbus's statement that he would be making another chart, implying as it did that he was already in possession of one. They deduced that Columbus had a clear idea of the route he would take, even though that route would violate Portuguese rights over both sea and land. Dyson was to conclude that Columbus was not a saint but an opportunist.

Nonetheless, three caravels, the Santa Maria, the Nina and the Pinta set sail for the unknown on August 3rd 1492. Columbus sailed in the largest, the Santa Maria, (100 tons). The Nina and the Pinta were slightly smaller. There was an overall crew of some 90 men. Land was first sighted on 10th October, by a sailor named Juan Rodriguez Bermeo. But Columbus claimed that he had sighted land in the early hours that morning and so deprived the sailor of a life pension. Columbus lied, swindled and betrayed many trusts. He may no doubt have had good reason to cook his logs. But what can also be discerned from the records, kept by himself and retold by others, is that he was possessed of an overwhelming ambition and megalomania. He was as cruel as he was pious.

His enterprise was to be the springboard for (in the words of the Dominican priest and historian, de Las Casas) 'the bloody trail of conquest' of what is now known as America. It is a supreme irony that Columbus, to his dying day, insisted that the lands he had 'discovered' were part of Asia. To this day the islands of the Caribbean Sea are known as the West Indies, and so I have been consigned to history as a West Indian, just as my own name had derived from a Scottish plantation owner.

Today, neither the ocean he had crossed nor the lands he had conquered bear his name, but the name he most used, Colon, strikes an uncanny chord. As we have seen the first attempt to set up a colony in the New World was by accident, but there had also been a symbolic end to that first voyage. On Christmas morning 1492 the Santa Maria had run aground off the island we now know as Haiti. The natives had been friendly and bore gifts to the unknown intruders. These peace-loving and gentle people acted with more Christian charity to the ship-wrecked bearers of the Christian message than they would receive in return. And so the first settlement in the New World was made, and a fort built made from the timbers from the wreckage of the Santa Maria. It was named Navidad, honouring the Day of Nativity on which it was founded. Columbus had returned home in triumph leaving a small group of Spaniards to consolidate the colony. But on this return the following year on a second voyage he had found the settlement completely destroyed and all his men massacred. Undeterred he sailed to the eastern section of Hispaniola, now known as San Domingo, to set up a new settlement which he named Isabella.

By 1495, the reign of terror on Hispaniola had reached unbelievable proportions. The Spanish had accepted the gifts of the natives, but gave nothing in return. If the Indians did not part with whatever gold they possessed or find it for their conquerors, they were mutilated, massacred, or made slaves. The only thing the Spanish gave were Spanish names for the islands they seized; an act of appropriation. The

'Discovery' ushered in an era of brutality and domination and for millions of people Columbus was a harbinger of death. Bartolome de las Casas, the bishop who was a witness to some of the barbarities perpetrated against the Indians, reported that the gallows were built low and wide, capable of stringing up 13 Arawaks at a time, their feet just above the ground so that burning wood could be placed under the soles. The precise number of each batch so hanged was *'in memory of Our Redeemer and His twelve Apostles'.* In two years half of the population had been killed or had killed themselves – 125-500,000 men, women and children. By 1515 only 10,000 were left; by 1540 they had all vanished off the face of the earth.

Columbus had described the indigenous Arawaks he encountered on his first voyage in a letter to the Spanish King and Queen thus: *'In all the world there can be no better or gentler people...all are of the most singular loving behaviour and speak pleasantly;... they are of good stature, men and women... and the houses are so pretty and with government in all, such as a judge or lord, and all obey him so that it is a marvel'* [Kirpatrick Sale]. But only a few years later when these gentle people became aware of the true purpose of the Christian emissaries from Spain and began taking to the hills, they were savages and cannibals to be pacified and enslaved or be massacred.

This image has persisted and was to shape European attitudes forever. Just over 100 years after Columbus, Shakespeare, no doubt inspired by a story published in England in 1609 (The Sea Adventure) about a ship-wreck of an English ship off Bermuda, wrote *The Tempest*. The play is located on an island in the Mediterranean that is more like the Caribbean.

> *There Prospero meets Caliban, son of the witch Sycorax, worshipper of the god of the Patagonian Indians. Caliban is a savage, an Indian of the type Shakespeare has seen in some exhibition in London: a thing of darkness, more beast than man, who only learns to curse and has no capacity for judgment nor sense of responsibility. Only as a slave or tied up like a monkey, could he find a place in human society; that is, European society, which he has absolutely no interest in joining.*
>
> [Eduardo Galeano]

This simple 'lover of Nature' could, like Nature itself, legitimately be exploited for the good of those who were clever enough to exploit by force of arms the rest of the world; those who because of their power were able to define the world and reality itself. Though Shakespeare seems to be analyzing the European lust for conquest and colonization, Caliban, the other, is portrayed as absolutely powerless and can be dispossessed with impunity; Caliban (Canibal), whose name appears after the list of characters, represents the fear of the unknown, chaos, the Wild Man of European myth: 'thou earth!', identified with sex and excess, a slave to his impulses, to be enslaved by the knights of light and order.

Despite his ugliness he has some saving graces, for he knows the secrets of nature, but by enslaving him you can gain some of these secrets for yourself. So Caliban must be civilized or sacrificed. By taming the wild man his claim to ownership of the land is nullified. Prospero, as a true representative of the human race, can legitimately appropriate it and Caliban can have no part in this brave new world – no future. Also by making him contemplate raping, that is, taking possession, of Prospero's daughter, Prospero is justified in taking possession of the whole island. In vain Caliban pleads:

This island's mine, by Sycorax my mother
Which thou tak'st from me. When thou cam'st first,
Thou strok'st me, and made much of me, wouldst give me
Water with berries in it;... and there you sty me
In this hard rock, whiles you do keep from me
The rest of the island.

According to the West Indian writer, George Lamming, *'Caliban is never accorded the power to see. He is always the measure of the condition which his physical appearance has already defined. Caliban is the excluded, that which is eternally below possibility, and always beyond reach. He is seen as an occasion, a state of existence which can be appropriated and exploited for the purposes of another's own development'.* [The Pleasures of Exile]

Lamming seemingly reinforces the general view initiated by Columbus but in a version of The Tempest (*Une Tempête*), by Aimé Césaire, Prospero does not in the end return to his Dukedom in Italy as in the original play, but remains on the island, because Prospero and Caliban are necessary to each other, *'Prospero can no more live apart from Caliban, than whites and blacks can exist independently in today's world.'*

Césaire is reported to have said that *'Caliban was the man who was close to his beginnings, whose link with the natural world had not been broken. Caliban could still participate in a world of marvels, whereas his master can merely 'create' them through his acquired knowledge.'* (S.Belhassen).This is true today – traditional peoples know the truth instinctively whereas the Western mind tries to rediscover it via science. Césaire's contribution is to 'deconstruct' the subject in the discussion. He shows us how to go beyond both Prospero and Caliban, thereby abolishing duality and allowing 'the poetic expression of the unspeakable' [J Michael Dash in 'After Europe']. This is a notion which shed light for me on the hybrid vigour of the Caribbean mentioned in the previous chapter and one to which we shall return to later. It certainly explained why I needed to get to the root of colonialism much as Fanon had done all those years ago.

After a third voyage in 1498 and persistent rumours of chaos in the new kingdoms Columbus was himself dispossessed by Bobadilla on orders from Spain and sent home in irons. He had not found much gold, but he started the gold rush. Many were to catch the fever – Cortez, Coronado, Soto, Pizarro, Raleigh, Hudson, La

Salle. Surprisingly he was to make yet another voyage, only to be stranded in Jamaica. Four years later he was to die a broken and disillusioned man. *'Christopher Columbus is going out (on his fifth and final voyage) knowing that there is no passion or glory that does not lead to pain. On the other hand, he does not know that within a few years the banner that he stuck for the first time into the sands of the Caribbean will be waving over the empire of the Aztecs, in lands yet unknown and over the kingdom of the Incas, under the unknown skies of the Southern Cross. He does not know that with all his lies, promises, and ravings, he has still fallen short. The supreme admiral of the ocean sea still believes he has reached Asia from the rear. The ocean will not be called the Sea of Columbus, nor will the new world bear his name, but that of his Florentine friend, Amerigo Vespucci, navigator and pilot master. But it was Columbus who found dazzling colour that didn't exist in the European rainbow. Blind, he dies without seeing it.'* [Galeano' Genesis] [20]

What is not in dispute is that Columbus' voyages (he made four between 1492 and 1502) heralded in an age of discovery and environmental destruction. He and his successors exploited the natural world and the people they encountered. Columbus' discovery was directly responsible for the decimation of entire peoples and was to shape the future of the known world. It was to impose definitions on the rest of the world, for instance, what constituted title to land, raising questions both about the ownership and possession of land.

Frederick Turner suggests that *'Columbus was what Jung would call the fully modern man and what others would call the hero of history: an individual who has somehow divined the urgently felt needs and aspiration of his time and intuited a means by which these might be satisfied. Such an individual, says Jung, has not only mastered the mechanics, facts and theories of his age, but has gone beyond them so that he must seem to his contemporaries eccentric, misguided, even dangerously deluded.'* Columbus may have been the instrument of great historical forces that had long preceded him. He was certainly sincere: *'believing to the end of his days that the enslavement, exploitation, and extirpation of these naked ritualists conferred strength and new vitality upon Christian civilization'*. [Beyond Geography] However, he has come to be seen as no more than an ambitious adventurer. According to Hans Koning, in *Columbus, His Enterprise*: *'Perhaps we will come to say that Columbus was not only a man of his time, but that he was a man of his race. The word race may no longer be accepted in science because it cannot be properly defined but let us say that Columbus was a typical man of the (...) West. And the West has ravaged the world for five hundred years, under the flag of a master-slave theory which in our finest hour of hypocrisy was called the 'white man's burden'... I am not ignoring the cruelties of other races. They were usually less hypocritical, though; they were not, in Marx's phrase, 'civilisation mongers' as they laid waste to other lands.'*

Columbus was to become as deranged as his detractors always thought him when he was seeking support for his first voyage. But maybe that derangement reflected the essential mind of the West - with all its warped religiosity, folklore, and the acquisition of technical skills that fuelled its hubris; its need to establish and celebrate its own superiority.

The same year that the fifth centenary celebration took place, the United Nations Conference on Environment and Development, The Earth Summit, was held at Rio de Janeiro, along the same South American coastline Columbus had sailed. It seemed that what he stood for was on trial. In his deranged state Columbus may not have been so wrong when he claimed that he had stumbled on an earthly paradise. On his third voyage he had sailed along the South American coast and encountered the strong current of the Orinoco River. He wrote to his sovereigns that this was probably the mouth of one of the four rivers of the earthly paradise in which God had placed the Tree of Life. The shape of this new hemisphere is not as others claimed but like a woman's breast. *'His body creaks with rheumatism, but his heart jumps for joy. The discoverer explains to Their Catholic Majesties that which is plainly evident; Earthly Paradise is on the nipple of a woman's breast... He realised it two months ago, when his caravels entered the Gulf of Paria.'* [Galeano]

The search for El Dorado, the City of Gold that followed Columbus, was no utopian ideal but a dream of plunder, for the centre of the world remained firmly in Europe. Despite the similarity of Copernicus' heliocentric system to the Aztec calendar and the fact that Muslim, Chinese and Egyptian astronomers preceded Galileo and Copernicus, the Eurocentric world view still prevails; other peoples and other cultures are still devalued.

In the wake of Columbus

According to Justin Winsor, American Columbus scholar and biographer (1891), the existence of Las Casas, the historian who witnessed Columbus' exploits at first hand, is the indictment of Columbus. But maybe it is the failure of history itself to interpret and evaluate what followed in the wake of Columbus, that is, the indictment of the Christian West. It seems that the West suffers from the presumption that no one would question its usurpation of the moral high ground. It clings desperately to causes it cannot truly believe in but which it dare not put in question. One day, before it's too late, let us hope that it may see like Prospero that what it most fears is within itself and say *'This thing of darkness I acknowledge mine!'*

It was in Haiti that the French were to continue what Columbus had begun. Black slaves from Africa replaced the indigenous Indian population which had succumbed to smallpox, brutality and greed. The blacks were to fare even worse. Families were separated; they were treated like cattle, sold, put in irons, burnt at the stake, the women violated. Words cannot express the brutality of the French. Black labour had converted the island into the richest colonial possession and the story of Saint Domingue under French rule is inextricably linked to the history of France and Europe.

But our history books rarely show this. In writing about the French Revolution and the universal concepts of human rights, no mention is made of the impact of the historic slave revolt in Saint Domingue on events in the metropolis and on the eventual abolition of the slave trade: events which demonstrate not only the relationships between European powers and colonialism, but also the immemorial nature of black resistance to white domination, as if blacks concurred with their own enslavement.

The abolition of slavery was not due solely to the humanitarian intervention of white Abolitionists. There were black crusaders as well living in England at the time; people like the ex-slave, Equiano, who was one of the leading political activists whose 'Interesting Narrative' was published in London in 1789. But the overriding reasons for the demise of the shameful trade were sound economic ones, e.g. the demise of the plantations in the Caribbean. Also, the final defeat of Bonaparte's 1803 expedition, and the establishment of the black state of Haiti, the first in the New World, is as alluded to earlier, generally unknown.

We must be careful not to construct historical 'models' which portray history exclusively from the top, as Christopher Hill has stated – models 'which all too often conceal unconscious (or conscious) 20th century assumptions. A whole ideology has been constructed around the concepts of modernisation, 'take off', and the assumption that modern capitalist civilisation is 'natural', that all societies strive towards it, but some are still 'pre-industrial and therefore 'backward." [Christopher Hill]

In the past, non-European societies did not strive to dominate nature; their technologies were simple and respectful of nature. Western culture owes a great deal to these other systems of knowledge, in medicine, mathematics and technology; to mention just a few; the magnetic needle, which was to cause Columbus so many problems, was a Chinese device; and the lateen sail was an Arabic invention, as were latitude and longitude.

Any system which sees itself as superior inevitably assumes attitudes of dominance and exploitation, interpreting events purely in this light, taking credit for 'civilised' values, while destroying entire peoples and the planet itself; celebrating 'discoveries' by appropriation. This includes the laws of nature and of physics as well as the facts of geography and history. Eurocentrism perpetuates perceptions and definitions on the rest of the world. It has dehumanised and devalued peoples and cultures in order to justify exploitation and dominance. The institution of slavery, for example, provided the wealth for the Industrial Revolution. The exploited are seen as 'others', not as part of the real world. Technology, it is assumed, confers leadership regardless of where the technology originated: the idea of a 'third world' only exists in a Eurocentric model of the world. Ironically, the term was coined in the West by those seeking a new system other than the Western concepts of Capitalism and Communism.

oooOooo

It so happened that I spent two months in 1958 on that same island that Columbus had made his first settlement. Its name had been changed to Saint Domingue by the French, and when in 1802 the revolt led by Toussaint L'Ouverture, a black slave, defeated the armies of France, it had reverted to the name the Arawaks had known it by – Haiti. I had been on location for the Italian film *Calypso* in which I played the leading role. This was during the time of the Ton-ton Macoute and Papa Doc. In this impoverished black Republic, the victim of five centuries of European exploitation, I had seen an impressive statue of Columbus, facing the harbour in the capital, Port-au-Prince. Even then it had seemed a powerful symbol of European enterprise and conquest. I have since read that when Papa Doc's son, Jean Claude, was overthrown in 1986, the statue was also toppled and dumped into the sea, still no doubt littered, as it was when I was there, with floating human turds. Someone had left a note in Creole on the pedestal, *'Pa de blanc en Hayti'*: no whites in Haiti. [Kirpatrick Sale, *The Conquest of Paradise*]

The history of Haiti is one of the most fascinating examples of colonialism and the struggle for freedom. Immediately preceding 1789, European writers and philosophers had been inspired by the new ideals of freedom which had promised liberation from the old political order, but at the outbreak of the French Revolution this liberation had not extended to the slaves in the New World. The Declaration of the Rights of Man was approved in October 1789 by the French National Assembly whose members had been guided by the ideals and experience of the American Independence fighters twenty years earlier. These ideals had in turn fired the imagination of the slaves in Saint Domingue and had forged a precarious alliance between black liberation in the New World and the Jacobin Republic in the Old.

It took a Caribbean writer, CLR James, to tell the full story of the slave rebellion in Saint Domingue. In his book, *The Black Jacobins*, James has put the record straight. The title derived from the extremist movement associated with Robespierre and the members of the Jacobin Club, characterised by its determination to carry through the Revolution at whatever cost and without compromise. Underlying this resolve was the idea, derived from Jean-Jacques Rousseau, French philosopher and political theorist, that the masses were incapable of making a successful revolution on their own. By extension the term was used by James to describe the leaders of the slave revolt in the latter half of the 18th century in Haiti (then St Domingue) – a leadership undertaken on behalf of all the enslaved on the island. The book tells the story of Toussaint L'Ouverture and the other leaders of the historic revolt, the defeat of Bonaparte's 1803 expedition to Haiti, and the establishment of the first black State in the New World. The theme of the book is effectively about the alliance, previously referred to, when the principles of liberty and equality had also become the catch words of the slaves.

It is clear from the writing of contemporary commentators that Toussaint was very highly regarded. Wordsworth was to write a poem about the fate of Toussaint, tricked and imprisoned in the Jura mountains by Napoleon. Writing in 1892, the American commentator and abolitionist Wendell Phillips wrote, *'you may think me* a fanatic tonight, for you read history not with your eyes but with your prejudices. But fifty years hence when Truth gets a hearing the Muse of History will put Phocion for the Greek, and Brutus for the Roman, Hampden for England, Fayett for France, choose Washington as the bright, consummate flower of our earlier civilisation, and John Brown, the ripe flower of our noon-day, then dipping her pen in the sunlight, will write in the clear blue above them all, the name of the soldier, the statesman, the martyr, Toussaint L'Ouverture'. It should also be noted that William Blake made engravings of the atrocities perpetuated against the slaves in the New World.

In his book, *The Overthrow of Colonial Slavery 1776-1848*, Robin Blackburn argues that *'the revolt in Haiti defended the gains of the French Republic against France itself. The eventual break with slavery provided the indispensable basis for the break with colonialism'*. Blackburn acknowledges the achievement of CLR James, whose book explores the extraordinary fusion of different traditions and impulses achieved in St Domingue in the 1790s. James' account *'illuminates the essential workings of capitalism, racialism, colonialism and slavery – and the complex class struggle to which they gave rise in St Domingue; it conveys a marvellous sense of the eruption of the masses in history. With a sensibility attuned to the cosmopolitan forces of the age he follows the transatlantic revolutionary impulse as it criss-crosses the ocean from St Domingue to Paris and back to the Caribbean again.'*

Most histories of the French Revolution fail to show that the many conflicting factions in France corresponded to those in Saint Domingue; that the most significant factor of the day, the power struggle between the major European powers (Britain, France, Spain and Portugal), had been the political and economic intrigue throughout the Caribbean and the Americas; that America herself was emerging as an independent power. So it is not surprising to find that in writing about the French Revolution and the universal concepts of human rights, no mention is made of the impact of the historic slave revolt in Saint Domingue; on events in the metropolis and on the eventual abolition of the slave trade: events which demonstrate not only the relationships between European powers and colonialism, but also the immemorial nature of black resistance to white domination, removing any doubt that blacks concurred with their own enslavement. The abolition of slavery, triggered by the active resistance of the slaves themselves, represents one of the most salutary achievements in human history. Yet the significance of that resistance through the ages is up to now hardly ever acknowledged or recorded. The abuses of Britain's imperialist past are still being ignored, just as some fascists are denying that the holocaust ever happened. Most Germans have faced up to legacy of Hitler; we are yet to make a similar breakthrough in Britain.

Also, in writing about the abolition of slavery, little if any mention is made of the resistance of the slaves themselves. The story of Olaudah Equiano, a British slave, is as little known as the story of Toussaint L'Ouverture but it illustrates how one-sided the recording of historical facts can be; and how easy it is to forget that there was a significant black presence in England as long ago as the 18th century.

In June1789, a month before the storming of the Bastille, a book was published in London under the title *'The Interesting Narrative of Olaudah Equiano, or Gustavus Vassa, written by himself'*. A total of nine editions were published during his life time and they are still being published – one of the latest in 1996 [included in *Unchained Voices:* An Anthology of Black Authors in the English Speaking World of the 18th Century; Vincent Carretta, University Press of Kentucky]

The story is about an African slave who managed to purchase his freedom for £40 (£16,000 in today's money) but whilst still a slave travelled the world – America, Canada, Europe, the Mediterranean. He served in the British Navy against the French, went on an expedition to the Arctic Circle, and became the first political leader of Britain's black community. His book has been described as *'a principal instrument in bringing about the motion for the repeal of the Slave Act'* [Thomas Digges,1791]

Equiano was born in Nigeria in 1745, the same year that Toussaint L'Ouverture was born in St, Domingue. Like Toussaint, he was a man whose life-work was an outstanding contribution of service to his community and the struggle against slavery. He saw the slave trade as *'a war with the heart of man'*. His book recounts his early years as a boy in Nigeria in the mid-18th century, giving us an idea of life in his community, the customs of his people, his capture at the age of twelve, the horrors of the middle passage and the slave trade, his travels in a ship of the British Navy off America, Canada, Europe including Turkey and the Mediterranean and the expedition to find a North West Passage. On his return to England having bought his freedom, he took part in political activities on behalf of those who were still enslaved as well as for those freedmen living in England. It was he who alerted Granville Sharpe to an atrocity which became known as the Zong affair. In 1783 the Captain of the Liverpool slave ship, the Zong, actually ordered 132 slaves to be thrown overboard in order to make sure he got the insurance money in the event of the slaves not surviving an illness which was sweeping the ship.

And it was a letter of his, written in 1788 to Lord Hawkesbury, that was used in evidence in the parliamentary enquiry into the slave trade. For the next nine years he was one of the most outspoken black people in the country opposing the traffic. There were many others living in England at the time who had spoken out against it – his friend, Ottobah Cugoano, for instance. He has said that enslaved blacks not only had a moral right, but also a moral duty to resist. Cugoano even went so far as to say that every person in Great Britain, by not speaking out against slavery is, in some degree, responsible.

Equiano travelled the length and breadth of the country speaking on behalf of the Abolitionist lobby. He visited Sheffield, Manchester, Nottingham, Bath, Devises, Exeter, Belfast and Scotland. No other issue had produced a greater number of petitions to Parliament. Granville Sharp, William Wilberforce and Thomas Clarkson had taken a stand for the emancipation of the slaves but black people were in the forefront of the movement. They had signed petitions and written about slavery – Ignatius Sancho, Ottobah Cugoano and also Ukaswsaw Gronniosaw. Historically slaves had always resisted and staged rebellions; they had not waited for the Abolitionists to free them – the Maroons in San Domingo and Jamaica, and the Bushmen in Surinam and Guyana, as well as the great escapes which took place in the United States of America bear witness to this.

The true story about the slave trade, slavery itself, the triangular circuit, abolition and black resistance is only just finding a place in our versions of history. Without black resistance throughout the time of slavery there would have been no abolition. There were other factors as well. It was not just by coincidence that the efficiency of slavery as a mode of production was in a course of decline. Commercial interests had always been paramount in shaping the nation's policies, without regard to humanitarian considerations.

Any version of history that ignores how prevailing social relationships have evolved, and adheres to a fragmented framework precluding the existence of other authentic cultures and histories has to be challenged. As does any system of beliefs in which the traditional cultures of the world are fit subjects only for anthropologists and museum curators. It had always concerned me that European religions and 'values' could have co-existed with slavery and exploitation, whilst indigenous peoples, converted and disinherited, their simple life styles, reminiscent of a lost Utopia, were laid waste.

Notes

Columbus's Voyages; 1492 3rd August – 12 October San Salvador (now Watling Island in the Bahamas.1493-96; Guadeloupe, Puerto Rico, Jamaica 1498-1500, Virgin Islands. Trinidad and South America

Greek knowledge of the world as a sphere: Enetosthens, in 3rd C. BC determined the earth's circumference quite accurately by deduction – he measured the distance between two points whose latitudes were known to him. There are 90 degrees between Equator and Poles. Similarly Longitude is distance in degrees between Meridians (N/S)

Compass: the Chinese had the compass in 12th century.

The normal diurnal rotation of the North Star, not visible in the Mediterranean, caused C & crew concern – appearing first to one side then later the other side of 'true' North determined by compass. Col. guessed (to allay their apprehension) rightly that the North Star moves like other stars & that the compass always points true (magnetic) North.

Portrait purporting to be Equiano at the Royal Albert Museum in Exeter most likely not of Equiano. A genuine portrait is on the frontispiece to his " Interesting Narrative"

References

After Europe; J. Michael Dash, Dangaroo, 1989

Beyond Geography; Frederick Turner: Rutgers University Press, 1990
The Conquest of Paradise; Kirkpatrick Sale: Hodder & Stoughton, 1990
Genesis; Eduardo Galeano: Methuen, 1986
Columbus, His Enterprise; Hans Koning: Latin American Bureau, 1976
The Columbus Conspiracy; John Dyson: T.V. Documentary, 1990
Black Spark, White Fire; Richard Poe: Prima Publishing, 1997
They Came Before Columbus; Ivan Van Sertima: Random House, 1970
The Pleasures of Exile; George Lamming: Allison & Busby, 1984
The Interesting Narrative of Olaudah Equiano; ed. Vincent Carretta: Penguin, 2003
The Black Jacobins; C.L.R.James: New York, Vintage, 1963
The Overthrow of Colonial Slavery; Robin Blackburn: Verso, 1989

Chapter 8 – An Ecology of Being

In my experience Nature cannot be dominated

Tao Te Ching

What a book a devil's Chaplin might write on the clumsy, wasteful, blundering, low and horribly cruel works of nature

[Charles Darwin, qt.The New Biology, Augros & Stanciu]

Race, Land & Culture

Columbus' voyages were to lead directly to the *colonisation* of great sections of the globe by European powers, extending the concept of racial superiority beyond their own shores. The very year Columbus set sail for his 'new world', Spain had expelled its entire Jewish population. Colonisation was brutal and barbaric and led to the genocide of the indigenous inhabitants. To replace them slavery was introduced into the Caribbean and the Americas. Millions of Africans had died in the holds of slave ships and on the sugar plantations. Performing Aimé Césaire's surreal masterpiece for over two years had kept the ancestral memory of the horrors of slavery very much alive for me:

We, vomit of the slave ship
We, hunted meat of Calabar....
I hear rising from the hold chained curses, gasps of the dying,
the sound of one who is thrown into the sea... the baying of a woman giving birth.
the scrape of fingernails advancing on throats
the sneer of the whip. the prying of vermin among weary bodies...

Or again:

The flogged negro who says 'Sorry, Master'
And the twenty-nine legally permitted strokes of the whip
And the cell four feet high
And the branched yoke of iron
And the hamstringing of my runaway courage
And the red-hot fleur-de-lys from the smoking brands
Bleeding on the soft flesh of my shoulder...

As the great grandson of a slave trapped within an alien culture it was only natural that I tried to understand what had led to my disillusionment. I had to try to understand the institution of slavery, what it meant not only for the enslaved and their descendants, but for the colonial powers whose wealth was built on their labour and suffering. Somehow the fall out of this unspoken and un-redressed first holocaust is still with us today – the debilitating psychological *collateral damage* – racism, cultural alienation; as well as issues regarding power and the ownership of land. I began to suspect that the Western spirit against man and nature stemmed from its need to control and dominate, sanctioned in part by the monotheism of the Old Testament, in which man is denied the fruit of the tree of knowledge but given dominion over the fruits of the earth and the animal species. '*Be fruitful and multiply, and replenish the Earth and subdue it, and have dominion over the fish of the sea, and over the fowl of the air, and over every living thing that moveth upon the earth*'.

This attitude underpins our present worldwide materialistic culture, from the Industrial Revolution and the writings of John Locke (1632-1704), David Hume (1711-76) and Adam Smith (1723-90) to the present day.

Locke believed that God had intended to give the world to humankind as a shared bounty... in perpetual partnership. What made something your property was the labour you put into acquiring it or making it. Locke also justified slavery. He was personally involved with slave owning American colonies, and contributed to racism by providing a model in which skin colour was seen as an essential property of human beings (H.M Bracken *Philosophy and Racism* quoted by Peter Fryer in his book *Black People in the British Empire*). He also disparaged the indigenous American. This was essential to his politics because their land was needed for the English settlers. The fact that these Americans did not' 'own the land' as Chief Seattle had stated, was sufficient justification for the European to appropriate it. To this American, as with most indigenous cultures, the idea of individual ownership of land was alien. The land was sacred. To the European, it was just wasteland to be tamed and exploited. As Ali Mazuri put it, 'European 'labour' made the land European property', even though the real labour was mostly done by non-Europeans.

Hume asserted that European culture was superior to other cultures and consequently race and culture are linked. Locke and Hume were also expounding a European 'enlightenment' and man's (European man's) right and duty to despoil the land. Smith also followed in this tradition. In his *Wealth of Nations,* he justified slavery and was openly racist. He claimed that black people were naturally inferior to whites, who held a monopoly on civilisation, art, science and talent (*Essays Moral, Political and Literary*). He thought that an individual (white), if allowed to promote his own interests freely within the law, often promotes the interests of society as a whole. And this has led to the present day materialistic, consumer society with its greed, over-production and waste.

These writers were among the main proponents of racist ideology. Others were the German philosopher, Hegel, (*Philosophy of History,* 1848); the German biologist, Ernst Haeckel, the French ethnologist; the Comte de Gobineau (*Essay on the Inequality of the Human Races*, 1853); and the English political philosopher, Huston Chamberlain (*Foundations of the 19th Century*, 1899). This ideology has sadly, also pervaded English literature. In Joseph Conrad's *Heart of Darkness*, Nature is untamed, 'red in tooth and claw', something ugly and terrifying; the title of that book, like Graham Greene's *The Heart of the Matter*, goes to the heart of the Western approach and can also be found in the work of Jefferson, Carlyle, Kipling, Haggard, Conan Doyle, Montserrat, Trollope, Coleridge and Lamb.

For Hegel (although considered a holistic and *'spiritual'* philosopher) the human mind constituted the nature of the Absolute – concepts, even racist doctrine, determining nature and mind! His insistence on the primacy of the practical and historical explanation was no more than a deliberate distortion of facts in order to bolster German nationalistic feelings of superiority and downright racism. His attitude to 'negroes' was very similar to that of Hitler towards the Jews and that of the present day English war historian, David Irvine, who denies that the Holocaust ever happened!

Whilst Conrad was writing about the 'bestial ugliness' of the natives of the Congo, Europeans were on the verge of discovering the beauty of African art. In his book *Hopes and Impediments,* the Nigerian writer, Chinua Achebe, analyses and attacks the racism that *The Heart of Darkness*, one of the classics of English literature, continues to propagate. Achebe noted that whilst Conrad's biographer ignored his blatant racism towards black people, he did not ignore his anti-Semitism.

The concept of race, that some races are intrinsically superior to others, has been applied to all Western studies, but especially to history, as the English scholar Martin Bernal points out. In the case of China for instance, as the balance of trade turned in favour of Britain and France, China came under attack and its ancient civilisation was devalued. A civilisation based on virtue and justice was undermined by the immoral Opium Wars waged by Britain in the nineteenth century. Similarly, the Ancient Egyptian civilisation, which had been seen to parallel that of China in the eighteenth century, suffered from the same need to justify the increasing European expansion and exploitation.

Bernal's book *Black Athena, The Afro-asiatic Roots of Classical Civilisation,* sent shock waves through academia when the first volume came out in 1987 (the second appeared in 1991, with the third and final volume announced in 2006) and continues to do so for bringing to light things that challenge the accepted view of history. But although his work has been attacked, no one so far has been able to disprove him. A professor of Government and Near Eastern studies at Cornell University, Bernal demonstrates that the ancient model held by the Classical Greeks themselves – that their culture was 'derived from the East in general and Egypt in particular' – had to be overthrown and replaced by something more acceptable. And this has led to the fabrication of Ancient Greece during the last 200 years. The fact that Egyptian civilisation was an African civilisation with many of the most powerful dynasties in Upper Egypt set up by black Pharaohs was obscured. The fact that, as late as the nineteenth century (when Egyptians led by Mohamed Ali and his son Ibrahim, were controlling large areas of Greece), Danaos the Egyptian had invaded ancient Greece was also denied.

My encounter with Bernal served to shore up what I had already knew of Fanon's exposition of the mechanism of colonialism. The latter had pronounced, 'Colonialism is not satisfied merely with hiding people in its grip and emptying the native's brain of all form and content. By a perverted logic, it turns to the past of the oppressed people and distorts, disfigures and destroys it.' If we are ultimately to arrive at a world view which is acceptable to everyone we will have to become aware of the distortions and biases of the predominant model of civilisation. If Bernal is right, we have 'to recognise the penetration of racism and continental chauvinism into all our historiography or philosophy of writing history... For 18th and 19th century Romantics and racists it was simply intolerable for Greece, which was seen not merely as the epitome of Europe but also as its pure childhood, to have been the result of the mixture of native Europeans and colonising Africans and Semites.'

Racism and deracination (of man from nature) are blood brothers. It was a short step from control of nature, rooted in the doctrines of the Semitic religions, to theories of racial supremacy and religious purges like the Crusades and the Inquisition. According to Ali Mazuri: 'because this monotheism limited the possession of a soul to homo sapiens, and sometimes for the pleasure of man almost without restraint … this is ecological racism'. Such theories permeate all aspects of Western culture, leading to the erosion of value and the spiritual and ecological crisis facing us today. This global mono-culture defines and imposes a conceptual framework and a world view that is inconsistent with the findings of the New Physics, but also with eastern religions and the traditional wisdom of other cultures.

This way of thinking was firmly established as orthodoxy in the seventeenth century by the English philosopher, Francis Bacon. His scientific method of induction or empirical generalisation was to contribute to the final rift between man and Nature despite the fact that he had written: 'Trial should be made whether the commerce between the mind of men and the nature of things… might by any means be restored to its perfect or original condition, or if that may not be, yet reduced to a better condition than that in which it is now' [quoted by Loren Eiseley, The Firmament of Time]

Today there are many who defend Bacon[19]. To these people he was the greatest English genius, some even ascribing the works of William Shakespeare to him (the Baconian Heresy[20]). But there are also many influential writers who claim that his new scientific method was anti-Nature, and there is an ongoing controversy as to where he really stood. William Blake was in no doubt: 'Bacon's philosophy had ruined England'. What is not in dispute is that he had set in motion a new scientific paradigm still with us today. As well as his own wide ranging intellectual insights he had considered that the three most important inventions to transform the world were paper and printing, gunpowder, and the magnetic compass. It is ironic that he did not know that these were all Chinese inventions hundreds of years before his time and that Chinese science never divorced itself from philosophy, ethics and history. It was even more ironic that Bacon himself had proposed that we can learn from the mistakes of history and that there should be a 'calendar of popular error'!

In the same century, Rene Descartes' dualistic philosophy established epistemology as the gateway to knowledge – that the world can be presumed to consist of two separate, irreconcilable substances, mind and matter, creating a dichotomy between the thinking human mind and unthinking matter – a determinist assumption of an objective reality based on separation of the subject from the material world. Animals have no feeling, no intelligence. These attributes only belonged to thinking man. *'As for the notions I had of several other things outside myself, such as the sky, the earth, light, heat and a thousand others, I had not the same concern to know their source, … seeing nothing in them which seemed to make them superior to me.'* [*Discourse on Method*] In essence this has led to the deracination of man from nature – that everything can be subject to mathematical analysis; and echoes Galileo's view *'that the undeniably empirical, but as yet non-quantifiable experiences of seeing, hearing, smelling, tasting, touching were mere 'secondary qualities' supplied by the mind to the real world of size, shape, motion, weight'*. [Roszak]

Almost two centuries after Descartes, the publication of Charles Darwin's *Origin of Species* (1859) introduced the orthodox theory of evolution, reinforcing Descartes' empirical, dualistic paradigm. But random selection has never been scientifically proven. One of its foremost advocates, Paul R Ehrlich, has even questioned its validity. He wrote *'that despite the persistence of Darwin's central idea* (that we are descended from apes) *evolutionary theory is not some sort of revealed truth to be believed without question'*. [*Human Natures: Genes, Cultures, and the Human Prospect*]

Many eminent scientists have contributed to the present 'scientific' view of evolution, the chief of these being Julian Sorrell Huxley [The Modern Synthesis 1943], Theodosius Dobzhansky [Genetics of the Evolutionary Process 1970], Ernst Mayr [This is Biology 1997], George Gaylord Simpson [The Major Features of Evolution 1953] and Ledyard Stebbins [In Defence of Evolution 1977]. But as we shall see there have been numerous dissenting voices and that is not to include the Creationists.

The whole concept was the final straw in the demotion of man from the pinnacle of creation. As Loren Eiseley expressed it in his elegant prose *'Earlier, man had seen his world displaced from the centre of space; he had seen the Empyrean heaven vanish to be replaced by a void filled only with the wandering dust of worlds; he had seen earthly time lengthen until man's duration within it was only a small whisper on the sidereal clock. Finally, now, he was to be taught that his trail ran backward until in some lost era it faded into the night-world of the beast'*.

Man had lost his elevated status in the sublime scheme of things. Social Darwinism was to undermine belief in anything sacred and determine the very nature of reality. It would provide the justification for imperialism and exploitation. The subtitle of *The Origin of Species* was *The Preservation of the Favoured Races in the Struggle for Life*. According to the American cultural critic Lewis Mumford, *'Darwin was in fact imputing to nature the ugly characteristics of Victorian capitalism and colonialism… This doctrine only unhappily offered a further touch of cold-*

blooded brutality, for it justified, in Darwin's own words, the "extermination of the less intellectual lower races by the more intelligent higher races" ' [letter to Lyell, 11 October, 1859: *The Pentagon of Power – The Myth of the Machine*]

The German biologist, Ernst Haeckel, justified racism, claiming that different races were a different species. *'He identifies human cultural differences with biological race and used the Darwinian concept of 'struggle for existence' to describe the violent conquest and race extermination carried by the European imperialist powers as a regrettable, but inevitable instance of the progressive workings of natural selection'.* [Ted Benton *Alas, Poor Darwin*]

Today it seems that evolutionary theory has become fashionable in the extreme. Darwin still reigns supreme where Marx and Freud are losing ground as interpreters of the human condition. Darwinian evolution is beginning to determine how all the life sciences are developing – underlying all scientific thinking from biology and medicine, psychology and psychiatry, DNA and the human genome, to computer technology and the workings of the human brain. Just a short time ago I read a review of a book *The Philosophy of Biology* (OUP 1998), in an issue of the Scientific and Medical Network Review, under the heading 'Biology as Controversy'. Whilst this heading was apt, as it illustrated the starkly conflicting views held by neo-Darwinists themselves (there is no consensus), it concluded that; *'The evidence for Darwinian natural selection was already overwhelming by the turn of the nineteenth century and our knowledge of the workings of DNA has only served to reinforce the new-Darwinian position.'*

In the past, few scientists have had the courage to question what has been accepted as gospel – the orthodoxy. Those who challenged it ran the risk of losing their status, their jobs and their credibility. But there is a growing body of scientists challenging its encroachment on their ground. *'Darwinism is everywhere... in the university, the ruling circles, the movies. It's the Matrix'* ... [there is a] *'tyranny of Darwinism over the Western mind...'* [Ted Hall, *Transcending the Matrix*] Another philosopher described it as *a "universal acid" which eats through all other understandings of not merely biological, but cultural phenomena'.* [Daniel Dennett: *Darwin's Dangerous Ideas: Evolution and the Meaning of Life*] Karl Popper said of it: *'I have come to the conclusion that Darwinism is not a testable scientific theory, but a metaphysical research programme – a possible framework for testable scientific theories... It is metaphysical because it is not testable'.*

Darwinism in all its guises has been challenged throughout the last century and today scientists from across many disciplines are challenging its reductionism particularly in the fields of socio-biology and evolutionary psychology[21].

To Have Or To Be

Ironically, it was the racist Ernst Haeckel, who first used the term 'ecology' (*oecologie*), recognising the interconnectedness of all things and mutual relations between all organisms and their environment – the spatial distribution of the population in relation to material and social causes as well as to other species of animals (including the plankton in the oceans and the rain forests); also *'the indissoluble connection between energy and matter.'* Having discovered Haeckel, it struck me that any imbalance in this relationship would be proof of the deep separation between man and Nature and that such a view was a refreshingly holistic and spiritual one in a increasingly mechanistic and materialist age, where one tended to define oneself by material possessions alone. At the after-Christmas sales in the West End of London in 2003, I came across a sign that read: 'I shop, therefore I am!' What we possess, it seems is what we are.

Césaire's masterpiece had made me aware that the West was locked in a duality that was at the very heart of all our modern problems – global economic and environmental domination which threatened its own survival, as well as that of the rest of the world. *Return to My Native Land* was not only a powerful deconstruction of colonialism but an impassioned plea by the poet for an imagined return to the Africa of his forefathers. It was a desperate longing to reconnect with the 'invulnerable sap', that state of total belonging that I was discovering in the Tao Te Ching. I began to suspect that the way of the West was contrary to the integral vision of the Tao; that despite the seeming paradoxes about us, these were not irreconcilable. Fanon of course pointed out that colonialism was an *ideological* rather than an economic project, for all its emphasis on material wealth. Hence my investigation of the ideologies that spring from Darwinism.

The recovery of history is vital in restoring erased memories but what to do with the results of my search for roots? For Fanon, resistance was the only way to empowerment but his work came out of real revolution in Algeria. He only identified the workings of colonialism, never prescribing the mechanics of any resistance and for this he is often mistakenly seen as an advocate of violence. However, many so-called 'post-colonial' commentators such as Homi Bhabha now envisage a 'third space' in which there can be a cultural resolution of what Fanon called the Manichaean split of colonialism. As the Tao had suggested, there can be *meaning* in the way we approach reality – concern for our planet and the future of mankind including our own grandchildren.

As we have seen, meaning was of the very essence of the ancient Chinese system of cosmology – it permeated all aspects of life – government, philosophy, art, medicine, our relationships with each other, even where to build our homes if we had the choice. As the authors of *The Universe Story* have put it: *'Only in this context was there any effective authority among humans, any social order and artistic creativity. The high expression of this intimacy of the human with the natural world is found in Chinese landscape painting of the twelfth century Sung Dynasty."* [Brian Swimme & Thomas Berry]

The great English scholar, Joseph Needham, has dedicated the greater part of his life to writing a monumental 25 volume treatise on Chinese civilisation: *Science & Civilisation in China* (Cambridge 1954 - ?). So far fifteen have been completed.

They document the genius of the Chinese, a civilisation like ancient Sumeria and Egypt, far in advance of the West. There is practically nothing that the Chinese did not first invent, even though modern Chinese, it seems, are not aware of this fact. According to Robert Temple in *The Genius of China* '*It is just as much a surprise for the Chinese as for Westerners to realise that modern agriculture, modern shipping, the modern oil industry, modern astronomical observations, modern music, decimal mathematics, paper money, umbrellas, fishing reels, wheelbarrows, multi-stage rockets, guns, underwater mines, poison gas, parachutes, hot-air balloons, manned flight, brandy, whisky, the game of chess, printing, and even the essential design of the steam engine, all came from China.*'

It is not surprising to learn that in the early fifteenth century, long before Columbus, a Chinese armada under Admiral Zheng of some 100 ships and 28,000 sailors had visited the coast of East Africa. Some of the larger ships were 400 feet long as compared to the mere 85 feet of Columbus' *Santa Maria*, the largest of his three ships! But unlike Columbus, Zheng's enterprise was not one of conquest [Kristof; New York Times 1999] And as Temple noted, without the genius of China, Columbus may never have crossed the Atlantic, Europe would not have established colonies and an Empire; there would have been no knights in shining armour; and printing would not have developed until much later in Europe. The circulation of the blood was already assumed in China; and the First Law of Motion was discovered by the Chinese and not by Isaac Newton.

One of the great paradoxes of the evolution of human/global consciousness is that recent Chinese political systems have turned their backs on this ancient wisdom. I suspect that it was because of the aggressive nature of European world domination that Chinese power went into decline. Today China has literally turned its back on its traditional values, harshly repressing any spiritual movements, such as the Falun Gong which it banned in 1999. [BBC Correspondent: *The Enemy Within*, 30 September 2001]

Ancient Chinese philosophy was urging me to return, like Césaire, to my own roots, the one that I most empathised with – Africa. Its animism integrated its way of life with the way of nature. By identifying with animals and trees and stones and water, Africans gained knowledge of the ways of nature, the medicinal properties of herbs, the changes in the seasons, the rising of the stars. They developed powers of prescience which though grudgingly admired by anthropologists was at the same time seen as evidence of their childishness.

A close relationship between man, Muntu, and nature extended beyond the family to the community. The African concept of a human being is that a person is always in contact with others in his daily life; *otherness* was a foreign importation with the advent, first of Islam and then of the West with its Christianity, later to be replaced by secularism posing as civilisation.

Prior to this period there existed a Nilotic concept of force unifying the whole of creation. According to Gabriel Setiloane, Associate Professor of Religious Studies,

University of Cape Town, in his *Introduction to African Theology*, *'This idea of a force permeating Nature and indistinguishable from God, is evident in other African cultures away from the Nile. In many African societies social groups have identified themselves with objects or other animals as symbols of solidarity... a sense of continuity between Nature and Man... (that) blur the distinction between Man and Nature, the divide between the living and the dead, the difference between the Divine and the human... A tree, a mountain, could have a soul. A river, in spite of its flow, could retain a soul. African religion is respectful of living creatures other than man.'*

The 'potency locked up in objects and beings' is also known as Modimo, and is immanent in all things, intangible and all pervasive. *'It is everywhere, it flows through all things, but it draws itself to a node or focus in conspicuous objects'*. Each human person forms one of these nodes or foci. According to the Sotho-Tswana *'the human person is that Energy or Force that is Modimo – Divinity.'*

The actual word used to describe the human person is the same as that used to describe the mysterious, all-pervasive energy force which is the source of life. So everyone possesses this quality of divinity. Setiloane explains that this force is positive, it unifies the relationships between the external and the spiritual worlds – the human, as well as the animal, the animate as well as the inanimate. They all radiate 'seriti'[22] which, like God himself, is everywhere. This force is also tangible and transferable. It was the same force or power which an African convert to Christianity would have understood when Jesus said, on the hem of his garment being touched by a woman, *'Someone has touched me for I perceive that power has gone forth from me'*.

Because this force is positive, it is called 'vital'. The human being is always interlocked with others and with nature in total participation. Animals as well as plants have 'seriti'. This belief was implicit in all the pre-Christian African legends. Modimo, the life force, is the source of all life and of all things. It is in every thing and it is every where, giving meaning to life.

It is the same potency that Bruce Chatwin and Robert Lawlor noted about the Dreamtime of the Australian Aborigine *'The shape of the land – its mountains, rocks, river-beds and water holes – and its unseen vibrations echo the events that brought that place into creation. Everything in the natural world is a symbolic footprint of the metaphysical beings whose actions created our world. As with a seed, the potency of an earthly location is wedded to the memory of its origin. The Aborigines call this potency the "Dreaming" of a place, and this Dreaming constitutes the sacredness of the earth. Only in extraordinary states of consciousness can one be aware of, or attuned to, the inner dreaming of the earth'* [*Voices of the First Day* Lawlor]

This is also the world view of the First Nation American. By entering into the unseen vibrations of rocks, trees, rivers, birds, animals and the entire landscape, they have an intimate perception of nature at many levels. It is not a relationship based on control but one of subjective experience, of harmony and balance, participation and obligation; an awareness of an immanent power or energy in all of creation, an energy that connected all living things and can be used to heal. It celebrated the diversity of the natural world; that chance and possibility were ever present, the circle never closed. In short, like the Modimo of African spirituality and the Dreamtime of the Australian Aborigine, life had meaning.

This concept of total participation with nature and the unity of all life existed in most ancient traditions and religions: the *boundless flux* of Tibetan Buddhists, the *ultimate indivisibility* of Zen, the *seamless whole* of Hinduism and the *web of connectivity* of the Kahunas of Hawaii. By contrast the West had moved away from so called 'mythological concepts' which ascribed any spiritual significance to nature. Instead it adopted a purely rational approach to the natural world. As Stephen Hawking has noted: *'The earliest attempts to describe and explain the universe involved the idea that events and natural phenomena were controlled by spirits with human emotions who acted in a very humanlike and unpredictable manner. These spirits inhabited natural objects, like rivers and mountains, including celestial bodies, like the sun and moon. They had to be placated and their favours sought in order to ensure the fertility of the soil and the rotation of the seasons.'* [A Brief History of Time]

William Blake, the great poet of the imagination, considered all life as holy, even a fly. Everything had value: *'Each grain of sand, every stone on the land, each rock and each hill, each fountain and rill, each herb and each tree, mountain, hill, earth and sea, cloud, meteor and star, are men seen afar.'*

John Ruskin also spoke of the *'spiritual power of air, the rocks and waters';* and for William Wordsworth…

An active Principle…
subsists In all things, in all nature; in the stars
Of azure heaven, the unenduring clouds,
In flower and tree, in every pebbly stone
That paves the brooks, the stationary rocks,
The morning waters, and the invisible air.
Whate'er exits hath properties that spread
Beyond itself, communicating good,
A simple blessing, or with evil mixed;
Spirit that knows no insulated spot,
No chasm, no solitude; from link to link It circulates, the soul of all the worlds.
This is the freedom of the universe

[The Excursion (Bk.IIX)]

DH Lawrence, true to the spirit of this earlier age, understood that true humanity *'consists in a relation with all things: stone, earth, trees, flowers, water, insects, fishes, birds, creatures, sun, rainbow, children, women, other men.* [Aristocracy, quoted by Keith Sagar in *Life into Art*]

For the Austrian poet Rainer Maria Rilke: *'The whole 'spirit world', death, all those things that are so closely akin to us, have by daily parrying been so crowded out by life that the senses with which we could have grasped them are atrophied. To say nothing of God'.*

Today some Western thinkers, psychologists and physicists are coming around to this point of view. Jung considered that the Western world view based on rationalism is <u>not</u> *'the only possible one and is not all embracing, but in many ways a prejudice and a bias that ought perhaps to be corrected.'* He believed that modern man has not truly looked into the great divide within himself, the great divide which separates him from wilderness and nature. He even went as far as suggesting that the symbols of indigenous peoples accord with archetypes of a collective unconscious – this is something the theoretical physicist David Peat takes issue with:

> *Jung's archetypes are too limited, too literal, and too impoverished to account for the vitality of Native American imagery… Indigenous knowing is a vision of the world that encompasses both the heart and the head, the soul and the spirit. It could no more deal with matter in isolation than the theory of relativity could fragment space and time. It is a vision in which rock and tree, bird and fish, human being and caribou are all alive and partakers of the gifts of Mother Earth…*

> [Blackfoot Physics]

According to Peat, indigenous science does not confine itself with trying to find the ultimate particle or theory to explain the foundation of its wisdom. Nor is it in anyway like the scientific empiricism of the West with its forever changing theories, devoid of intuition and that special knowing that comes from accepting the true integral nature of reality, of belonging and non-duality.

In *Wholeness and the Implicate Order*, another theoretical physicist, David Bohm, has given us the most intellectually challenging theory on the nature of reality in his holographic view of the universe: the interconnectedness that exists between subatomic events: that an electron is not an 'elementary particle' but only the name given to the *holomovement* as he called it. Subatomic particles only seem to be unrelated; they are not separate but part of a cosmic web in which everything is connected; there is an implicate order, a deeper reality that underpins our ordinary existence. Everything is part of a continuum, echoing the African idea of a force permeating Nature: *Even a rock is in some way alive, for life and intelligence are present not only in all matter, but in "energy" "space", "time", "the fabric of the universe" and everything else we abstract out of the holomovement and mistakenly view as separate…*

For Bohm the holomovement was 'life implicit' – the ground both of the 'explicit' and inanimate matter; life and inanimate matter are not separate, one is an outcome of the other. He maintained that scientific investigation has been grounded in the *explicate* order, on analysis, on separating the parts from the whole. As a result we have failed to see that everything is connected, that we are part of nature, that what we do to our environment we do to ourselves; and by failing to see the connection we create psychological problems for ourselves as well as jeopardising the future of the planet.

As we have noted the rise of Western civilisation coincided with the supplanting of feelings of gratitude towards nature and the vital interdependence of all things by notions of dominion over nature. These sentiments became walled off from organic harmonies and became defined in terms of opposites, as though they were absolutes in themselves and not merely aspects of the larger entity of life. [Joseph Campbell] It was only when certain seasonal regularities were seen to take place regardless of the intercessions of man that Western determinism was born. Now we have lost our beliefs in the transcendental but are no wiser about the how and the why of the universe. The Western world ignores or denies the existence of an internal or subjective consciousness to all things and creatures except humans. Desperately seeking a simple, rational system to explain the mysteries of the universe, of life and of natural phenomena most Western philosophers and scientific thinkers turned their backs on everything that could not be empirically proven, i.e. all that was not readily quantifiable.

In his book, *Radical Nature, Rediscovering the Soul of Matter,* Christian de Quincey explores the ontological gap between two radically different views, the Cartesian view of reality and that of shamanic, Taoist and indigenous traditions. He also shows that many early European traditions had much in common with the latter, from the non-duality of Pythagoras and the philosophy of Thales (*Nature was full of Gods);* to Leibniz's *monads (the ultimate substantial constituents of the world);* Spinoza's *monism* and Teilhard de Chardin's *radial energy (an interior source of universal attraction).*

For de Quincey all things have a mind or consciousness: *'The entire world of nature tingles with consciousness. Nature literally has a mind of its own. Nature feels and responds to our presence… all bodies, from atoms to humans, tingle with the spark of the spirit'* This *panpsychism* holds that all objects, including those we normally classify as inanimate possess an interior, subjective reality – that mind cannot emerge from something that is mindless, a view that our present day science does not acknowledge.

By ignoring the world view of the traditional cultures of the world, Western science rejected the one thing that could save her. By concentrating solely on splitting the atom, she has created a split in the very psyche of mankind. By replacing the myths of the world Europe has become the first of the lost tribes threatening to take all other tribes with it. Today, the central challenge facing the West is the split between the psychological and the ecological. The urban industrial way of the West runs counter to the way of Nature. The ancient wisdom of traditional cultures as well as that of poets and visionaries of all ages attest to the spiritual and psychological transformation necessary to heal the rift.

As Robert Lawlor has noted, the *Dreaming* of the Aborigines is an alien concept in our culture and so we degrade and despoil our environment and enslave animals. This alienation from nature can be traced to the 'cradle of western civilisation'; Greece. Socrates' assertion that 'trees and the open country won't teach him anything' [*Phaedrus*, Plato] was responsible for the move away from the previous participatory identification with the natural landscape of Homer's epic ballads, a sentiment shared by DH Lawrence. The early attempts of mankind to harmonise itself with nature changed with the Greeks and Romans to '*produce a mental cunning and a mechanical force that would outwit Nature and chain her down completely, completely, till at last there should be nothing free in nature at all, all should be controlled, domesticated, put to man's meaner uses.*' [*The Escaped Cock*]

As we have seen the African did not separate faith and practice, belief and ethics and, as far as I can discern, there is no African word for 'religion'. At best it is translated as 'a peoples' way' or 'customs' – something lived and practised, not discussed or discoursed about. Like the Tao, it cannot be stated. The presence of Modimo, or Divinity, is in the totality of life. So it was very easy for the African to see Christianity as coming from God, and adhere to it whilst denouncing Western civilisation. '*What African theology objects to in Western theology is the accretion of Western civilisation and culture which has come to be considered as inseparably part and parcel of Christianity.*' [EW Smith, *The Christian Mission in Africa*, quoted Setiloane]

In his book, *The Healing Wisdom of Africa*, Malidoma Somé writes about the wisdom of the Dagara cosmology of Burkina Faso in West Africa. He explores the gap between the traditional African paradigm and that of the Western materialist paradigm. He believes that in the West we have lost all connection with the world of *spirit*. For the Dagara, a relationship with the natural world imbues every aspect of life and culture. It defines the very nature of existence in which everyone is an integral part of creation and each has to find his/her life purpose. This relationship is kept alive through ritual and by enlisting the help of the ancestors and the spirits of the *other world*. For Somé, the tree, the river and the landscape '*are all golden hieroglyphs capable of bringing a deep understanding to those willing to pay attention*', reminding me of Césaire' tree of consciousness '*Look, the tree of my hands is for all*'.

Somé, however, believes that Dagara philosophy is inclusive of the West. Like the Tao, everything is part of the whole; the West is here to stay. He believed that there could be two types of knowledge; that the indigenous and the modern could co-exist without '*the deliberate narrowing of reality in modern thought*'. The indigenous knew that different laws operate in the different dimensions of reality.

He believes that the West, similarly, needs to recognise that the indigenous view of reality is also here to stay and will not go away. That already a large number of people in the West are turning to traditional cultures; but that the indigenous paradigm, may have to be 'redefined in Western 'scientific terms. I would rather say that the Western scientific paradigm would have to change to accommodate the indigenous.

In the late 19th Century and throughout the 20th century, Western man has begun to be increasingly conscious that there is something profoundly amiss in his culture and civilisation. There is *evolving* a growing consensus that we have become deracinated, uprooted, from Nature. We are slowly beginning to rediscover the connection between ourselves and our planet. It is not just a concern for environmentalists but for us all. As Theodore Roszak warns; *"Our sense of being split off from an 'outer' world where we find no companionable response has everything to do with our obsessive need to conquer and subjugate. How clearly we understand the world depends on the emotional tone with which we confront the world. Care, trust, and love determine that tone, as they do our relationship to another person."*

Many of today's deep ecologists, though loudly advocating the preservation of wilderness, are somehow unaware that lack of respect for nature cannot be divorced from a lack of respect for those who respected nature. Natural resources include human resources. You cannot be green and racist at one and the same time. We will not protect our environment, or wild life and the flora and fauna so essential for our survival, if we dehumanise our fellow humans. In denying the other half of the symbol for wholeness we deny ourselves – in denuding our environment we denude our true selves.

It was Lawrence Van Der Post who claimed *"[that].. before we can close our split natures we must forgive ourselves. We must, we must forgive our European selves for what we have done to the African within us. Even the Spring is a re-beginning because it is sheer, utter forgiveness and redemption of the winter land and its murder of leaves."*

Europe was blessed by a rich geology which provided a seemingly inexhaustible supply of natural resources and which it exploited to the full. By also exploiting the resources and peoples of vast sections of the world, it developed its dominant position in the world and continues to perpetuate the rift between humanity and nature. Now that all these resources are drying up Western technology remains dependent on a level of supply that is no longer sustainable. The West still needs the resources of a third world but not its debts – but who are the debtors? Concern for the rest of the world is in reality, concern for one's own survival.

What is urgently needed is a change in our world view for one similar to that of the Indigenous peoples of the world : respect for the ecology of the planet which includes us all. Anti-racism besides being a powerful catalyst for personal change, is a necessary first step towards that radical change needed to reconstruct our future relations with our planet and with each other. It will take nothing less than a complete psychological transformation to quell the discontent at the very heart of industrial societies. We need to develop a new resource within ourselves, *"a new science of the soul that must minister to that discontent as something that is more and other than sexually based, family based, or socially based. In our time, the private psyche in its search for sanity needs a context that embraces all that science has to tell us about the evolution of life on Earth, about the stars and the galaxies that are the distant origin of our existence."* [Theodore Rozak]

References

The Voice of the Earth; Theodore Roszak: Bantam Press, 1995

Voices of the First Day, Awakening in the Aboriginal Dreamtime; Robert Lawlor: Inner Traditions International, 1991

The Genius of China; Robert Temple: Prion, 1998

Introduction to African Theology; Gabriel Setilione: Skotaville, 1986

The Tao te Ching; Gia-Fu Feng & Jane English: Wildwood House, 1073

A Brief History of Time; Stephen Hawking, 1988

The Song Lines; Bruce Chatwin: Picador, 1988

The Healing Wisdom of Africa; Malidoma Some: Tarcher/Putman, 1997

Hopes & Impediments; Chinua Achebe: Anchor, 1990

Black Athena; Martin Bernal: Free Association Books, 1987

Blackfoot Physics; F David Peat: Fourth Estate, 1996

Beyond Geography; Frederick Turner: Rutgers University Press, 1990

The Spell of the Sensuous; David Abram: Vintage Books, 1997

The Holographic Universe; Michael Talbot: Harper Collins, 1996

Wholeness & The Implicate Order; David Bohm: Routledge & Keegan Paul, 1980

Radical Nature; Christian de Quincey: Invisible Cities Press, 2002

Life into Art; Keith Sagar: Penguin, 1985

The Firmament of Time; Loren Eisley: University of Nebraska Press, 1999

Discourse on Method; Rene Descartes: Penguin Classics, [first published] 1637

Pentagon of Power; Lewis Mumford: Harcourt, Brace Jovanovich, 1970

Alas, Poor Darwin; Ted Benton: Jonathan Cape, 2000

The Africans; Ali Mazuri: BBC Publications, 1986

Part 3

Towards a holistic reality

Chapter 9 – Universe

The universe is a teaching and learning machine. Its purpose is to know itself. Knowledge is freely available in the universe like every natural resource. It is there for everyone who is willing to make the effort to take it. We can poke around in our sequential objective time-space, or we can take the intuitive, subjective time-space route. Both are needed to get us there

Itzhak Bentov Stalking the Wild Pendulum

...most of us live a very restricted circle of their potential being. They make use of a very small portion of their possible consciousness, and of their soul's resources in general, much like a man who, out of his whole bodily organism, should get into a habit of using and moving only his little finger

William James

As Jung has pointed out, the way of the West, based as it is on rationalism, is not the only possible paradigm; but because it has been developed over centuries, an orthodoxy has been established that would be hard to overturn. One of its leading exponents, the media-popular Darwinist scientist Richard Dawkins, has also suggested that long held beliefs, or *memes* as he labels them, are as deterministic as our genes. He is notorious for claiming that our genes are like Chicago gangsters in a highly competitive world that is ruthlessly selfish [The Selfish Gene]; a concept of savage competition, ruthlessness, exploitation and deceit that has informed all our sciences. Recently, Dawkins has gone further, reinterpreting the old model in a television programme [The Big Question: Why are we here?: Channel 5, 7.1.04]: "In plants and animals reproduction appears to be the driving force, their purpose in life. [But] in human evolution our brains were the most important part of our development; our goals have changed as our brains have developed, allowing us to choose our purpose in life." For humans, in other words, our evolution has nothing to do with our genes but only with our brains, our purpose. However, these so-called special human 'good qualities' are still anti-nature – competition and survival still drive the technological machine. He implies that our developed brains will allow us to conquer *new worlds*, a blinkered conclusion in the face of the ecological crisis that threatens the very process of evolution and our survival here on Earth. It is this sort of Colombian *enterprise* that underpins the prevailing Western paradigm which we have observed in the last three chapters; the type of world view which will allow us, inter alia, to spend countless trillions on space exploration and colonisation whilst despoiling our own habitat.

The continuing ecological dilemma facing mankind stems from the dominance of the West – in political, ideological and economic terms – whose tendency as we have already explored, is to ignore the wisdom of other cultures and the possibility that they may have anything of value to offer in the great scheme of things. Western thought, by and large, has not acknowledged its debt to highly advanced ancient civilisations like those of China, India, Africa (especially Egypt) or the Middle East (Sumeria) that preceded and laid the foundation of its science and the relationships that made those civilizations great. As we have seen the ancient Chinese did not separate science, politics, religion and art into watertight compartments; each was a facet of a whole reflecting an overall natural philosophy: a holistic world view not dissimilar to the *holomovement* or cosmic web of David Bohm in which everything is connected in an implicate order.

In the Taoist tradition, balance and the reconciliation of opposites inform all its followers' sciences. Everything, everyone is part of the mystery. There is only the Impersonal Tao, which cannot be named. Naming it would create separation – them from it. Followers of this way do not have the problems we have regarding ideas of God (whether monotheism, or the existence of many gods). Their philosophy or way of life lay claim to no *divinity*, which the West first *identified* by 'naming' but now rejects, only to be replaced by Secularism and a Science which does not recognize the existence of anything but itself. Western thinking has even moved away from the beliefs of the great mystics of both East and West and, ironically, from that of the founders of its own discipline – the philosopher/scientist, Aristotle, who saw Nature as one unified whole and Sir Isaac Newton who was devoutly religious as well as a practising alchemist.

I have suggested that we need to reassess almost everything we have been taught in our schools and universities. The old paradigms have to be replaced by a new one of belonging and caring. Every choice we make and every belief we hold exerts influence upon the whole of life. As a first step, I believe that we have to look deep within our souls and rediscover our true relationship with wilderness and nature. As Lewis Mumford has so aptly stated: *"the wilderness that Western man had failed to explore was the dark continent of his own soul, that very 'Heart of Darkness' which Joseph Conrad depicted, released by its distance from Old World sanctions, throwing off archaic taboos, conventional wisdom, and religious inhibitions, and obliterating every trace of neighbourly love and humility. Wherever Western man went, slavery, land robbery, lawlessness, culture-wrecking, and the outright extermination of wild beasts and tame men went with him: for the only force that he now respected--an enemy with equal power to inflict damage on him--was lacking, once his feet were firmly established on the new soil"* [Pentagon of Power]

This book is an attempt to understand why we are in the predicament in which we find ourselves. As an outsider in England, I have been forced to try to make sense of it all and address some of the burning questions facing us today. It may be a harsh read for some: no one wants to have his gods overturned, his culture put under the microscope and found lacking but if we can see that we are the product of our past and that we have the power to change ourselves and our situation, then we may be able to make a better future for our children and for the survival of our species as well as other forms of life.

The previous discussion has pointed out how it is the West comes to be locked in a dualism that defines its orthodoxy: its science is compartmentalised, there being no overall ethic that supports the findings of them all; each is a separate and distinct part of the body of scientific enquiry that fails to see the whole picture. In this chapter, I want to look at why a unified interdisciplinary approach would be more likely to understand how evolution takes place and how our Universe operates; that we are very much part of the 'It'.

Most of our problems stem from this Eurocentric paradigm of division, competition and conquest, for it is only when we *fragment the world into parts* that we fail to see the whole. On the one hand we have great art – music, literature, paintings architecture, and great scientific and other discoveries; on the other, the seemingly irreversible march towards self-destruction – warfare, genocide, pollution of the planet, deforestation, extinction of other species. We lack any coherent philosophy that makes sense of our world. We demand empirical proof for everything but all we end up with are theories: endless theories all of which can invariably be disproved with the passage of time and new discoveries.

According to Thomas Kuhn 'normal science' is scientific endeavour that restricts itself to operate within the clearly defined parameters of the orthodox paradigm of the moment (The Structure of Scientific Revolutions). A purely scientific resolution is almost impossible where science has taken the place of religion. But a purely religious answer is inconceivable – there are too many religions, too many sects, too many philosophies. There should be no dichotomy between Science and Spirit, knowing and unknowing – polarity only exists when we are stuck in one or the other, for there is only the One Nature. This is the hurdle to be surmounted by all who question the assumptions of modern science, or seek open exploration in science and human experience. A purely scientific paradigm resists paradigm change, excluding, as it does, the invisible elements, the duality, the Mystery.

Scientific theories come and go. At most they involve formulating hypotheses and testing them *empirically,* i.e. if something can not be measured by external instruments, it is not a fit subject for Science. What the empiricists do not take into account is the fact that the human body itself is a measuring device of remarkable complexity. According to the Oxford Reference Dictionary, empirical proof relies on observation and experiment, and not on theory; but at the same time it defines empiricism as the *theory* that regards sense-experiences as the only source of knowledge. How, we may well ask, can scientific proof be based on an empiricism which is only a theory?

One of the most renowned scientists, Stephen Hawking, has even acknowledged that Scientists have no idea how the world really is – all they do is build models with which they hope to prove their theories. In his *A Brief History of Time*, he claims that *"most scientists have been too occupied with the development of new theories that describe what the Universe is to ask the question <u>why</u>? On the other hand the people whose business it is to ask why, the Philosophers, have not been able to keep up with the advance of scientific theories".*

This is the great dilemma posed by the perceived dichotomy that exists between science and intuition. Scientists demand empirical proof but the fact is that scientific method is not suitable to all fields of study. We need both science and intuition, both the left and right brain – they are not polar opposites, but part of the whole.

Science & Music

One way I believe we can demonstrate this dilemma brought about by a reliance on a so-called empirical knowledge, is by considering music and our 'empirical' sense-experience of hearing in regard to the phenomenon known as the Pythagorean comma. I make this digression into a field close to my heart but which, by synchronicity, I hope will bring us full circle to, or should I say, to the next rung of the evolutionary spiral of, the latest scientific paradigm – string theory, the possibility of a unified theory of everything!

I first came across the strange creature known as the Pythagorean comma, when I was asked by Macmillan, in 1995, to write a book about the steelpan of Trinidad and Tobago. The publisher wanted a simple, large format picture book to tell the story about the evolution of 'pan', as the instrument is called. From the very start of my research I realized that I was dealing with something very special and quite magical: the *mythic* story of the only acoustic instrument to be invented in the 20th century. It was the story of the transmutation of industrial waste material into a musical instrument, which led me to explore the nature of sound and the harmonics of music.

In making steelpans the top of the drums are sunk into a concave surface. This is followed by marking the notes and grooving, all of which disturb the molecular and crystalline balance of the steel which is corrected by tempering – the drums are heated for a specific time over intense heat to make the metal stronger and more ductile, the *soul* of the material lingering on, induced into liquid iridescent sound colours or overtones. In Trinidad, in the middle of the last century, discarded oil drums were transformed into a highly tuned percussion instrument without its innovators being aware that they were alchemists. Alchemy involves a base metallic material, the outward form of which has to be first destroyed, the energy released and reunited. Then heat is applied, blackening the substance, something known as *nigredo*. The goal of Alchemists was not just the materialist transmutation of base metal into gold but of a deeper understanding of the processes of transformation and creation. Much despised at first, the steelpan is now the national instrument of Trinidad. It has healed a divided society and it is played by all races. Today the music of pan resonates around the world.

According to a recent computer generated hypothesis, the primordial matter of the Universe arranges itself, because of gravity, in thin filaments, which the cosmologists describe as a *Cosmic Spider's web*. It is a strange coincidence that one of the earliest versions of the steelpan which spawned the modern tenor pan, was known as a spider web pan. The primordial matter of the Universe is none other than the *prima materia* of the Alchemists from which all things evolve.

In my book[23], I proposed that the universal appeal of steelpan music may be due to its special harmonic structure, although I made it clear that research still had to be done into the acoustics of the instrument. I also suggested that steelpan music produces healing natural harmonics [*unstruck* vibrations] by virtue of its unusual and complex acoustics and tuning (the harmonics or partials are tuned in). What seemed certain is that the sound the instrument makes follows the rules of Physics which are universal. The *overtone series* is *pure sound* and not the product of Western *tempered* tuning. It may well be that steelpan music bridges both and that an exploration into the world of pan will not only be about steel drums, but also about the true meaning and significance of the word *pan* ('all' in Greek) – it has certainly led me to an understanding that everything in creation has a harmonic base, that metaphysics is part of reality.

I no longer agree as I did in that book (p95 para1), with Joachim-Ernst Berendt's statement that the 'ears' of the world experience the teleological nature of the Western system of harmony. Although I stand by the main tenet of the book – that the creation of the steelpan was an alchemical process, I did not at the time quite understand how I myself was being transformed by studying the underlying principles of the harmonics of music.

The study of harmonics can be traced back to Pythagoras, the 6th Century BC Greek philosopher and if pursued, will take us to that mysterious *comma* which was named after him. His theory of the *harmony of the spheres* was itself most likely derived from the Egyptian *sidereal* musical scale. As already noted, he had studied for 21 years in Egypt and the school which he later set up in Crotone, Southern Italy, was based on Egyptian mathematical and religious (*pan* theistic) principles.

In his book on the life of Pythagoras, the historian Iamblichus, describes how the Greek philosopher, was walking past a brazier's shop, when he heard 'hammers beating out a piece of iron'. The hammers were producing sounds that 'accorded' with each other. Going into the shop he found that those that sounded well together had weights that were related – twice, three times or half the weight of one another. He applied what he had discovered to various instruments, to pipes, reeds, monochords, triangles and to instruments known as patellae or pans. He had in fact discovered the *overtone series*. The sounds he heard – 'hammers beating out a piece of iron' – have resonated down the centuries: some Trinidadians still refer to playing pan as beating iron!

In the overtone scale, also known as the harmonic series, the notes rise in exact numerical relationships to the fundamental. Taking the fundamental as the first note, the second note is twice its frequency (an octave); the third note is three times the fundamental (a fifth in musical terms); the 4th four times the frequency (the next octave) and so on. As we move further away from the fundamental, the intervals between the octaves become progressively smaller (i.e. the ratios between the numbers become smaller and smaller the greater their number).

Overtones are in pure mathematical proportions, or whole number ratios, and the most consonant of these are the octave (2/1) and the fifth (3/2). But no matter how many times you put a fifth on top of a fifth you will never reach an exact octave. A succession of twelve musical fifths is almost the same as seven octaves, but not exactly. Starting, for instance, from a fundamental C, a series of twelve perfect fifths will arrive at B#, which is slightly higher in pitch to that of the original C. This discrepancy in pitch is known as the Pythagorean comma[24], because Pythagoras was thought to be the first to discover it. A comma is the interval between two almost identical notes. To bridge this discrepancy, Western music, since the Seventeenth century, has adopted what is called *equal temperament* in which commas do not exist; the interval between each of the twelve semitones of the octave is exactly equal. Apart from the octave, all the notes are out of tune to the natural principles of resonance. The introduction of Equal Temperament has forced the natural spiral of perfect fifths into a circle[25] of imperfect fifths by the process of flattening them 1/12 of a Pythagorean comma, thus equalizing the B# and C. It has eliminated the problem posed by the Pythagorean comma and allows for chord changes and shifts in key.

Despite the obvious advantages, Western music has moved away from natural harmonic resonances and has threatened the music of other cultures. Accepting the comma would be to admit the limitations of the human intellect, that empirical proof is only an illusion of science. Perhaps the symbolic value of the Pythagorean comma, is that infinite and intangible side to our world that we cannot explain. *E.T.* is indeed an alien in that it does not accord with the laws of physics. If physical laws can be ignored there can be no such thing as empirical proof. At the very time empiricism first was introduced in Enlightenment Europe, clocks were becoming commonplace and the first Astronomer Royal, John Flamsteed, [1646-1720] claimed that *"The clocks have proved rational conjecture to be a very truth"*. Clock faces are divided in twelve equal hours just as the circle of musical fifths has replaced the natural spiral of the Pythagorean comma. In 1752 the Gregorian calendar was adopted in Britain, this being another symptom of our disconnection from the natural, our 'organic' sense of time, that is lunar time.

The switch to equal temperament at the end of the 18th century began in earnest with the Industrial Revolution and the standardization of pianos and organs. Today, the New Oxford Companion to Music (1983) actually defines Just Intonation[26], a system of tuning instruments derived from the natural Harmonic Series, as a system of tuning in which the notes furthest from the fundamental *"are severely out of tune, hence the introduction of Equal Temperament as a substitute for the 'natural' non-tempered scale."* One can safely speculate that Equal Temperament is part of the foundation of modern Western civilization, based on technology and has contributed to our separation from nature and to the ultimate triumph of science – rationality now supersedes reality... And so we have lost that sense of magic the ancient Greeks once embraced. Considered to be irrational, the Pythagorean comma is of no import, because we need to be in control, not only in the sacred realm of music, but of time itself.

When equal temperament was first implemented it was generally considered inharmonious, producing *'a harmony extremely coarse and disagreeable'* (Robert Smith 1759). The father of scientific acoustics, Hermann von Helmholtz (1821-1894), who had proposed the first scientific theory of consonance and dissonance, claimed that equal temperament *'had a deplorable effect on music practice.'* Since its introduction much of early music by the great composers is no longer heard as it was written e.g. J.S. Bach's vocal and organ music and Handel's works for clavichord and harpsichord which were written in the mean-tone[27] system. All this was to change when, in 1723, Bach himself adopted the system. His *Wohl-temperiertes Klavier* (Well Tempered Clavier) covers all twenty four major and minor keys and *'enabled compositions in all keys to be played without disagreeable discords'*. [Sir James Jeans: *Science & Music*] It also facilitated modulation and transposition. Resisted at first, equal temperament gradually caught on and spread dramatically, swamping the music of all other cultures. It should be noted that the tempered scale was in fact proposed as early as 1492 by the Spanish musician, Bartolo Rames, and by the French mathematician Marin Mersenne in 1636. [Jeans]. It was also proposed by Chu Tsai-Yu[28], a Chinese Prince, over a hundred years before Bach adopted it. The Chinese, however, have stayed with the natural intervals as sacrosanct to the relationship between man and the Cosmos.

In the West, we learned to hear the inexact intervals of equal temperament as true. As I mentioned in Chapter 1 – El Dorado, I was brought in a musical family. My mother taught the piano and I myself could play *Für Elise* by Beethoven, and some of the relatively easy pieces for students of the piano. My ears were entrained to equal temperament as my mind had been to Western versions of history and, more importantly, to the dualism that underpins the Western paradigm, a subject explored in more detail in Chapter 12. In tempering the musical intervals we have tampered with nature, claiming the product as the real thing – reality. Perhaps that is why the world is in the state that it is in today.

Herman Hesse in his book *Musique*, seems to be saying the same thing: *"The music of a harmonious epoch will be calm and serene and the government will be moderate. The music of an agitated epoch will be shouting and loud and the government will be wrong. The music of a State on the decline is sentimental and sad and the government will be in danger".* [qt. Fabien Mamam: *The Role of Music in the Twenty-First Century*] This corresponds with the view of the ethno-musicologist, Alain Danielou, who believed that for the world to be in a state of equilibrium, its different elements need to be harmonized. *Music expressed the relations between human and cosmic order and* must respect the exact intervals on which these relations are based. *"Disregard for such an obvious law necessarily leads to a breakdown of equilibrium and social disorder;.....by allowing such aberrations as equal temperament, the lack of a proper theoretical foundation will in all probability drive the European classical system to complete decadence."* [*Music & The Power of Sound*]

If I learned anything from studying the Tao Te Ching, it is that life is paradoxical and true knowledge or wisdom elusive; that there is no consonance without dissonance. The tempered scale and the natural scale are all contained within the holographic whole. Commas are part of the harmonic fabric of natural resonance. As we have seen, a series of Pythagorean fifths create an infinite spiral not a closed circle; and the Pythagoras Comma (expressed in numerical terms, 1.0136) was none other than the *tiny gap* or sacred number of the gods of the ancient Egyptians which applied not only to music but to astrology and cosmology. The Well Tempered Clavier is wonderful music; my ears do not hear the slight dissonances. Indeed, the noted British scientist, Sir James Jeans has stated that *"The indisputable dissonances of equal temperament no longer distress us in the way that they seem to have distressed our more fastidious predecessors."* [*Science & Music*] Nonetheless, because of the importance that I attach to the 'comma', I should like to set out some of the ways the natural scale has been employed over the years, by cultures both western and eastern.

The universal consonance and appeal of early music has been known to have a healing effect. This was demonstrated by Dr. Alfred Tomatis, a French physician and researcher in the field of audio-psycho-phonology (a science of re-educating the ear) when he demonstrated that the reason monks in a monastery in France were becoming lethargic and falling ill, was due to the fact that their normal routine of chanting had been suspended for some months. When the practice was re-instituted they became well again. Tomatis believed that sacred chant, rich in high frequency harmonics has a neuro-physiological, transformative and healing effect on mind and body. The Tomatis method employs an *Electronic Ear* especially invented by Tomatis over very many years of research, in which sounds – *particular kinds of music,* are filtered to emphasize the harmonics. By hearing these higher frequencies the ear can be re-educated and many conditions, like autism and schizophrenia, *inter alia*, cured.

Through a study of Sacred Geometry[29] I first became aware of the relationship between sound and form, that a harmonic structure underlies all creation – not only in the field of mathematics, geometry, architecture, philosophy, physics and many other natural sciences (to our body structures and sense organs) but also to sound and music therapy. The deep structure of music is the same as the deep structure of everything else. The musicologist, Rudolph Haas, discovered that "harmonic proportions exist in chemistry – molecules strive for symmetry." The irrational Pythagorean comma may be beyond the grasp of whole numbers as is the Fibonacci series in the spiral growth patterns we see in nature[30]. The irrational numbers, the intangibles, are the Mystery which cannot be grasped by Science alone.

> *Beyond form, it cannot be seen*
> *beyond sound, it cannot be heard*
> *intangible, it is not to be grasped*
> *indefinable, these three merge into one*

Tao Te Ching

Instead of seeing things in irrational numerical terms, we must somehow grasp them without being able to describe them in words.

Shape clay into a vessel It is the space within that makes it useful

Tao Te Ching

The space within is none other than the *tiny gap* or sacred number of the gods of the ancient Egyptians. Remarkable as it may seem, it has been demonstrated that perception and awareness depend on myriads of neuronal interactions within the brain. All nerve impulses have to jump a *tiny gap* (a synapse) between the *axons and dendrites*[31]. How we interpret what we see may depend on how we perceive them.

Sir Isaac Newton discovered the full colour spectrum of light by viewing the light of the sun through a narrow slit between curtains, filtering it through a prism. The rays of the colour spectrum are to *light* what the harmonic series is to *sound*. Overtones are always present although not always filtered out by our hearing. But the *rainbow of sound*, the overtone series, can be heard, for instance, in the magical art of overtone singing. This kind of singing was first introduced to the West through the recent interest in world religious practices and music, for instance in the chanting of Tibetan monks and the many toned singing (known as throat singing) of the Tuvan people from Mongolia. It has led to a revival of interest into the nature of sound.

The great Sufi master, Hazrat Inayat Khan, has said that what we simply refer to as music *"is only a miniature from the music or harmony of the whole universe which is working behind everything, and which is the source and origin of nature. It is because of this that the wise of all ages have considered music to be a sacred art. For in music the seer can see the picture of the whole universe..."* For him *"The cosmic system (works) by the law of music, the law of harmony; and whenever that harmony in the cosmic system is lacking in any way, then in proportion disaster comes to the world, and its influence is seen in the many destructive forces which are manifest there".*

The ancient Greeks were deeply aware of this cosmic relationship of music to science and culture. They knew that the mathematical laws of music were the same as the laws that regulated harmony in all matters, from the growth patterns of plants to geometry and good government. This *magical* connection between sound and all aspects of manifestation, including form, was integral to many cultures and a way of restoring harmony at all levels of society. They used various modes for calming, stimulating and creating desired moods. These modes resonate with the endocrine system of the body.

Music was also integral to every aspect of ancient Chinese culture and government. According to the Yue ji, *"under the effect of music, the five social duties are without admixture, the eyes and the ears are clear, the blood and the vital spirits are balanced, habits are reformed, customs are improved, the empire is in complete peace".* [qt. Danielou] This was to a lesser extent true of the music of Arabia, Persia (Iran), Turkey, Japan, Tibet and Africa. African Music was said to be *"divine expression… is medicine. Its intensity, its pitch, its timbre all translate the power of the gods into action among human beings and the physical world. Thus music can charm a person, send her/him into an altered state of consciousness: it can heal someone.."* Dr. Anthony Ekemezie Mereni The British Journal of Music Therapy Vol.10 No.1.

Indian classical music is modal (each piece being based on a single scale or mode [raga] and not on chords which are constantly changing), with a fixed ground tone, but finding its true expression in improvisation, tone colour, embellishments and intervals that are not found in Western tempered scale. In Hindu musical theory there are two kinds of sound, ahata nada, struck sound, and anahata nada, unstruck sound. The former corresponds with our scientific understanding of sound vibration, the latter with the Pythagorean. In *Shabad Yoga*, the Sound Current (also referred to as the Audible Life Stream) equates to the concept of limitless sound, the WORD, or Divine Creative power, or LOGOS. This yoga of the Divine Word utilizes Anahad Shabd or unstruck[32] sound as an aid to spiritual development and liberation from the bonds of mind and matter while living here and now on earth. In the teachings of the *Saints* (Sant Nat), the *soul* (Surat) merges with the *Word* (Shabd) and is carried to the Source, the Godhead. It is a system of meditation that takes its followers to the highest attainable states of spiritual development and consciousness by developing the Audible Life Stream or Sound Current. The principle behind Dhrupad, one of several styles of giving voice to the cosmos, for instance, is that of *advaita,* non-duality, that the individual soul (atman) is not separate from the universal soul (Brahman).

Improvisation is at the very heart of Indian music as it is in jazz, which is also modal in character. Thus music can be a communication linking both performer and audience to the cosmic forces. The art of improvisation, which is no longer found in the Western classical musical tradition, connects the musician to the *subtle bodies* or auras (the higher harmonics of his physical body) by activating the psychic centres, or chakras, of his body. Indian classical music has been making these connections for three millennia and as Joachim-Ernst Berendt says, knowing this *"might make Western music lovers become more humble about their generation-old pretension of having a monopoly on musical culture and on 'classical music' in particular."* Except for the atonality of Schoenberg, Berg, Webern, et al, Western music has come to incorporate key signatures related to scales and with a tonal centre; in general it comprises tension and resolution away or towards that centre. Early Western music, on the other hand, employed modes which did not have a tonal centre but produced music with that timeless quality found in plainsong and Gregorian chant. These intervals have a universal consonance and appeal as in early Christian music and are still to be found in Eastern Church music. What I have sought to show, by the many examples set out above, is that modal music has a *spiritual* 'feel-good' quality, connecting us to something greater than ourselves, the cosmic order and tranquillity.

Metaphor or Quantum Reality

In his book *Temperament*, Stuart Isacoff, a prominent music critic sets out to show *'How Music became a battleground for the great minds of Western civilization'*, documenting the controversy that has raged through the centuries. The book sets out to justify equal temperament as a natural progression in the development of Western music. He concedes, however, that equal temperament is impossible to attain on a modern piano *'because of the permanent out-of-tuneness of the strings'* (due to the variations in materials, temperature changes etc. etc. etc.). On the very last pages of the book, he recounts his experience at a private recital by the composer and pianist Michael Harrison on his 'microtonal' *harmonic* piano, which left the invited audience completely spaced out.

> It sounded like a jumble at first – a drone, or a room full of drones. Then, from within the din, high-pitched sounds seemed to rise and float towards the ceiling...... he seemed to free an angelic choir above..... musical concords seemed to emerge and shake hands above the fray.... I though of Huai Nan Tzu, his temperament theories and his ascent to heaven..... And I thought: Perhaps Pythagoras was right after all

He seemed to be conceding that non-tempered music may reflect the 'great cosmic dance' of the latest and hottest scientific 'Theory of Everything', String Theory, which holds that everything in the universe *is* composed of infinitely vibrating strings – that what were once described as different elementary particles are really just different notes in an enormous celestial symphony.

This is exactly the position of Brian Greene, a leading string theorist. In his book *The Elegant Universe,* he states that throughout history, scientists had collectively sought the song of nature *"in the gentle wanderings of celestial bodies and the riotous fulminations of subatomic particles"* – in other words, musical *metaphors* take on a startling *reality*. String theory suggests that *"the microscopic landscape is suffused with tiny strings whose vibrational patterns orchestrate the evolution of the cosmos. The winds of change, according to superstring theory gust through an Aeolian universe".*

It is extremely relevant at this point to note that Max Planck, one of the founders of modern quantum theory in Physics and the originator of wave/particle duality (that objects manifest properties that are both wavelike and particle-like) had been greatly interested in music. He worked out his quantum theory on the basis of the overtone series of natural harmonics. He observed that notes jump from whole number to whole number and was able to deduce that *"'particle energy' in the atom changes not gradually but in 'jumps.'* For Planck the term matter implied a bundle of energy which is given form by an intelligent spirit, [*Nada Brahma*, J. Berendt] a concept close to the Pythagorean metaphor of the Music of the Spheres which has guided inquiry through the ages.

Wave-particle duality is central to String theory, a tantalizingly promising unified *theory* of everything (TOE). Although no analogy is made between waves and strings it is nevertheless inferred – the tiny vibrating strings that make up the particles that make up the atoms that make up matter (and which Einstein's Equation $E=mc^2$ shows to be interchangeable with energy) constitute the *wave*like properties of quantum theory.

Today, a great many physicists believe TOE is in all probability the grand unified theory they have long been looking for. Also known as M theory (M for Matrix, Mother, Membrane), string theory is described as a theory of super symmetry and mathematical beauty – a unified, elegant and overarching *theory* of the very nature of our Universe – all the principles underlying the physical universe as well as the forces of nature, reconciling gravity with Einstein's General Relativity Theory, Quantum Mechanics and Electro-magnetism and the Strong & Weak nuclear Forces. It proposes that the Universe is comprised of tiny vibrating *strings* (or energies) each with its own resonant pattern or fundamental, just as in music each string on a violin, for instance, has its fundamental note which includes the natural harmonics or overtones. [Two strings of equal length sound harmonious, or when one is plucked at ½, ⅔ or ¾ of the other's length i.e., in proportions expressible in the smallest whole numbers – ½, the octave, ⅔, the fifth and ¾ the fourth] These are the same ratios as in the overtone series and which accord with the laws of physics. This is a marvellous analogy supporting my own preoccupation with the nature of Sound; that the world is sound – *Nada Brahma*. Indeed, Pythagoras had proposed a mathematic and therefore musical structure to the Universe despite the irrationality of the Pythagorean Comma which cannot be explained empirically.

Although String Theory claims to accommodate all previous scientific theories and specifically acknowledges duality as an essential ingredient, it still does not acknowledge that Science and Philosophy are not irreconcilable: that would not be *scientific*. It still has difficulty accepting the philosophical implication of its own findings. Any truly unified theory of everything must be integral: a purely dualistic approach cannot comprehend the Mystery, the mind of God [Stephen Hawkins]. There can be no unification of scientific or other theories that excludes the individual, who is part of the Universe. Both left and right brain hemispheres are linked, as by a string (or mobius strip). It may well be that the strings of string theory are not just 'open' lengths with free ends, or closed loops of vibrating energy as claimed, but interconnecting energy particles that speak to each other suggesting a different, holistic Reality – that of a non-dual Universe. Scientists, it seems, only find the kind of reality they set out and so deserve to find.

String Theory also proposes that there may be as many as eleven parallel universes! If it can be proven that there are indeed more that just one Universe, then the philosophical implications would be profound, foremost of which is that they will all exist within a Reality, a greater whole, that goes beyond what we can comprehend; the unnameable Tao. It should be obvious that even within our present universe/reality there exist the different (parallel?) realities or beliefs of the majority of mankind – those of the ancient Egyptians, the Taoists, the Hindu, the Maya, the Hopi and of the other indigenous peoples we encountered in Chapter 8 – An Ecology of Being.

Holons and Holograms

The question we are forced to consider is, is there some other approach to understanding our Universe which surpasses all empirical systems and epistemologies and which is capable of providing us with an 'implicate order' or grand unified theory which embodies all the laws applying to different spheres of activity and existence and which we have to understand before we can make any sense of our *ordinary* world?

Sting theory does indeed provide a materialist concept that approximates to a new holistic paradigm. All that is needed is a point of view no longer entrained to a purely scientific approach. And this I believe has been taking place gradually over the past three decades – in fact with the emergence of Quantum Mechanics itself. No theory is worth an ounce of salt if it cannot provide us with a sense of meaning in our lives. There have indeed been many worthwhile systems of knowledge: we certainly know enough to prevent ourselves from falling over the edge of the earth, and to apply Newton's laws of physics to take us to the moon and back and It was not so long ago that Stephen Hawking predicted that soon we will be able to read the mind of God, presumably the monotheistic god of the Semitic religions, out there somewhere, who can be empirically proven or discounted – a god of a purely material and physical universe.

Scientific theories follow each other in quick succession – from gravity and Newtonian physics to atoms, electromagnetism, general Relativity Theory, Quantum Mechanics (with its Uncertainty principle and probability theory) singularities, black holes, the big bang, parallel Universes, String or M Theory and finally to dark matter, dark energy and neutrinos. What seems certain is that we will never find a purely physical explanation of the nature of Reality, until we realise that theories follow theories in an evolutionary spiral like that of the Pythagorean musical spiral of fifths. We may never find the answer to our questions in purely measurable terms.

According to Itzhak Bentov, *"Knowledge moves in an ever-expanding upward spiral, which allows us to see from the higher turns of the spiral our previous knowledge in a broader perspective. Thus, Newton's mechanics have become a 'special case' within Einstein's theory of relativity"* [*Stalking the Wild Pendulum*]. In the same way, Einstein's theory of relativity has become a 'special case' in an endless spiral of cosmological theories leading to the latest 'special case' that strikes a cosmic chord – String Theory, the grand unified theory of everything. A failure to see the spiralling nature of the evolution of knowledge, is what Ken Wilber termed, *flatland* – a fragmentary view of reality and *"a failure to grasp ... the full spectrum of consciousness."*

I quite like Arthur Koestler's idea that evolution progresses by making and discarding hypotheses. He had coined the word holon to describe a whole within a whole, that Reality is composed of holons (universes within universes?), that reality is holistic. If this is so, there should be no dichotomy between science and intuition, rational analysis (so often limited by exclusively materialistic reasoning) and intuitive insights.

Even before the advent of String Theory, the new physics and its acceptance of probability theory, attested to this fact. Its findings have sounded remarkably like the sayings of Eastern mysticism. For example, Heisenberg's *Uncertainty Principle*, states that at the atomic level, the position and momentum of a particle cannot be determined with limitless accuracy simultaneously. And Bell's *Theorem*, says that the very act of observation affects the results of any quantum event -- that an object may at one time be seen as a particle, at another as a wave. [Local *hidden variables* are incompatible with quantum mechanics, i.e. they are in fact nonlocal – John Bell]

We cannot be certain what it is until we observe it and yet the very act of observation will affect our findings. In sub-atomic physics, electrons and neutrons 'EXIST' although they can only be deduced to exist. And so at the most, in considering the nature of reality, we can only attempt to deduce the nature of the intelligence which holds our Universe together and which connects our minds and our feelings and our bodies and the ecological system to one another. In so doing we cannot state it in material, or finite or numerical or quantitative terms. Reality can only be thought of in metaphysical terms, beyond scientific definition.

One scientific theory which attempted to resolve this seeming dichotomy was put forward by the theoretical physicist, David Bohm in which he treats the totality of experience as an unbroken whole. For instance, the strange behaviour of an object as both wave and particle can be explained when both aspects are understood to be enfolded in a quantum whole. [*Wholeness and the Implicate Order*] Bohm provides a scientific critique of the fragmentation that so bedevils our outlook at all levels of activity, replacing it with a holistic model of interconnectedness. *"In terms of the implicate order one may say that everything is enfolded into everything. This contrasts with the explicate order now dominant in physics in which things are unfolded in the sense that each thing lies only in its own particular region of space (and time) and outside the regions belonging to other things."*

Orthodox scientific thinking, locked in fragmentation (in the explicate order), still finds it difficult to come to terms with this approach. As Fritjof Capra put it over thirty years ago, *"It is indeed ironic that the Physicists themselves do not seem to realize the philosophical and cultural implications of their theories, for many of them actively support a society still based on the mechanistic and fragmented whilst their science points beyond such a limited view to one of wholeness, of the oneness of the Universe which includes not only our natural environment but also our fellow human beings. [The Tao of Physics]*

And there are many other distinguished thinkers and scientists who seem to support Bohm's quantum theory of an Implicate/Explicate order in which he describes the universe as a *holomovement.* One of these was the neurophysiologist, Karl Pribram, who made the discovery that memory was non-localized in the brain; that it was not stored in a particular section of the brain. In other words that the brain was holographic. He also believed that every part of our body is a reflection of the whole.

In his book, *The Holographic Universe,* Michael Talbot links both the theories of Pribram and Bohm. *"Considered together, Bohm and Pribram's theories provide a profound new way of looking at the world: Our brains mathematically construct objective reality by interpreting frequencies that are ultimately projections from another dimension, a deeper order of existence that is beyond both space and time: The brain is a hologram enfolded in a holographic universe."*

This was also the view of Itzhak Bentov, a practical thinker and inventor with an open mind not constricted by the straitjacket of an orthodox *scientific* education His revolutionary concept of the human brain as a hologram in a holographic Universe, echoes the theories of Bohm and Pribram.

Another theory that seems to validate Bohm's *holomovement* in which everything is enfolded in everything else, is Fractal Geometry, proposed by the French mathematician, Benoit Mandelbrot[33]. He suggests that patterns in nature repeat themselves in different scales – that they are merely fractions or fractals of each other, and that this encoded phenomenon can be seen in solid structures; i.e. that the earth is modelled according to these principles. [*The Fractal Geometry of Nature*]

Referring back to evolutionary theory, briefly discussed in the last Chapter, It is perhaps worth noting that one of the leading Neo-Darwinist biologists, Paul R Ehrlich, once suggested *"that evolutionary theory was not the only possible explanation of observed patterns in nature, just the best explanation that has been developed so far. It is conceivable, even likely that what one might facetiously call a non-Euclidean theory of evolution, one that is beyond our current imaginations, lies over the horizon."* [Patterns & Populations, Science 137: 652-7, 1962]

Not only has Bohm's holographic universe been supported by Pribram, Bentov and Talbot, but Mandelbrot's mathematics also seems to validate it. *"A decade after Mandelbrot... some theoretical biologists began to find fractal organisation controlling structures all through the body."* [James Gleick, Chaos: Making a New Science]

Both fractals and holograms can be understood by considering the ripples and interference patterns caused when one or more stones are thrown into a pond. When one stone is thrown, the ripples are fractals of each other, different only in their size. When two stones are dropped into the same pond, their ripples will pass through each other creating irregular ripples known as an interference pattern, as on holographic film taken by a laser. The film is a holographic record containing the encoded image of the object photographed but which is dramatically transformed into a three-dimensional image of the object when another laser is shone on it.

The 1982 experiments of the French experimental physicist Alain Aspect, demonstrated that the web of subatomic particles that comprise our physical universe also supported the concept of the holographic nature of quantum reality–

that there was an unbroken wholeness or interconnectedness in the Universe that transcended space-time. Aspect's experiments *empirically* demonstrated that *photons* (correlated grains of light) influence each other across space without exchanging signals, something that is now known as quantum non-locality. This finding, incidentally, completely reversed Einstein's space time locality – that there is a finite time for an object to travel through space. Einstein, probably our greatest scientist, was to die disillusioned. Quantum physics had made his ideas outdated even though he himself had fathered it.

David Bohm had endeavoured to explain the connection between two particles without violating Einstein's special relativity, by an analogy of a fish in an aquarium being monitored on a television projection of the fish seen from the front of the tank and simultaneously from the side. For someone who had never seen a Television split screen image or indeed a fish in a tank, it might appear that they were two fish responding to each other's movements without being able to communicate with each other – the only communication was at a deeper level of reality.

It may now be possible to see that it is consciousness that converts possibility into actuality. According to Amit Goswami, a distinguished professor of Physics, non-locality is the transcendent domain of Reality. In his book, *The Self Aware Universe*, he acknowledges the view of the physicist, Henry Strapp, who as early as in 1977, concluded that things outside space-time affect things inside space-time, and which, incidentally, accords with the psychologist, Stanislav's Grof's transpersonal psychology and with his own theory that matter is not the primary stuff of the universe as held by classical science, but that consciousness is the ground of all being.

Perhaps through the groundbreaking findings of the early classical scientists, like Einstein, Newton *et al*, to those of the scientific explorers of the New Physics, Niels Bohr (complementarity principle), Max Planck (who discovered the quantum and its relationship to the overtone series in music) and the quantum leaps made by Werner Heisenberg (the uncertainty principle) and Erwin Schrodinger and others like Henry Strapp and John Bell, we can now envisage a new integrated philosophy that transcends the reality of a purely scientific materialistic theory of everything in which things are seen as separate and independent.

The Tao Te Ching – a return to primordial wisdom

Amit Goswami's *non-locality as the transcendent domain of Reality* really strikes a chord with me. I am not a physicist but it seems to me that the concept of non-locality is applicable to the primordial wisdom of the Tao beyond science, beyond religion or any man made concepts This book is merely a layman's attempt to understand the philosophical implications of what the New Physics may be saying. Most of its theories are profoundly difficult to grasp, but it does appear that Science, generally, has created separation instead of the primordial non-duality of reality. Absolute knowledge, if there can be such a thing, may well be a non-intellectual experience arising in a non-ordinary state of consciousness. In the words of William James *"Our normal waking consciousness, rational consciousness as we call it, is but one special type of consciousness; whilst all about it, parted from it by the flimsiest of screens, there lie potential forms of consciousness entirely different"* [*Varieties of Religious Experience*]

William James' potential forms of consciousness are akin to in D.H. Lawrence's intuition in *The Escaped Cock* *"Every real discovery made, every serious and significant decision ever reached, was reached and made by divination. The soul stirs, and makes an act of pure attention, and that is a discovery."* And again in Apocalypse. *"It was a great depth knowledge arrived at direct, by instinct and intuition, as we say, not by reason. It was a knowledge based not on words but on images. The abstraction was not into generalities and into qualities, but into symbols. And the connection was not logical but emotional."*

It required insight and intuition to lead Einstein to formulate his theories and properly viewed these are not purely material concepts. 'Matter' as energy, in philosophical terms, bears a striking resemblance to the ancient traditional African belief in a potency locked up in objects and beings which is called Modimo – Divinity. Einstein was able to predict a certain state of things through an intuition nurtured by an inner absorption with how things work. Observation and intuition led him to divine, or predict a certain scientific theory.

Deep down in the Western psyche is the knowledge that something is wrong in our approach to finding answers to the fundamental questions of existence. *Homo sapiens* has not the wisdom to see that by fragmentation and separation we have created all of our problems. Perhaps we will have to go beyond paradigms altogether and adopt a Zen or Taoist approach in this kind of enquiry. When we can see that there exists no dichotomy between Science and Spirit, Knowing and Unknowing and that polarity exits only when one is stuck in either one or the other, or in limited belief systems (scientific or religious), we may know that Nature includes everything and our approach to understanding her secrets will not be specialist, fragmentary or purely secular.

The intuition behind the Physicists' interpretation of the sub-atomic world in terms of the quantum field, closely parallels the philosophy of the Tao Te Ching, supporting both the paradox and the interdependence of all existence. This very ancient philosophy, based on a similar form of divination that comes from observation of Nature (including human nature), does not limit itself to a formulation which is without meaning. As we have seen, it does not claim its authority from empirical proof nor from Divine revelation or religious dogma. It does not exclude intuition, that faculty of the mind which in the West has been relegated to the unscientific: a faculty which can only be cultivated through an attitude to life which does not, among other things, seek to dominate and manipulate Nature, accepts it for what it is – as the very nature of existence and to live in harmony with it.

I believe that we have to leave our academic, scientific training behind when we approach the mystery of the Tao. We tend to want to analyse and look at knowledge, *what is*, in a Western 'objective', scientific and discursive way (a construct of materialist dialectics) which immediately separates us from reality. The ultimate answers to existence are not to be found in intellectual, scientific or philosophical concepts but rather on a level of direct non-conceptual experience. We should no longer confuse the indivisible nature of reality with conceptual categories of language. The meaning of the language of the Tao Te Ching can only adequately convey the meaning if related to personal experience, i.e., experiential self-exploration.

The very first lines of the Tao Te Ching state that *"The Tao that can be spoken is not the Eternal Tao"* meaning that the Tao cannot be caught by words. One cannot discuss it in ordinary language; it is ineffable; it can only be *experienced.* That is the paradox. The Tao is impersonal yet can only be known by personal experience. One could but try to live it and be in a state of complete *nowness*, one with the primordial wisdom. Very few can attain this state, so who would dare expound it? One can but meditate on its precepts: reconciliation of opposites, non-duality, non-attachment, without desire for accumulating material things.

Discovering the Tao is about discovering what is intrinsically good about human existence and how to share it with others; that there is a vast, unchanging primordial wisdom that supports all life – a sanctity that is never tarnished or diminished by the confusion that bedevils the phenomenal world e.g., the materialistic construct of the prevailing world view, nationalistic hubris, alienation from the natural sustaining environment threatening ecological disaster for our planet, economic embargoes and warfare, racism and unconcern for the poverty and suffering of the majority of mankind, It is a wisdom that predates everything in existence.

Special Note on Sound

The physical vibration of matter – a string or a column of air in a pipe produce musical notes as well as natural overtones, a sound spectrum similar to the colour spectrum of light If you depress a string on a violin at the mid-point between the nut and the bridge the sound generated is the octave above the fundamental (the note of the string) – the 2nd note in the overtone series and twice the frequency of the vibrating whole string, a ratio of 2/1. If you press at a point 1/3 of the string, the other 2/3 of the string vibrates at 3 times the frequency of the whole string, the 3rd note on the overtone series and a perfect fifth, a ratio of 3/2 This interval is a perfect fifth, the most consonant one. The next harmonic or overtone is 4 times the frequency of the open sting (another octave by the way) and so on.

In *The Crystal Sun, Robert,* Temple speculated that the Pythagoras comma, expressed in decimal terms (1.0136), a universal constant having a mathematical relationship to Erdington's *Uncertainty Constant* of 9.6 which is found in physics. "It is part of the fabric of the Universe, as fundamental as Heisenberg's Uncertainty Principle......... *fundamental to the deep structure of the universe'.* And in his book The Deep Forces that Shape the Universe, Martin Rees suggests that a tiny number governs everything – 0.007. Temple suggests that this describes only half of the process. Double it and we get 0.014, the rounded off expression of the *Particle of Pythagoras* (i.e. the raw number regardless of the scale of the Pythagoras Comma) and "which in turn is related to the physicists' dearly beloved 'fine structure constant', which is also related to the hydrogen/helium process"

References

Science & Music; Sir James Jeans: Dover Publications, 1939
Music & The Power of Sound; Alain Danielou: Inner Traditions, 1995
Temperament; Stuart Isacoff: Faber & Faber, 2001
The Role of Music in the Twenty-First Century; Fabian Maman: Tama Do, 1997
The Music of Life; Hazrat Inayat: Khan Omega, 1983
The Crystal Sun; Robert Temple: Century, 2000
The Holographic Universe; Michael Talbot: Harper/Collins, 1996
The Elegant Universe; Brian Greene: Vintage, 2000
Critique of Economic Reason; Andre Gorz: Verso, 1988
Varieties of Religious Experience; William James: Touchstone, 1997
Brain States; Tom Kenyon: United States, 1994
Ring of Steel; Cy Grant: Macmillian Caribbean, 1999
Wholeness and the Implicate Order; David Bohm: Routledge & Keegan Paul, 1980
The Pentagon of Power; Lewis Mumford: Harcourt, Brace Jovanovich, 1970
A Theory of Everything; Ken Wilber: Gateway, 2001
The Self Aware Universe; Amit Goswami: Tarcher/Puitman, 1993

Chapter 10 – The Unity of Life

...we must always renounce the lesser for the greater, the finite for the Infinite, we must be prepared to proceed from illumination to illumination, from experience to experience, from soul-state to soul-state. Nor must we attach ourselves to the truths we hold must securely, for they are but forms and expressions of the Ineffable who refuses to limit itself to any form or expression.

Sri Aurobindo

Until we successfully re-examine the implicit "nuts and bolts" of the philosophical superstructures that condition the way we think... we will continue to programme ourselves to repeat the same kinds of mistakes. A major element... in the conceptual and perceptual matrix that shapes our worldview is our scientific attitude to consciousness and its relationship to the world of matter. For, from this view, we look out on a world devoid of any real intrinsic value, or any inherent purpose, meaning or feeling.

Christian de Quincey

As we have seen, today's physicists are claiming that they may have finally arrived at a grand unified Theory of Everything – String Theory. In 2000, via the Human Genome Project, it was the biologists who had proudly announced that they had unravelled the secrets of the Book of Life. Both of these scientific theories remind me of the charming Anancy stories, or fables, I had heard as a child in Guyana beginning with the words *"Once upon a time…."*. Anancy (or, Ananse) stories are the Caribbean version of African folk tales and in those days, with there being no television, listening to them was one of the great pastimes. One in particular reminds me of the ontological dilemma we have in trying to understand reality, a theme that keeps recurring throughout this book.

Once, a very long time ago, Ananse, the wise spider man of African lore, thought that the world's wisdom needed to be kept in a safe place so he decided to gather it all up in a large pot and leave it at the top of the tallest palm tree he could find. Unfortunately he tied the pot in front of him and this hindered him as he struggled to climb the tree. When he was just half way up, the pot became dislodged and fell to the ground scattering all the wisdom he had so painstakingly collected. He should, of course, have tied the pot to his back. And ever since then mankind has been scrambling to pick up the pieces which they proceeded to put in libraries all over the known world – from Alexandria to Timbuktu.

I had also been aware of the biblical story of the Garden of Eden. My father, you will recall, was a Christian minister. Today when I think of these two stories I can see that they have something in common, i.e. our misinterpretation of the true nature of the tree of knowledge. The Garden of Eden was the location of Paradise, representing peace and the unity of all life. After Adam's fall from grace, it has become a place of conflict and duality – good and evil, man and god, man and woman; and so a rejection of the life giving principle, unity in diversity. The biblical *Genesis* is now the physicists' Human genome Theory – the book of life – gene therapy, and genetic engineering.

The garden revealed another powerful symbol – the snake. It has played a central role in the unfolding drama of the evolution of consciousness. We know from the last chapter that at least one scientist, the physicist, David Bohm, viewed the totality of existence, including *matter* and *consciousness,* as an unbroken whole, but still it seems strange that the snake, so universally feared, has played such a central role in human cultures. Snakes were sacred to Apollo, for whom they symbolised transcendence (as mediator between one way of life and another) as well as healing. In most cultures[34], the snake symbol has been interpreted in a positive way, for instance the Sumerian entwined serpents of Enki and the double *Cosmic Serpent* of the ancient Egyptians – 'the provider of attributes' which held the key of life; the opposing serpents of the Navajo Indians leading to integration – the two halves of the double spiral which meet at the spherical vortex; the anaconda of the Desana of the Colombian Amazon – a serpent separating the two hemispheres of the brain; and also the Serpent Lord in human form depicted on an old Mesopotamian seal and represented by the double helix symbol.

It is obvious that in cultures where the serpent represented two opposing energies of good and evil, the double helix symbolizes the life principle, its spirals resembling two snakes coiled around each other. In his book, The Cosmic serpent, Jeremy Narby quotes Joseph Campbell: "whenever nature is revered….and so inherently divine, the serpent is revered as symbolic of its divine masks." [*The Masks of God*: Occidental Mythology]

The intertwined snakes of the Caduceus comprised the therapeutic symbol of the Roman god of medicine, Aesculapius. Today, the caduceus has been adopted by the medical profession as its symbol. To heal was to make whole and the snake represented both death and life and the mystery of death and rebirth. By shedding its skin it was born again. It is now possible to see that these ancient symbols of double serpents are none other than the physiological symbol of the DNA double helix.

The crystalline structure of DNA (deoxyribonucleic acid), known as the Double Helix, was *discovered* in 1953 by James Watson and Francis Crick – an achievement for which they were awarded the Nobel Prize (The real work however, was done by Rosalind Franklin, a young English researcher at Cambridge University[35]). DNA molecules are in the form of two spirals, which comprise the structure of the genetic code and the system by which DNA (and RNA) molecules carry genetic information. The spirals are connected, as on a ladder, by rungs of complex organic compounds.

Since that time (in the 1980's) genetic scientists have concluded that all races originated from a common female ancestor in Africa, the so-called mitochondrial Eve. (mt.DNA,) This was a significant discovery. When I was growing up, such an idea would have been considered sacrilege. Yet the knowledge that all human beings share the same DNA and so are members of the same human family, has not prevented the phoney science of Eugenics[36] from resurfacing (even though it is now discredited), carried on under the new name of genetic engineering.

The announcement of the completion of the mapping of the human genome and the discovery that human beings share the same four basic molecules of the DNA code with a one-celled animal called the tetrahymena, is also significant. There is only one source of DNA for all life on earth – everything that lives has the same DNA: human beings, animals, insects and plants. We have evolved from the humblest of life forms, a fact which clearly demonstrates the unity of all life, and most likely the most positive thing to have come out of the project.

Genes are the stretches of DNA that direct the production of amino-acids and proteins and each gene consists of thousands of letters They however, represent only 3% of the human genome – the genetic information of an individual; the other 97% science has relegated to the dust bin – just gibberish or 'junk DNA' as it has been termed. Also, the genetic code consists of only four elements to transmit information: a four letter alphabet A,C,G & T, the initials of the four nucleic acids (Adenine, Cytosine, Guanine, Thymine) which spell out all life on earth and which combine to make just 64 three-letter 'words' with only 22 possible meanings. In other words it seems that DNA is only a random collection of words.

Restricted as the language of the genetic code appears, the problem with the genome project is that genes can work together to produce many more proteins. Genetics cannot explain the complexity of life forms and attributes. Scientific orthodoxy fails to see that there can be no such thing as genetic determinism. It still maintains that it can find genetic explanations for the mystery of life. But at the very most genetics can only tell us about our material bodies – who we are. There may well be other things, not related purely to our material well being, that the other 97% may tell us about ourselves; for instance, functions relating to environmental and cultural inheritance – who we are and our place in the cosmos.

What came as a surprise to the scientific community was the announcement that the human genome contains just 30,000 genes and not the anticipated 100-140,000. That figure had been the subject of great controversy, involving many issues such as the delaying of medical testing as well as the interests of the drug companies for whom more genes mean the targeting of more drugs. Gene prediction has always been precarious but there appears to be some sort of consensus now that there are some 26-30 thousand which code for proteins and which have the same function as the genes found in all life forms.

But what really shook the scientific community was that of the 30,000 or so genes of the human genome, only 300 distinguish human beings from mice. Also, it appears that about the same number are missing in the invertebrate stage on the evolutionary tree of life – perhaps justifying the claim by Zacharia Sitchin that at some early time in our history humans were upgraded by the Anunnaki from the planet Nibiru (*Genesis Revisited*); and not unlike the theory put forward by none other than Francis Crick that the molecule of life was the deliberate activity of extra terrestrial forces! ["Directed Panspermia" paper – 1973]

This rather strange theory comes from the scientist who had previously supported the 'central dogma' – *"that genetic variation can only come from errors in the duplication process"*. If the missing genes did not come from extra-terrestrial sources one can only speculate that there was a sideways insertion of these missing genes from bacteria.

This may well be the case, for bacteria also share the same DNA as humans and as Lynn Margulis, pioneer of an evolution theory called 'Symbiosis', has observed, all organisms are equally evolved. Bacteria support the whole biota, all of life. Instead of evolution being seen as survival of the fittest it should be regarded as a symbiotic relationship between bacteria and all other life forms. *"A single bacterial cell – is a monument of pattern and process unrivalled in the universe as we know it."* [Resurgence #206, May/June 2001] Although she developed the Gaia theory with James Lovelock, she nevertheless denies that Gaia means *singular and sentient.* supported by Bruce Lipton's theory of fractal evolution [see *The Fractal Evolution Centre* – www.biofractalevolution.com

oooOooo

The discovery of the human genome is credited to the American Francis Collins who saw it as a revelation, a map or book of life – the language God used to create life and meant to be a synthesis of science and religion and a cure for all disease; science finally usurping creation. But despite the fact that it is patently none of those things and that genes represent only 3% of the human genome, the Scientific community still promotes the genome as if it were sacrosanct, the Holy Grail. The problem with this assertion is the relationship the Human Genome Project has with the corporate world of bio-technology – pharmaceutical companies – and the links between big business and University Research programmes.

My concern is that in future this may lead to genetically engineered humans, a reconfiguration of the human species (by a process called germline genetic engineering) into two types of humans, which supporters of the idea have already termed the "GenRich" (a small elite class) and the "Naturals", a separate underprivileged class who will be dominated by the former. The result would mean a further alienation of man from the natural world. Since the cloning of a sheep, Dolly (1996), other animals have been cloned – goats, cows, mice, pigs. cats, rabbits etc.; and embryonic cells kept alive in laboratories and proposals to transfer somatic genes to foetuses. Even if genetic engineering were only to be limited to the prevention of disease (somatic genetic engineering) and so to become 'socially acceptable,' it would still echo the worst aspects of eugenics and pave the way for germline reconfiguration of the human species. This false concept of 'enhancement' is already being actively promoted, and if adopted would lead to another disastrous new epoch for humanity. Already there is a book, *Remaking Eden, How Cloning and Beyond Will Change the Human Family*[37].

This to my mind is a vision of a catastrophic mutation of the human species in line with orthodox (Darwinian) evolutionary theory; survival of the fittest, the richest, the most privileged. Such a future would see genetically engineered humanoids lording it over the naturals (the non genetically engineered), the transformation of the natural habitat, of plants and animals, and genetically modified 'frankenfoods', whilst creating a technological wasteland. Such a scenario would deny humanity its greatest assets: the beauty and diversity of Nature, its art and music and spirit – a soulless Universe where the only goals would be the continued pursuit of excessive pleasure. personal freedom, money and power; the world of meaning and of the sacred disappeared forever.

Another claim of geneticists is that our genes determine our behaviour and that we are here by accident. One notable geneticist (and we have come across this in our earlier discussion) actually postulates the existence of a *selfish gene* and we tend to go along with what these scientists claim. The fact is that scientists have little idea of how to make sense of the genetic code. Genes alone do not provide the text of life. There is no script waiting to be read. In each cell there are regulatory networks of proteins which sense and adapt to changes in the cellular environment *"There are dynamic-epigenetic networks (which) have a life of their own… not specified by DNA… The programme location is the cell as a whole, and the cell, through signalling pathways, is connected to larger wholes and to the external world"* [Richard Strohman *Scientific & Medical Network Review* #75 April 2001]

The prominent Neo-Darwinist evolutionary biologist Paul R Ehrlich, although supporting the central concept put forward by Darwin, is also opposed to genetic determinism based, in his view, on what he considers a fundamental misunderstanding of evolution. In his book *Human Natures: Genes, Cultures and the Human Prospect,* he proposes that it is culture and environmental variations, as well as our genes, which determine behaviour. There are just not enough genes to support the generally accepted theory.

The cell biologist, Dr. Bruce Lipton, believes that gene therapy, based on the primacy of DNA, is mere dogma. In 1983 he made the breakthrough discovery that Benoit Mandelbrot's fractal geometry, as the principle behind physical design in nature, could be extended to include biological evolution. Studying the behaviour of a single cell under his microscope it suddenly dawned on him that the single cell had all the life support systems of the human body, that a single cell was a *fractal* of the human body. He proceeded to develop his theory of bio-fractal evolution. A former medical school professor, his completely new holistic biological science of evolution severely challenges the outdated academic 'state' science ushered in by Darwinism (Classical & Neo) which forms the corner stone of Western thought, and is responsible for the divorce of Western man from Nature. [*Biology of Belief*, Mountains of Love, 2005]

Lipton's theory shows that cell evolution is based on more and more intelligence building up in a cell in the form of frequency receptors or integral membrane proteins (IMP's) in cellular membranes. ["The IMP complexes select frequencies from the environment and transduce these to inner domain"] When no more information could be stored in a single cell, there was a pause in evolution followed by the appearance of the first multi-cellular organisms all over the world. [see *Welcome to the Future*, Ted Hall, http://globalvisions.org]

Genes, according to Lipton, are only the third step in the process of creation, the first being intelligence coded in the environment and the second the IMP's. His Bio-fractal Evolution theory suggests that life is not a mechanistic process but an ongoing holistic one, the choreography of which depends not only on the DNA but on the cells of the body and also on the mind and environment in a sort of feed back process. It is a theory that is both revolutionary and transcendental, and one I believe that has the potential to change every aspect of our thinking and to usher in a new social and scientific paradigm in the West; one which is not dissimilar to that of the earth-centred Indigenous cultures of the world in which people experienced themselves as an integral part of a whole living biosphere. This theory is based on pure science by a biologist who has had a long and distinguished career in his field; one that accords not only with David Bohm's holographic theory of an Implicate order, but also with Michael Talbot's Holographic Universe and Benoit Mandelbrot's fractal design in nature. Bio-evolution is fractal replication, repetition on different scales of magnitude, from unicellar to multi-cellar organisms. Human evolution, instead of being seen as survival of the fittest and of competition, can now be seen as dependent on a holistic, co-operative, interactive environment.

At a personal level, this knowledge is healing in the broadest sense of the word as we become aware just how much our thoughts and perceptions actively affect our health and behaviour, giving us a sense of belonging and identity, of caring and community; of freedom, yet knowing that we each have a responsibility for the preservation of life on our planet and the future of our children. A single cell is a fractal of the human body and human beings are inseparable from the flow of nature. Our brains link us to the mind of the planet; even our dreams keep us in touch with this emerging consciousness –that we are one with everything else. It is a theory that is capable of uniting all doctrines, all branches of specialised knowledge, thereby giving meaning to our lives. Along the way, we may have to forego some of our sacred dogmas, our scientific bigotry which have created division and separation. We will have to cultivate an open mind, like the ancient Sage, who knew that all minds are one mind. We will have to reassess entrenched views of how we see ourselves and reality. It would usher in a new consciousness that could literally transform our world. In *Beyond Freedom and Dignity* [New York 1971] B.F. Skinner suggests that *"We need to made vast changes in human behaviour, and we cannot make them with the help of nothing more than physics or biology, no matter how hard we try."*

Although they would never acknowledge it, scientists in seeking to unravel the secrets of our world are embarked on the same quest as the philosophers, mystics and psychologists. Any inquiry into the nature of reality, seeking to find that grand unified theory, is a spiritual activity. The neuroscientist Candace Pert, whose ground breaking book the *Molecules of Emotion* established the link between mind and body, acknowledges this: *"I have come to believe"*, she says, *"that science, at its very core, is a spiritual endeavour. Some of my best insights have come to me through what I can only call a mystical process. It's like having God whisper in your ear… It's this inner voice that we scientists must come to trust"*. She acknowledges that the world we receive from our five senses alone is not enough; quantum physics and information theory suggest that there are other ways of knowing.

Nevertheless most scientists still deny the metaphysical dimension to reality despite the fact that there is an extraordinary degree of research employing 'scientific' methods of proof into areas such as paranormal and psychic phenomena, from psycho kinesis to telepathy, precognition, remote viewing, out of body and near death experiences and a host of other unusual phenomena. Science itself is divided into different categories which are in water-tight compartments, a scientist from one discipline finding it impossible to understand what one from another discipline is talking about. There are experts in every field of knowledge but no overarching system linking them to a reality much greater than the sum of the parts. This limitation in itself relegates the purely *scientific* investigation to a kind of materialist rationalism which views animate reality as if it was inanimate.

Rene Descartes' dualistic philosophy assumes much of the responsibility for this split in Western thinking. Mind and matter, body and soul were pronounced separate entities: Science was to become mere Scientism, something apart from intuition and this has alienated scientific investigation from the natural world for the last three centuries.

In *The Cosmic Serpent*, the anthropologist, Jeremy Narby, addresses this issue in an unusual way. He links DNA and the origins of knowledge to the claims of the shamans of the Amazonian rain forest, that by the use of hallucinogens, they can communicate with the animate essences which power all life; they can communicate with plants and learn their secrets for healing: an interesting hypothesis as genetically, human beings have the same make up as plants. *"Modern biology"*, he says…*".is founded on the notion that nature is not animated by an intelligence and therefore cannot communicate"* and points out that seventy four percent of the modern pharmacopoeia's plant baseremedies were first discovered by 'traditional societies' and that by taking their consciousness down to the molecular level shamans have access to the 'reality of molecular biology' and the 'hidden unity of nature'.

Another anthropologist who studied the shamanistic powers of the Amazonian Indians is Michael Harner. After taking a hallucinogenic concoction made from the ayahuasca or *soul* vine, he saw a dragon-like creature emerging from his spine who communicated to him in 'thought-language' that they resided in all life forms. Although he did not know about DNA at the time (1961), in retrospect he considered that what he had seen had been a visual manifestation of the double helix.

Narby came to the conclusion that in order to reconcile two seemingly irreconcilable ways of looking at reality (the purely scientific as well as Indigenous wisdom), it is necessary to defocus the mind. Although he was an anthropologist, a scientist, he decided not to dismiss the seemingly unscientific claims of the shamans but to treat them as their truth. This, I think is the way of arriving at a deeper understanding of reality. I also believe that it is necessary to defocus the attention from the purely visual language before a larger reality can emerge. This is not unusual in science but it is not generally acknowledged. The tendency is to ignore the role that intuition plays in any discovery. Most scientists believe only in what is before them; what they can see and touch and measure like those men in Plato's cave unable to see beyond the darkness of their cave.

It is generally accepted that he brain has two hemispheres. On the left is the analytical and logical hemisphere dealing with syntax and language; and on the right the intuitive. Like the yin and the yang they complement each other, each having aspects of the other. The left yang hemisphere is the rational side, whilst the right, the yin is the seat of the hidden codes of creativity capable of resolving paradox. We need both sides in order to perceive a holistic reality.

A purely analytical left brain approach can never unlock all of the secrets of life and the Universe or make sense of the nature of reality. Scientific and other revelations can only surface when the empirical, measurable gaze is defocalised, allowing the right brain to come up with the answers which are already encoded at the molecular level of our consciousness. DNA is within the human brain and is both single & double (RNA), the source of information from both hemispheres, male and female, from within and without -- the vital principle.

We do not have to be geniuses to understand how this happens. Take for instance the anagram YNELUSLIVRA. Look at it for a minute or so. If you have not unscrambled the word in that time, read on to the end of this page; then return to it. The word would probably jump out at you after a short while. Your right brain would have solved the problem without the effort you were putting in when you first looked at it. It seems that in problem solving we first use our left brain, but it is the right which comes up with the answer.

As we have seen in Chapter 9 – Universe, the neurophysiologist Karl Pribram considered the brain to be holographic, interconnected to all part of our bodies. A theory borne out by Candace Pert's concept of a 'mobile' brain' – *"an apt description of the psychosomatic network through which intelligent information travels from one system to another."* Pert was referring to the interconnectedness of all the body's systems, but I believe with Itzhak Bentov that there are systems outside our physical bodies which form our bodies – that our *"physical bodies are end products, the result of the interaction of our subtle, non-physical "information bodies."* [*Stalking the Wild Pendulum*] These non-physical information bodies are in turn linked to the Universal brain, a microcosm of the macrocosm. We only consciously use a very small percentage of our brains even though the unconscious larger part is forever in touch with cosmic consciousness. The question is how can we learn to access it?

Some of the most important scientific discoveries have been made when the mind is no longer focused purely on solving the problem. Suddenly the solution *mysteriously* surfaces. This was the case with Newton and the falling apple; Einstein day dreaming in a tram as it approached another (relativity); James Watson riding a bicycle having viewed Rosalind Franklin's radio photographic work (the DNA double helix); and the dream[38] of August Kekule which led to the development of organic chemistry.

Science only investigates the physical, material nature of the Universe and so only gets answers in mathematical terms – how many molecules, or genes there are in cells, for instance. It cannot explain how information jumps the synapses in the brain, or how something can be both a wave and a particle at the same time. I knew this of course, but never thought of posing the question that we see only what we expect to see or want to see and that our beliefs determine what we want to see. If we believe that there is no meaning in the universe, then of course for us the Universe will have no meaning. And if there is no meaning then it is possible for us to believe in the existence of a selfish gene. The two go hand in hand, for we create our own universes.

Whatever we discover is only a small part of what there is to discover. It is never the whole reality that exists. If we think our discoveries can make us make definitive conclusions about anything, then we are deluding ourselves and we deserve our selfish genes. See a selfish gene, and out goes concern, community, compassion. Seeing ourselves as separate, we create division. The Universe is only without meaning if you expect it to have meaning and can find none. We expect things to be either one thing or another; but the reality is that the Universe is impersonal. Consciousness flows downwards impartially to everything on earth, to all of us, whether we make use of it or not and all things partake of the abundance of Nature.

In a *quantum* reality where the consciousness of the observer affects the reality of a sub-atomic particle, scientific enquiry is no longer merely a matter of materialist reductionism but a participatory event. This was the method employed by Narby and Harner, on their separate encounters with the Amazonian shamans. They did not just observe them but entered into their world with open minds, partaking of the hallucinogen themselves in order to gain insights their training would not have expected them to find.

The Universe contains all. We take from it what we want. We make of it whatever we want to create. We are the Universe, the creators. We have the choice to create what kind of world we want to live in, at a personal level as well as a species and it may well be that we deserve the meaningless Universe which we have created. But we have a choice: simple as that. We have a choice whether we go down the road constructed by the Human Genome Project in collaboration with genetic biologists and big business. We have the choice to insist on the imposition and implementation of standards regulating genetic engineering and the cloning of ourselves and our children.

Change our thought and we change the Universe we inhabit. It's not a matter of dark or light, but of seeing that dark and light complement each other: they are equal parts of the ingredients of reality; they need each other. If we deny other dimensions, or levels, we will never find them. If our vision is limited our discoveries can only be limited. If we limit our vision to the purely physical, material world we can only hope to discover those secrets expressed in purely mathematical terms or as symbols.

Our task then, is to interpret those symbols. As we have seen, the human brain, like our earth has two hemispheres representing the analytical (Western) and the intuitive (Eastern) mode. Einstein was aware of this. He saw the connection between matter and energy. He saw that we were not separate from the rest of creation. Science has been responsible for unlocking many of the secrets of the Intelligence that underlies the creative process. But science is not that Intelligence. It seems inconceivable that science can still disclaim the existence of an intelligence beyond itself; that it fails to see the philosophical implications of what it has uncovered and that there may well be other ways of knowing.. The paradox is that the intelligence is not out there but within us. We are fractals of the crystal of creation. Our DNA is the same as it is for all life – the vital principle connecting us to ALL.

Genetic engineering is based on a wrong interpretation of the double helix symbol which carries genetic information. The information is applied only to the physical substrate of the code: manipulating genes to improve the health of a person. It treats the parts but not the whole person, an extension of orthodox medical practice. But the double spiral of DNA is a symbol of wholeness. Mind and body are not separate. As Pert points out [*Molecules*], there is a communication network joining every part of our body, from the nervous immune and endocrine systems to the brain – another example, it would seem, of a holographic brain linking us to a holographic universe. In *Healing with Love,* Leonard Laskow also sees that there is no duality: *"the mind cannot be explained in physical terms alone; it also consists of nonmaterial substrate composed of the information that is flowing in and around it. The physical brain might be likened to a radio receiver, while the information that constitutes the mind is like the radio waves around it. Clearly, not all communication and understanding occurs at the mental or intellectual level. There are additional levels of awareness, which we call the intuitive and spiritual, that help us complete the picture."* Good health would be better achieved by an understanding of the psychosomatic relationship between the psyche, or soul, and the body. Fortunately this is already taking place – there is an emerging field of medicine called psycho-neuro-immunology.

If we really knew who we were we would not need to be artificially engineered. Somewhere along the way Western culture has lost that wisdom of wholeness that had once flourished; when science and healing were not separate, when physics was practical, in the sense that there was no distinction between philosophy, physics and healing. Indeed the word physician has the same root as the latter. Now the need is surely to transform our ideas about who and what we really are.

Philosophy, the love of wisdom, is about love – love of ourselves and of each other and of all creatures who share the same DNA. It is not just rational thinking. Something else is involved, call it intuition, or revelation. It comes out of a state of being beyond reason, or empirical proof. We only use one percent of our brains. What does this say about perception based on reason? As Peter Kingsley notes in *In the Dark Places of Wisdom,* "All distinctions between rational and irrational are only valid from the limited standpoint of what we call reason."

The story of the biblical garden of Eden where a serpent tempted Eve, is an example of this misconception of who we really are. The serpent goddess, the symbol of the mystery of life was rejected. A false tree of knowledge has taken root and the concept of polarisation has continued to plague Western thinking: male and female, good and evil, dark and light. And so we have created our own fragmented reality.

What the entwined spirals of the DNA symbol can teach us, is that there are two ways of knowing, two ways of being which when integrated can make us wise; make us whole. We are now equipped to learn a new way to perceive ourselves.

References

The Cosmic Serpent; Jeremy Narby: Phoenix, 1995
Wholeness and the Implicate Order; David Bohm: Routledge & Kegan Paul, 1980
The Holographic Universe; Michael Talbot: Grafton, 1991
Biology of Belief; Bruce Lipton: Mountain of Love, 2005
Human Natures; Genes, Culture & the Human Prospect; Paul R Ehrlich: Island, 2000
The Power of Myth; Joseph Campbell: Doubleday, 1988
Genesis Revisited; Zacharia Sitchin: Avon, 1990
In the Dark Places of Wisdom; Peter Kingsley: Element Books, 1999
Healing with Love; Leonard Laslow: Harper San Francisco, 1992
Beyond Freedom & Dignity; B.F Skinner: Hackett, 1971
Molecules of Emotion; Candace Pert: Pocket Books, 1997
Stalking the Wild Pendulum; Itzhak Bentov: Destiny Books, 1988
Welcome to the Future; Ted Hall [www.globalvisions.org]

Chapter 11 – The Seven Pillars of the Prevailing Paradigm

What sets worlds in motion is the interplay of differences, their attractions and repulsions. Life is plurality, death is uniformity. By suppressing differences and peculiarities, by eliminating different civilizations and cultures, progress weakens life and favours death. The ideal of a single civilization for everyone, implicit in the cult of progress and technique, impoverishes and mutilates us. Every view of the world that becomes extinct, every culture that disappears, diminishes a possibility of life.

Octavio Paz

The events of September 11 2001 were a defining moment in human history. For the first time it was obvious to the world at large that there was an irreconcilable rift between the outlook of the West and that of the rest of mankind. A month or so later I attended a lecture by Rabbi Michael Lerner entitled, *The Globalisation of Spirit versus the Globalisation of Capital* which outlined a new strategy for radical social transformation. Lerner is a leading eco-spiritual visionary of the growing "Politics of Meaning" movement in the US as well as here in Britain. He was at one time an advisor to both Bill and Hilary Clinton. His vision is of a world based on what he calls a *community of spirit*, on grass roots renewal and ecological, ethical and holistic values.

Lerner believes, as I do, in *Change* – that it is possible to bring about change for the better if enough people want it. He mentioned, for example, the change brought about by the Women's movement, pointing out that in the 1960's no one would have foreseen the remarkable changes that have taken place because of it. I believe that a strategy for radical social transformation would require something much more radical than that – a change of heart at the very centre of our thinking; our epistemology, our perceptions. At a psychological level, it would mean challenging deep-rooted assumptions about the very nature of the Universe, about ourselves and the culture in which we were raised. It may even mean that we may have to revise the very way we look at reality.

My long life has brought me to the view that, as in the mystery of the TAO, balance is all; and that the West is driven by a rationality that destroys that balance. So what in any realized completeness is an essential *duality* in absolute harmony, has in the West at this time been replaced by a *dualism,* in other words, an imbalance that results in elemental discord.

This chapter will attempt to bring together the main themes I have attempted to address in the previous chapters, in order to demonstrate this point. The themes expounded so far are *inter alia,* scientism, empirical proof, the split of matter and spirit, secularism, monotheism, ruthless competition, domination, imperialism, historiography, hubris, hegemony, ecological destruction, epistemology, fragmentation of knowledge, language, division, suppression of the female, genetic engineering and globalisation. Whilst a certain amount is inevitable in any summation, I shall attempt to avoid repeating myself unduly.

The expression of imbalance is the current prevailing paradigm that the West in its hour of dominance seeks to impose on the world. This paradigm can, with painful irony, be imaged as a tower block, unstable and remote from the earth, and supported by what I see as its own seven pillars. In my view these would be:

- Dualism as Reality
- The Control of Nature as *Divine* Mandate
- Science as Absolute Knowledge
- Technology as Progress
- The West as Best
- Globalisation as Civilisation
- This Paradigm as the Only Choice

Dualism as Reality

The first pillar, 'dualism as reality', is indeed the central pillar of the prevailing Western paradigm. It can be traced back to the story of the Garden of Eden, the tree of knowledge and man's fall from grace. (But, as we shall see, all the pillars that support the prevailing Western paradigm only reinforce the same *polarity* that shapes our world-view). It has led to the fragmentary manner in which we approach knowledge and is also responsible for our separation from Nature and from each other. Our differences divide us into 'them and us,' 'long and short,' 'right and wrong,' 'good and evil' and 'white and black'. What we do not see is that all these are only aspects of each other; they depend on each other. There can be no light without the dark.

How can this apparent duality be resolved? The New Physics of quantum mechanics of the last Century, seems to suggest that we live in an interconnected, holistic, non-dual world; but that this *reality,* or way of seeing things, has somehow not changed the way we think. In the 17th century, Rene Descartes put forward his dualistic philosophy ("I think therefore I am") which is still with us and which established *epistemology* as the gateway to knowledge. Henceforth the world would be presumed to consist of two separate, irreconcilable substances, mind and matter, creating a dichotomy between the thinking human mind and unthinking matter [*Discourse on Method*]. Descartes pronounced on many issues from the movement of the planets to tidal waves and music. Although he was tone deaf he wrote his Compendium of Music (1618). Ironically, he was opposed to the tempered scale of Western music (discussed in Chapter 9 – Universe), as against nature.

Early in the last century, Einstein's *General Theory of Relativity* put paid to Descartes' narrow interpretation of reality. The theory which underpins all work on atomic energy, postulates the constant velocity of light which led to his famous equation relating matter and energy, $E=mc^2$, with 'c' being the speed of Light. It has now been established that matter and energy are interchangeable and that how we perceive our world and ourselves determines our reality. The New Physics tells us that our physical world is made up of sub-atomic particles revolving at great speed within a huge void; and that these particles are also waves or energy within a space-time continuum. It even tells us that our bodies are not made of solid matter, but are the end products of subtle information fields. '*The physical body just happens to be where the wave function of the organism is the most dense*' [Mae Wan Ho of the Open University – qt. Hempel The Natural Resonance Revolution]

I still find it difficult to understand many of the principles of the New Physics, for instance, that something can, at time same time, be defined both as a *particle* and a *wave*; that at the sub-atomic level, matter does not exist with any certainty at definite places, but rather shows a tendency to exist; that the *observer* changes what is being observed simply by the fact that he is observing it. It seems that the Cartesian split between the 'I', and the world out there, does not exist when dealing with quantum reality. Now it appears that we are not our thoughts, although our thoughts may determine who we are at a certain level of awareness. Our true selves may well be beyond our ego-centric view of the world, an awareness of an *existential self* at the very core of our being.

The New Physics has ushered in a new way of looking at our world, a holographic model – that there exists an implicate order in which everything is enfolded in everything else and that everything is part of a continuum. In the past scientific investigation has been grounded in the *explicate* order, on analysis, on separating the parts from the whole. As we have seen, David Bohm pointed out that perhaps the biggest stumbling block to our understanding of the nature of reality is our language – the *Subject/Object* structure of phonetic European languages.

For Bohm, it is our minds that create conceptual barriers between pure energy and the physical phenomenal world. European scientific thinkers in the 17th century confronted with the baffling complexity of nature, elected to cut away the portion of the world that proved more elusive to observation and more difficult to quantify: In the Tao te Ching we read,

> *The five colours blind the eyes*
> *The five tones deafen the ears*
> *The five flavours dull the palate.*
> *Chasing after things madden the mind.*
> *Therefore the Sage concerns himself with inner nourishment*
> *and not with outer objects.*
> *He lets go of one and cultivates the other.*

By withdrawing from the external five senses of perception, an adept can restore the primordial unity of matter-energy, body and mind. This unity cannot be described in words: it can only be experienced by a return to a higher state of consciousness, to wholeness. This Chinese concept provides a non-dualistic cosmology for going beyond the conventional Western separation of matter and spirit, mind and body.

Beauty is seen as beauty
only because there is ugliness
and good as good, only because there is evil
To have or to be, arise together,
difficult and easy complement each other,
long and short contrast each other,
high and low support each other,
before and after are in perfect sequence.

The Control of Nature as *Divine* Mandate

The second pillar supports the theory that Nature must be controlled. As already stated, this stems in part from the monotheism of the Old Testament common to the Semitic religions. It has been a mandate for Western man's continued desire to dominate nature and of all life on the face of the earth. The alienation from nature can also be traced back to Greece, the so-called *'cradle of western civilisation'*. The early participatory identification with the natural landscape of the Pythagorean tradition of non-duality had changed by the time of Socrates. In his book, *Ancient Philosophy, Mystery and Magic, Empedocles and Pythagorean Tradition* [Oxford University Press 1995], the Greek scholar, Peter Kingsley, has noted that most scholars had deliberately left out the connection between magic, alchemy and mystery in Greek philosophy and 'science', dismissing them as *irrational* and so distorting the evidence. It is not surprising that that the much misunderstood and underrated English novelist and thinker, D.H. Lawrence, could state that "*any attempt of man to harmonise himself with nature, and hold his own and come to flower in the great seething of life, changed with the Greeks and Romans into a desire to resist Nature, to produce a mental cunning and a mechanical force that would outwit Nature and chain her down completely, completely, till at last there should be nothing free in Nature at all; all should be controlled, domesticated, put to man's meaner uses.*" [*The Escaped Cock*]

This ethos underpins our present world-wide materialistic culture, beginning as we have seen, with the Industrial Revolution and the writings of Francis Bacon, John Locke, David Hume and Adam Smith. Bacon, one of the great thinkers of his time and the founder of *empiricism,* (the basis of our scientific method), went so far as to suggest that Nature was hostile; and had to be conquered or controlled; "*it must be hounded, raped, placed on the rack – forced to reveal its secrets.*" Rene Descartes, also subscribed to this view, stating that, "*Knowing the force and action of fire, water, air, the stars, the heavens and all other bodies that surround it, men can be masters and possessors of nature.*" This rationale is commensurate with the archaic and atavistic drive of males for dominance over nature and the repression of the feminine. The rehabilitation of the feminine principle will be a necessary first step towards restoring balance to our world. Male dominance stalks all walks of life – in the home, in commerce, politics and government. It has set nation against nation and is the root cause of racism and warfare, both sanctioned by Darwin's evolutionary theory of competition and survival of the fittest. Nature, women and all those who are considered *others,* are somehow of less value and so can either be dispensed with or subjugated. Descartes and Darwin have much to answer for; their theories are central to the prevailing Western paradigm of conflict and materialism.

The indigenous peoples of the world, on the other hand, lived in harmony with nature. The hunter-gatherers and nomadic people were egalitarian and adapted to their environment, believing that everything was alive and imbued with a force or spirit that pervaded all creation. For many African peoples, community extends beyond the family, the clan – the exclusion of the 'other' simply because he is different, is just a Western concept. The ancient Chinese Taoist philosophy was concerned with maintaining balance and harmony in all things – in personal life as well as within the State: based on respect for, and on observation of, Nature, the *Tao Te Ching* states that:

> *In my experience, Nature cannot be dominated*
> *The Universe is sacred, and cannot be improved*
> *Trying to improve it, destroys it*
> *Trying to grasp it, is futile.....*

The words, T*ao Te Ching,* can loosely be translated as *The Way of Nature* and might easily form the basis for a new eco-philosophy to replace our out-dated and fragmented philosophical ideas. The drive to control nature has led to the deracination of man and Nature – a psychological rift deep at the heart of our materialistic culture. C.G Jung, the Swiss psychologist, and one of the leading figures in modern psychoanalytic theory observed that "*Modern man has not truly looked into the great divide within himself, the great divide which separates him from wilderness and nature. And there is so much in Nature which can fill us, day and night, through plants, animals and flowers, with the eternal in life, and the eternal in man. The more uncertain I have felt about myself and life, the more has grown in me, through Nature, a feeling of kinship with all things.*" [qt. Van Der Post Wilderness, Resurgence #96]

Modern man has lost all connection with wilderness, with the land and the mysterious interrelationships of all things. Writing about the dreaming of ancient aborigine people of Australia, Robert Lawlor noted that the Western world *"denies an internal or subjective consciousness to all things and creatures except humans. The rest of nature, we believe, has no dreaming and consequently we feel justified in cutting down trees, gouging the earth, and killing and enslaving animals as if they were all empty souls."*

Instead of feelings of gratitude towards nature which provides us with everything that we need, these sentiments became walled off from organic harmonies and became defined as opposites, *"setting apart all pairs of opposites, as though they were absolutes in themselves and not merely aspects of the larger entity of life"* Joseph Campbell [qt. William Turner]

As Theodore Roszak, has so aptly put it: *"We ignore the greater ecological realities that surround the psyche – as if the soul might be saved while the biosphere crumbles. The context of psychiatry stops at the city limits; the non-human world that lies beyond is as great a mystery as the depths of the soul… The great changes our runaway industrial civilisation must make if we are to keep the planet healthy will not come about by the force of reason alone or the influence of fact. Rather, they will come by way of psychological transformation."* [The Voice of The Earth]

Science as Absolute Knowledge

In the 18th Century, the Enlightenment, or the Age of Reason, replaced orthodox authoritarian beliefs by rational scientific inquiry. Out went traditional religion to be replaced by science and individual liberty. Francis Bacon had already ushered in *empirical proof* and Descartes *epistemology,* the separation of mind and matter. The separation of science and religion was now complete. Thereafter, the profound wisdom of spiritual traditions of all cultures was discredited; from Christian mysticism and the wisdom of the Kaballah and of Islam, to Sufism, Buddhism, the great Ayurvedic tradition of Indian philosophy and medicine, the Taoist cosmology of ancient China and the overarching wisdom and achievements of ancient Egypt – all of which had evolved over centuries of research and experimentation just as rigorous as that of the scientific method.

The traditional wisdom of the great sages over the ages has all but been discounted; a wisdom that recognises the interconnectedness of all things and all life; a truth which has since been validated by Quantum theory in which merely observing a phenomenon changes the nature of that phenomenon. Science has been divided into different categories which are in water-tight compartments, a scientist from one discipline finding it impossible to understand what one from another discipline is talking about. At the same time there is no institutional body to oversee all the research and develop an ethical and egalitarian policy for the good of all. As one commentator put it "Today there are specialists who cannot understand each other; economists who *add the price of the sale of a bushel of wheat to the gross national product whilst forgetting to subtract the three bushels of topsoil lost to grow it."* [David Orr]

Scientists develop technologies in the pursuit of knowledge regardless of where they may lead: the Atomic bomb to Hiroshima and Nagasaki; the munitions industry to *international* terrorism; over-production to waste and food mountains; agricultural policy and pesticides to BSE, foot and mouth and GM food; genetic engineering to human cloning. At our current rate, scientific companies will own the genetic blue prints of everyone of us, as well as all life forms on the planet; eventually determining, it seems, the very process of human evolution. A well-known chemical firm, for instance, is rapidly converting public goods into private profit, seeking a monopoly to control agricultural seed and water in many areas in the world. They may soon control the entire food chain as well as the very basis of life on earth. Humanity itself has been divided into different races through the study of anthropology and *eugenics*, both justifying policies of divide and rule, and exacerbating racial and tribal tensions, warfare and genocide.

The Intelligence that underlies how our bodies work and many of the things that science has uncovered, transcends polarity of any kind. Which takes precedence? The Intelligence or the Science? It's like putting the cart before the horse – putting science before the intelligence it studies. We need synthesis not just analysis. Intuition plays the greater part in any scientific inquiry. In a *quantum* reality where the consciousness of the observer affects the reality of a sub-atomic particle, scientific enquiry should no longer be merely a matter of materialist reductionism but a participatory event. It is we who have created division, locked as we are in duality. The Intelligence underlying all creation has been marginalized by Science and replaced by Scientism, a new religion which in turn replaces, but isn't much different from all the other fragmented religions. Today secularisation has become the orthodoxy that dare not be questioned: an orthodoxy that disclaims any spiritual dimension to life. People begin to shift uneasily if one makes any statement which might be interpreted as having anything to do with the 'S'-word.

The pursuit of science as the only way of knowing, leads to the dualism between the *secular* and the religious and is allied to the fragmented religious dogmas which were also aimed at control above all else. Instead of being controlled by religion, we are now controlled by secular fundamentalism – we exchange one form of control for another – a false sense of freedom in place of the opiate of the masses. This point was vividly borne out to me when I watched the final episode of a recent BBC documentary: *The Century of the Self*. The programme focused on the effect of marketing and PR on post-Thatcherite Britain in which individuality is vigorously catered for. Secularism is based on Freudian concepts of man as somehow bestial – a creature with no higher qualities; endowed only with desires that have to be satisfied and by satisfying them he can be controlled.

This is the *raison d'etre* of Big Business – how to get us to spend more and more – and the belief that technology will pave the way to a golden future. Ultimately, living becomes the pursuit of endless commodities we could well do without, whilst walling ourselves off from the so-called ravages of nature We move imperceptibly away from the world of nature to create virtual environments becoming cut off and alienated from nature losing any sense of true community and of caring.

According to the eminent psychotherapist, Stanislav Grof, "*Material profit and increase of the gross national product are considered the main criteria of well-being and measure of the standard of living. This ideology and the economic and political strategies resulting from it bring humans into a serious conflict with their nature as living systems and with basic universal laws.*" Pandering to all those so called needs is simply what it is all about. Now Governments have adopted the marketing strategies of big business in order to stay in power[39], promising to pacify the selfish needs of a insatiable population forever wanting more; without regard for the less fortunate, the poor, the peoples of other cultures, the future of our children and the survival of other species. The Western privileging of business and technology stems directly from the myth of science as absolute knowledge. Ironically, what is said to liberate merely binds...

Technology as Progress

The belief that technology represents progress is indicative of the *masculine mode* of thought – the hallmark of development and status of any society. We are led to believe that technological sophistication is the measure of man's progress. The majority of scientists still claim that all our problems, including those involving energy, sickness, social violence and ecological damage will eventually be solved by better science and improved technologies. Progress is linked with linear time, i.e. things get better with time. But the world is not getting to be a better place for any of us, even though it brings more material comforts for a small percentage of mankind.

The idea of linear progress presumes that the more knowledge we have, the better the world will become. This was the view of the so-called Enlightenment; and although we may be gaining knowledge in some areas, we are losing knowledge in many vital areas, e.g. knowledge of the land, of traditional arts and crafts, and the healing plants of so-called primitive cultures. One of the greatest losses is that we have forgotten how to live sustainably on the earth.

Unlimited growth literally means the depletion of non-renewable natural resources (fossil fuels), the accumulation of toxic waste, deforestation and pollution by chlorofluorocarbons (CFC's). The earth's resources are not infinite and technology will not solve our problems. The knowledge we gain from it has failed to manage the earth. Common sense tells that It would make more sense to reshape ourselves to fit a finite planet rather than attempt to reshape it or control it to fit our infinite wants.

The general view still is that all problems can, and will, only be solved when we solve our economic problems. Progress is seen purely in materialistic terms. But greed and envy and our so-called indisputable right to individual freedom to indulge ourselves in every conceivable way surely cannot lead to any solutions to the problems that face mankind. It is time we start taking ourselves seriously as human beings instead of merely as consumers. As Andre Gorz [*Critique of Economic Reason*, Verso 1989] puts it *"The right of everyone sovereign to pursue his or her advantage implies that no constraint or restriction should be imposed upon them in the name of the 'higher interests' of society or transcendent values"*. We cannot have rights without responsibilities.

What, to my mind, is lacking is our inability to utilize all the knowledge that is readily available to us, to see beyond our received and culturally fragmented models and to make the necessary fundamental changes to our conceptual frameworks or mind-sets. A tall order I admit, but is there any alternative? The so-called primitive peoples of the world arrived at their ideas simply by observing Nature and they lived in total harmony with her. The Australian Aborigine knew this. But then came

Captain Cook. Nature was far kinder to the Aborigines than Western civilization ever has been. The similarity of their ideas to Taoism, the product of one of the oldest and most advanced civilizations on earth, is quite extraordinary. Following the spoor of Nature, they lived their lives with a sense of belonging to their immediate world – whatever they did affected everything about them – accepting the vagaries of Nature as part of the natural order of things.

The constant need for change and a belief in material progress was something absent from indigenous societies. They valued things that brought long lasting peace and happiness. They treasured balance, harmony, and tried to live in accordance with the seasons and the passage of time. The way to earn respect was by service to the community. Their technologies were simple but effective. For them linear progress and unlimited growth were a false ideal.

But these ideas have not been seen as being relevant and so applicable to the problems of the modern materialistic developed world. With the advent of the scientific age and the mechanistic concepts of Darwin, Descartes and Newton, Western thinking has become increasingly rational and linear. In grappling with non-linearity, the West still employs the linear mode when confronted by and trying to describe it. Noting the unpredictable nature of natural phenomena, like the weather, instead of accepting the reality it observes, it creates a science of Chaos to explain these non-linear systems.

The indigenous cultures saw time as cyclical. Their rituals honoured their relationship to a higher order. Their sciences did not seek to control nature but to stay in harmony with it as it revealed its secrets. As we have seen, knowledge moves in an ever-expanding upward spiral, just as the Pythagorean cycle of musical fifths reaches upwards in an infinite spiral. So it seems does consciousness[40]. The knowledge of the indigenous peoples has either been appropriated (74 % of the modern pharmacopoeia's plant based remedies were first discovered by them) or has been discredited as mere superstition. Chinese herbal medicine has also been looked at askance; it took a very long time for the efficacy of acupuncture to be recognised. The latter discipline is based on restoring balance to the system and the theory that illness is due to an imbalance in the body caused by blockages in the flow of vital energy (or chi) through meridians in the body. Chinese medicine is holistic; it treats the cause of the disorder and not the symptom as is generally the case with Western medicine. I, for one, have had personal experience of this in regaining balance to my system in cases relating to my health.

In the case of music, not only have we tampered with the natural laws of physics but we continue to create new technologies which we hope will solve all our problems. Today in the West we live more comfortable lives and have a great many things to entertain us and give us a sense of what we call security, at the same time depleting the resources of the earth. Though technology has improved the quality of life for a minority, particularly in some aspects of health care and hygiene (we all live longer), our lives somehow lack meaning, isolated as we are from ourselves and each other.

Technology has become a kind of religion. Our reverence for the knowledge technology can seemingly bestow on us, is leading to our own extinction. We now know how to blow ourselves up and the rest of the world as well. Bio-technologies have made the possibility of biological warfare a present threat to the survival of our species and all species. Even our genes are threatened and our biology in danger of being modified. We seem to be at the threshold of becoming the wrong sort of hybrids – our notions of what life really is, threatened. Genetic technologies are altering the food we eat and even our DNA yet our present understanding of DNA may also be only a point on the spiral of knowledge arrived at by the Human Genome Project, just one Chapter of *The Book of Life*.

In our quest to conquer and dominate nature, we have lost all sense of the wonder and awe of being alive. We no longer have time to consider the mystery of life. We no longer ask the fundamental questions of existence: who we are, and why are we here? According to the ancient Tao Te Ching, *"When men lose their sense of awe, disaster is not far away."*

The West as Best

The fifth Pillar encompasses the belief that it is the manifest destiny of the West to lead the world. It accounts for the religious zeal of Christendom from the time of the Crusaders, to the Christian missionaries in Africa and to all colonial territories; missionaries to China; the Spanish conquest of Central and South American, the bible in one hand and a sword in the other. Even today we've had Christian missionaries to Afghanistan.

But the main tenets of Christianity are completely irrelevant; the Church having no moral authority over the State condoned a brutal slave trade – in the 16th to the 19th Century – and colonisation. Exploitation of non-Europeans became the norm, kept alive by racism, the false science of Eugenics and claims that the rest of the world contributed nothing to human knowledge and advancement.

But this would not be the case, were we to acknowledge the debt we owe ancient civilizations. The Sumerian civilisation, for instance, (4000 BC) probably invented writing (although the Chinese also lay claim to this). It was in Sumeria in southern Mesopotamia – the region between the rivers Tigris and Euphrates known today as Iraq – that what we, ironically, today refer to as civilization, is thought to have been founded. Foundational status notwithstanding, it invented printing, mathematics, astronomy, the clock and the calendar. It also had a legal code and traded extensively with its immediate neighbours. Indeed, Arab countries led the way in most of today's sciences: Astronomy[41], Mathematics, Medicine & Surgery and Chemistry. The first world map and globe were also Arabian. Indian mathematicians developed a system of names for the successive powers of 10 to describe very large numbers and the grammatical principles of Sanskrit (analysed between the 7th & 4th centuries BC) laid the basis for the science of linguistics in the 19th century.

In the first Volume of his monumental work, *Black Athena*, Martin Bernal has shown that Greek culture was permeated by Egyptian influence and that the current Aryan Model incorrectly replaced the Ancient Model held by the Greeks themselves – their culture was the product of Egyptian and Phoenician colonists. It is indeed strange that whereas Europe traces its culture and civilization back to Greece, the ancient Greeks themselves traced their culture back to Africa, to Egypt specifically, as Herodotus had noted. Pythagoras studied for twenty-one years in Egypt resulting in his non-dual philosophy, which was later deliberately distorted by Aristotle and Plato. Thus was created the dualism that has formed the cornerstone of Western civilisation.

We also know very little about ancient Chinese civilisation, a civilization that had developed a binary system used to mediate between the individual and cosmic forces. Their mysterious book on divination, *I CHING,* which is the source of all Chinese metaphysical thinking holds that all manifestation issues from two concordant principles, the *yang* (the positive, male and spiritual) and the *yin*[42] (the negative, female and material). In the West the yang has lost its spiritual aspect. What is in essence duality in harmony has been replaced by dualism, imbalance and discord.

The ancient Chinese binary system was the inspiration for the co-founder of calculus, the German rationalist philosopher, Gottried Wilhelm Leibniz (1646-1716). It is also the language of our modern day computers. As noted in Chapter 8, the English scholar, Joseph Needham, has undertaken to write a 25 volume treatise on Chinese civilisation [*Science & Civilisation in China,* Cambridge 1954 -...]. In *The Genius of China*, Robert Temple has revealed some of Needham's research about the inventiveness of the Chinese – there is hardly anything you could name that they had not first discovered; something present day Chinese are seemingly unaware of.

The fact is that the West knows very little about prehistory and its debt to ancient civilizations. We know very little about the Phoenicians, Minoans and other civilizations of the Mediterranean; just as we know little of the Harappan in the Indus Valley [Pakistan] or of ancient civilizations of the Aztec and Incas. Nonetheless, an evolution of consciousness is taking place. East is no longer just East, nor West just West. We are beginning to appreciate the gifts of other cultures. Today in the West more and more people are reading about the indigenous peoples and their way of life. Environmental issues and concern for poverty in the world are now on the agenda of an increasing number of people. More of us are turning to alternative remedies and practices to heal the division and fill the void of a purely materialist culture. More and more people are taking up yoga, tai chi, chi kung, overtone singing, meditation. More and more of us are enjoying the diversity of other cultures, their arts and crafts, their Carnivals, their Festivals, their music (so-called world music), their cuisine and their sense of caring and community; their sense of being. The issue as we shall see in the next Pillar, is that what we most desperately need is not the globalisation of Capital, but the globalisation of Spirit as Michael Lerner has so aptly termed it.

Globalisation as Civilisation

The ultimate goal of political and economic globalisation as it is generally perceived in modern Western society, is that every place on the face of the earth should be more or less like every other. Whether you are in Taiwan or in Timbuktu, you will order the same hamburger and the same diet coke, even if coconut palms laden with coconuts are swaying in the breeze outside your window. The same music will be piped to you in the lifts of your hotel; everyone will be wearing the same designer jeans, driving the same automobiles and dreaming the same dreams of making a fast buck and to hell with his neighbour It is a pauperised nightmare scenario – a seamless sameness only serving the greed of the global corporations for whom diversity is their greatest enemy. Western corporate state institutions are derived from closed linear western knowledge systems based, as I have already outlined, on control of nature, false notions of progress, dualism, the primacy of science and on the beliefs and hubris of these systems.

Today with the spread of consumerism with its seductive technology, the West dictates world trade and markets, exporting its technology, its political systems and institutions which stifle the diversity of creation; completely ignoring its indebtedness for all the things it has borrowed from these early civilizations -- their contributions to science, art and most importantly, for their resources, raw materials and labour without which it would be unable to sustain its extravagant life styles. The traditional virtues of community and caring, the true hallmark of democracy have been replaced by the desire for more and more comfort, and self interest: values to which the West claims the moral high ground.

Globalisation is violence against nature and against humanity. The violence of the corporate state is as reprehensible as the violence of those who hate. As Martin Luther King said, *"The ultimate weakness of violence is that it is a descending spiral, begetting the very thing it seeks to destroy. Instead of diminishing evil, it multiplies it. Through violence you may murder the liar, but you cannot murder the lie, nor establish the truth. Through violence you may murder the hater, but you do not murder hate. In fact violence merely increases hate. So it goes. Returning violence for violence, adding deeper darkness to a night already devoid of stars. Darkness cannot drive out darkness; only light can do that. Hate cannot drive out hate; only love can do that."*

The Sufi mystic, Ibn'Arabi has said *"Every cause is the effect of its own effect."* Every action we take has a reaction, a consequence; and conversely, behind every action is a cause for which it was the effect. This is karmic or cosmic law, the law of cause and effect – our own interest can only be secured if the interest of all is served – a lesson we will surely have to learn. It can provide us with a new, holistic paradigm based not on dualism nor on division but on unity: a unity of science and spirituality, and the knowledge that all life is connected; that what we do to each other and to the earth affects us in like measure.

A culture based exclusively on self interest goes counter to natural law – which is not based on the survival of the fittest as our orthodox theory of evolution claims, but is one of co-operation and balance – and, like the domination of nature for purely materialistic objectives, is unsustainable. A capitalist, materialist monoculture, which privileges the rich, thus creating a life of misery and poverty for the majority, is in no way a worthy aim for any civilised society. What is required is nurturing what is best and noblest in the human spirit – a compassionate, life affirming culture that embraces all of humanity.

Diversity is the defining characteristic of Nature. The Universe is continually in a state of diversification, or getting to know itself. The evolution of consciousness is taking place from moment to moment. Despite the arrogance of globalisation and the disharmony and resentment that it generates, the evolution of consciousness continues apace. It is nature's way of maintaining balance. In an article titled, *Education for Globalisation*, David Orr, a professor of Environment Studies, questions the whole thrust of Globalisation. He argues that Education is taking us in the wrong direction – preparing us for a purely technocratic, materialistic and fragmented world, instead of preparing us to start the long process of undoing the damage that has been inflicted on ourselves and our planet. *"Education should not be turning students into efficient corporate units but rather into curious and open minded adults."* [*Ecologist* May/June 1999] He stresses that the planet does not need more successful people but people with moral courage to make the world a better place.

We desperately need world leaders with integrity and moral courage and fibre, possessed with a strong vision of what is possible – not men or women who can be bought, bribed or bullied to succumb in the face of political and economic pressure. We require leaders who can eschew 'special relationships' with countries which denounce global agreements of merit to all – such as those on global warming and an International court for war criminals – opting instead for the type of technocratic globalisation questioned by Orr and others. The American Star Wars project, for instance, is seen by many (even in the West) as the ultimate goal of a military industrial complex. Code-named 'Masters of Space', it has the ability to control everything on the planet; what we eat, what clothes we wear, how we think, genetic determinism and discrimination.

Also typical of this form of globalisation is a country that will spend 400 billion dollars each year on its arms industry (the only business in that country that is not in recession), whilst billions of people in the third world starve; one that talks about making the world safe for democracy and freeing the world from terrorism whilst being one of the greatest exporters of terror in the history of mankind. Meanwhile very few of us, and only a handful of journalists have the courage to be at variance with the tribe lest we lose our jobs or the security that comes with our sense of belonging, seemingly oblivious to the fact that terror only breeds terror.

This Paradigm as the Only Choice

In his Dimbleby lecture in December 2001, Bill Clinton referred to the struggle between, what he termed the Western *pluralistic vision of community* and that of the rest of the world – inferring that political and economic globalisation was the only choice for mankind and that all cultures must adopt the Western paradigm. In other words, the way of the West is democratic and just; a secular world view is the only reality worth striving for. He stated correctly that nobody has a monopoly on the truth. But what he was really implying was that if anyone did indeed have such a monopoly that it would be the West. Jung would have taken issue with that assessment. He had long come to the conclusion that the Western world view based on rationalism is *not "the only possible one and is not all embracing, but in many ways a prejudice and a bias that ought perhaps to be corrected."*

Clinton intimated that the West must now show more concern for the rest of humanity, the poor and dispossessed. He claimed that we have already moved a long way from the days when Crusaders could burn down a synagogue and massacre the population of an entire city. But whilst in office he had ordered the bombing of the poor and vulnerable in the Sudan in a vain attempt to stave off impeachment. Today the most powerful state in the world can bomb with impunity the poorest countries with hardly anyone in the West lifting an eyebrow. It still employs weapons that cause genetic mutations to the offspring of innocent civilians decades later. We spare three minutes of silence in remembrance of the dastardly murder of thousands of ordinary people, and a lifetime of silence in denial of the crimes against humanity.

The events of September 11 2001, have made it quite clear that we desperately need to change the imposed paradigm. I believe that it is too early to know exactly what went down apart from those two twin towers. The dramatic collapse of those towers of duality is etched on our memories for all time – a poignant and symbolic defining moment in human history. Ground Zero is not just a burial ground for thousands of innocent people, but of ideals which cannot be sustained by the evolutionary spiral of planetary consciousness.

The idea that we do not have a choice in determining our future is totally unfounded. Choice will be forced on us: when a situation becomes untenable we will be forced to take action. I believe that the very need for change is itself changing consciousness. Soon we may all know that we are part of a whole, that there is a universal primordial wisdom that transcends the boundaries of separation and limitation. We have all witnessed what took place in racist South Africa towards the end of the last century and in order to achieve a similar world wide movement towards peace and reconciliation we must exercise our birthright to choice and all take responsibility for change. The Universe is holistic: we, as part of the whole, have access to a greater reality; we have the power to activate the potentiality inherent in the true nature of our place in the world. The choice should not be difficult – our survival depends on whether we can summon the compassion for all life on earth, for the eighty percent of the dispossessed in our world, but also for our future generations, our children and grandchildren who will inherit the world we have created.

There are, indeed, other ways of knowing than the purely scientific and scientists themselves are acknowledging the big part that intuition plays in the process. There are also many people committed to change; to improve conditions in the third world and to cancel its debts; people opposed to a global capitalist domination who speak out against the corruption and self interest of corporations and governments. The escalating crime and violence in modern day Western society surely reflects the division and spiritual bankruptcy at the very heart of our culture. To find a remedy would involve radical change in the way we think and how we look at our world. It would mean discarding entrenched belief systems. We urgently need to address the underlying cause of the disease then treat it and not the symptoms. Eradicating poverty and disaffection means addressing the ethos that the more we have the better our lives would become.

Our Governments keep promising to tackle the rising crime rate whilst the Police talk about enforcing zero tolerance, the emphasis being only on the symptoms instead of the causes of crime. Millions of pounds are spent on the provision of more police officers, prisons and detention centres. The British Government talks about establishing global peace whilst the single biggest arms manufacturer is a British company. In Chinese medicine, healing requires balance. Such a holistic approach derives from Taoism and applies equally to all knowledge and to healing society's ills: undoubtedly it could be adopted by the West in dealing with social and political issues, plagued as they are by division.

The Tao contains all; science and spirituality. We are all included in the same human journey. A Return to balance or to our Native Land, is none other than a return to that Source, which like the Tao, cannot be named. To name it would be to create separation, and so make it impossible to return. We are already there, if we but knew it – facets of the hologram of reality. By naming it we create duality, we divorce ourselves from it whether we call it Tao or God, Gaia or Mother Nature, Science or Technology... We are all part of the mystery that cannot be spoken..... the oneness that includes all opposites, yet seeks, and will ultimately and in its own time find its own balance, regardless of human hubris, greed, ineptitude or just plain stupidity.

Despite the confusion that exists in our present day situation we will come to recognise that special intelligence that operates at all levels of the phenomenal world regardless of nationhood, race, culture or belief – an intelligence linked to the primordial unchanging wisdom of existence that benefits all without condition or favour: a wisdom that regulates all of our systems for survival. We take them all for granted – but without our breath we would expire. Whether rich or poor, prime minister or scoundrel we all have this gift of life. There is something sacred here. When we acknowledge that sacredness without wishing to possess it we will cease wanting to impose our ideas, our philosophy on to others, we will cease polluting our earth, our home; we will cease wanting to control others by force. We will recognise our debt to human resourcefulness throughout the ages, the knowledge passed down by men from all cultures into a pool of knowledge that informs and enlightens us. That is the primordial wisdom, the primordial goodness of existence which existed before man-made concepts, before history itself. Our technology is not our technology, we do not own it. It has always been there. We are just now tapping into it because of the spiral of consciousness which is our true evolutionary path. This is the way of the Tao and the way is great:

> *Something mysteriously formed*
> *existing before heaven and earth*
> *silent and void, it stands alone*
> *unchanging…pervading all.*
> *Is this the Mother of all things?*
> *I do not know its name*
> *I shall call it Tao*
> *For lack of a better word,*
> *I call it great*

[Chapter 15 Tao Te Ching (my paraphrase)]

References

Education for Globalisation; David W Orr: The Ecologist, Vol.29 No.2 May/June 1999
Blackfoot Physics; F David Peat: Fourth Estate, 1995
The Adventure of Self Discovery; Stanislav Grof: State University of New York Press, 1988
Wholeness and the Implicate Order; David Bohm: Routledge & Kegan Paul, 1980
The Holographic Universe; Michael Talbot: Harper/Collins, 1996
Molecules of Emotion; Candace Pert: Pocket Books, 1999
Anatomy of the Spirit; Caroline Myss: Bantam Books,1997
Stalking the Wild Pendulum; Itzhak Bentov: Destiny Books, 1988
The Genius of China; Robert Temple: Prion, 1998
Black Athena; Martin Bernal: Free Association Books, 1987
Homage to Pythagoras; ed. Christopher Bamford: Lindisfarne Press, 1982
The Fractal Geometry of Nature; Benoit Mandelbrot: W.H Freeman, New York, 1983
In the Dark Places of Wisdom; Peter Kingsley: Element, 1999
Music & The Power of Sound; Alain Danielou: Inner Traditions, 1995

Chapter 12 – Negritude Revisited

Know the white
But keep the black

Tao Te Ching

that very ancient yet new being, at once very complex and very simple who at the limit of dream and reality, day and night, between absence and presence, searches for and receives in the sudden triggering of inner cataclysms the password for connivance and power

Césaire: Poetry and Knowledge – essay.

In summarizing the main themes of my book in the last Chapter, I did not include the concept of negritude which had led me to undertake my search for identity and meaning. At first it had seemed that the issue was one of colonialism and racism, or at the very least, the pigmentation of one's skin. Later I was to realise that it was more to do with mankind's deracination from Nature and the fragmentary way we look at reality. But it was not until I had explored all the issues surrounding the prevailing Western paradigm, that I became aware that it was this dualism that was responsible for the *blackness* at the very core of our culture; and that the mystics and sages of all ages and all cultures had understood that there can be no light without the dark – without the invisibles. It seems appropriate then to discuss this topic more fully.

When in 1988, I was invited to give a talk at the Dartington Conference "What future for the arts?" I was not quite sure how to approach the subject so I consulted with my good friend John Moat, who suggested that as the Cahier of Aimé Césaire had so profoundly shaped my thinking that maybe I should show how it led to me setting up Concord in the first place. It was John, you will recall, who had invited me to do a Concord festival in Devon. What started out as a possible weekend event as had been the norm, turned out to be a county-wide festival (Concord in Devon) which lasted for 4 months in 1986. It was a phenomenal success and sealed a friendship which has lasted to this day. It is possible that my invitation to speak may have been because of the success of that Festival.

Whilst touring around the county we had long discussions about the importance of what we were doing and about that strange word *negritude* and what it meant. It was John who had drawn my attention to the book by Peter Redgrove, *The Black Goddess and the Sixth Sense,* a book which seemed to challenge the whole Western intellectual tradition and led me to re-evaluate the whole concept of *negritude* and the role of the Black Goddess in the human psyche.

As we have seen, Europe first encountered the wealth of other civilizations when it embarked on its voyages of exploration. As a result of centuries of domination, European values have virtually determined global values. This is reflected, for instance, in the Group Eight Economic Summits that take place every year to protect the interests of the richest nations in the world – the so-called 'developed world'. The inhabitants of 'the third world' are worthy only as recipients of 'aid' and as providers of raw materials and labour.

Globalisation is an ideology of supremacy, indiscriminately imposing rampant consumerism as an ideal for all to aspire to. This hubris had given us not only one version of history but also a distorted interpretation of what it means to be civilized. It is time an unbiased history be told, the story of all peoples and all cultures; a record of the entire human journey including the contribution of so called 'prehistoric cultures'.

We should, by now be aware that our Planet is one interconnected eco-system. And that there are links between economics, race and ecology; that we pay a heavy ecological price for the way we mismanage our global resources. And there are other lessons to be learned. In most traditional cultures there is no real distinction between art and life – 'art' celebrates life itself, rites of passage, sharing and participation. Unlike the role of the arts in our own industrial culture, the 'arts' of Africa, for instance, are related to a meaningful pattern of beliefs and values which define a way of life and delineate the world in which men act, judge, decide and solve problems, creating a framework for the different aspects of daily life. African traditional life is essentially religious and ritualistic. The relationship of its cultural concepts, religion, ethnic identity and a sense of community are closely interwoven. Everything has meaning. Traditional African art forms are not 'art in isolation', but functional within particular social contexts. And the Balinese once said *"We do not have any art, we do everything as well as possible, we do all things properly."* I believe that Europe can learn from the arts of other cultures. It is only when one system imposes its priorities and its values on the rest of the world that the whole is thrown out of balance.

When Picasso first saw the magnificent cave-paintings at Lasceaux he declared that we (modern man) had invented nothing. An intuition amply borne out by the genius of the ancient Chinese and of the civilizations that arose around the Mediterranean sea.

Not all of us, perhaps, are aware of the pre-historic hunting and pastoral frescoes in the Tassili and elsewhere in the Sahara, which according to Terrence Mc Kenna [*Food of the Gods*] were the source of the high civilisation of pre-Dynastic Egypt, *"the motifs and stylistic concepts associated with Egypt were first introduced into Egypt by dwellers of the Western desert."* Nor are we aware of the equally magnificent rock paintings of the Bushmen of the Kalahari. The Bushmen, nomads, hunter-gatherers, concentrated much of their artistic expression on portable and necessary items, such as the engraved ostrich egg-shells they used to carry or to store water. But in their rock paintings we can see a people who lived in total harmony with nature and with themselves, something very few of us have experienced. Yet, as Laurens van der Post has written in his *"Testament to the Bushmen"*, *"I know of none who have written on Bushman art, for instance, who thought it necessary to acquire in depth a knowledge of symbolism, comparative mythology and psychology."* He went on to argue that our sense of continuity and of the totality of history depends on our ability to recognise that the Dream is the "gateway to the meaning of our pre-historic past". This is something the Australian Aborigine stress in their claim to the return of their *native* land for they believe that the land is sacred and that a person's very identity is tied to the tracks across the land made by their ancestors in *Dreamtime*; a dream time which had been shattered by the arrival of Captain Cook on their shores. The Dreaming, wrote James Cowan, should be *"seen for what it is: a metaphysical statement about the origins of mankind as a spiritual being."* [*Mysteries of the Dream-time*]

Writing this book is a record of my search for meaning and an attempt to understand the world about me. It was only when I started to meditate in 1975 that I began to realize that there could be an alternative way of being in the world; but that it would entail complete dedication and strong discipline. It soon began to transform the way I was to relate to the *real* world out there – the world of the intellect and of science, of business and advertisements, of dominance and power, political and social; of desires and frustrations.

Finding the Tao te Ching had been the final jewel. I began to comprehend the nature of perceived duality. I found that by withdrawing from notions of striving to be someone special, craving for success and recognition, I was feeling more at peace with myself. I became aware of a reality beyond all that had confronted me – the 'intellectualising' of knowledge, the fragmentation, the purely materialistic rationale of the Western culture, its need to dominate, and its profligacy of natural resources. Whilst still part of that world, the outlook had seemed extremely black, if I were to use the currency of the language.

The word *black* I was to discover was pregnant with meaning. Now I can see that the seeming duality in nature, in creation, is essentially non-duality; yin and yang are not exclusive of each other, they each contain essential aspects of each other and are complementary to each other. This allows for meaningful relationships and change for the better. It represents the true nature of things: day and night, positive and negative, man and woman, rational and intuition, the dark and the light. It began to shed light on the blackness of my dreaming soul. I could see that the darkness was my own ignorance of who and what I was, a darkness that entraps us all.

I also began to suspect that the darkness of ignorance and prejudice of the European mind was projected onto Africa, the cradle of civilization. We now know that the Ancient Egyptians were non European, a belief which has been denied in Europe since about 1830's. Whereas the West traces its cultural roots to Greece, the Greeks of the classical age, as we have seen, not only acknowledged the primacy of Egyptian civilization, but they affirmed that Pharonic culture had derived from inner Africa – the country of the blacks, as Herodotus referred to the Ethiopia of his time. Today, books by both black and white historians have been setting the record right. For example, Peter Redgrove [ibid] states that Gerald Massey's *"insistence that Africa was the cradle of humanity has been vindicated by modern research and will, I suspect, be further vindicated on the cultural level,"*

As we have seen, recent research in molecular biology also suggests that we are all directly linked through maternal genes to an African mother. Egypt, Sumeria and China, were all advanced civilizations whilst Europe was still in its dark ages. Yet this is hardly ever acknowledged. We owe a great deal to the genius of China, for instance. Western hubris, hurtling out of control like an asteroid, threatens all life on the planet. By some supreme irony, the rehabilitation of the black is the only hope. Perhaps, it is in the darkness, the wilderness, the invisibles of which we are all a part, that we can discover our true selves and our true home.

Redgrove traced a transition in human consciousness in the powerful symbolic presence of the Black Goddess – a symbol of all the things we could know in the blackness beyond visible light – a return to the black Mother, the Earth, Gaia, a return to the womb, the dark senses which are aware of the invisibles. And it is significant that Sartre called the poetry of the black poets in his introduction to Leopold Senghor's Anthology of Black Poetry, published in 1949, an 'orphic journey'. The Anthology included portions of Césaire's long poem. Van der Post would also have us look at the Odyssey. *"The deepest of all the patterns in the human spirit is one of departure and return, and the journey implicit in between. The life of man is the journey, a voyage such as that of Odysseus, a travel downwards into cataclysmic depths like Orpheus in search of Eurydice."* [*JUNG & the Story of our Time*, L.Van der Post]

For Redgrove the symbolic presence was the black Goddess; for D.H. Lawrence, that 'pilgrim in search of truth', the symbol was the dark god. Lawrence's search was to find union in duality. It is probably not surprising that he glimpsed his dark god in the Australian bush. Although making no reference to the aborigine and of the rainbow serpent, his vision of the rainbow is uncannily similar: *'the iridescence which is darkness at once and light, the two-in-one, the crown that binds them both.'* [*The Crown*, Phoenix II] Lawrence's 'fulfilling god' is dark and unknowable as he strove to return to his own true nature, to a union where all duality was resolved. This aspect of Lawrence has not been fully acknowledged because he was a critic of Western values and culture, its materialism and lack of spiritual values. Instead he has been attacked for his sensuality and his true spirit obscured.

Christianity perceives light as equated with good and dark as equated with evil. "Let there be light" necessitated the banishment of darkness and of the dark senses like intuition. As a friend confided in a letter to me: *"We are cut off from our darkness and the feminine, conditioned by centuries of emphasis on sin and guilt, on being saved only by grace, on the need for control of nature because our feelings have been so controlled, not understanding what has made us what we are. We are still only semi-conscious, not aware of what has been lost or of the reasons why it was lost."* [Anne Baring]

What can be seen is the only acceptable proof, science the only God. Out go intuition and all the *'invisibles'* as Redgrove calls them. Yet everything is invisible until brought to light. It was Heraclites who claimed that the invisible connection is stronger than the visible, and this is borne out by quantum theory – that all things in our Universe including ourselves are part of a whole organic pattern. Everything is connected in an intimate and immediate way, the visible and the invisible, the dark and the light, forming a continuum, a web of Reality reflecting everything else. A return to wholeness means recalling the knowledge of connectedness that we have lost – it is a return to the homeland – the home of the spirit, and for Africans this meant the home of the ancestors.

The necessity for undertaking the journey into darkness was known throughout the ages by the poets and the mystics – Blake, Ruskin, Rilke, Dante, Novalis, Valery, Graves, Yeats, and Goethe among the poets. According to Paracelsus, the Swiss physician, *"our animal soul is the lost daughter, the Kingdom of Heaven on Earth"*. Jung's collective unconscious also bears this out and in the Song of Solomon: the Queen of Sheba proclaims her blackness with pride, *"I am black but comely...."* Dante found that the hells he encountered on his journey were within himself. Shakespeare's Prospero recognised Caliban at last in the line *'This thing of darkness I acknowledge mine!'* What is clear is that this journey, although not specifically expressed in terms of black and white, is none the less a search for reconciliation with, and acceptance of, our dark side, the shadow, the feminine, the magical and the intuitive.

Until we reconcile these opposites we are not truly whole. Egyptian civilization knew this. Symbolically the Sphinx with its black features was the embodiment of both the male and the female. The pagan cult of Isis and her son Horus had been incorporated into early Christianity at the time of the Roman persecution. All over Europe supposedly scorched statues of the Virgin and child are reminders of this – the Black Madonnas (*Jung, The Wisdom of the Dream:* Segaller/Berger). Not only do we have to face up to the substance of our origins but we must also confront the shadow in order to experience the integration of the whole personality – the Return to the Self – the other mind in us, the true centre.

Philosophy & Truth

In the book, Homage to Pythagoras, edited by Christopher Bamford, there is this quote: *"Pythagorean thought is the seminal mystery of Greek civilization and recurs everywhere, impregnating almost all religion, poetry, philosophy, music, architecture, not to mention the 'sciences' which in many ways are still those of today."* What is not mentioned in the book was that Pythagoras had learned all his 'mysteries' during his twenty-one year long sojourn in Egypt. On his return to the country of his birth, the first thing Pythagoras did was to found his own school, known as the Cenobites or Pythagoreans. Its teaching was based on Egyptian mathematical and religious pantheistic principles – that in order to achieve harmony with oneself and with the kosmos, or universal order, one must follow the disciplines of arithmetic, geometry, music and astronomy. According to the Greek Philosopher,

Iamblichus, Pythagoras was the first to call himself a philosopher. A philosopher was someone with a love for wisdom, a science of *objectified truth.*

Pythagorean philosophy was holistic and thus, non-dual. Aristotle had stated that *"Plato and Pythagoras think that being and unity are not something else, but that this is their nature; namely that their essential being is just to be one and to be being".* However, Peter Kingsley, in *Ancient Philosophy, Mystery and Magic,* suggests that it was Aristotle himself, along with Plato, who 'consciously corrupted' this non-dualism. Dualism inevitably became the fingerprint of the Western paradigm and its purely scientific and quantitative approach to Reality.

To Pythagoras, truth and beauty were the same thing, something that the poet John Keats expressed in his *Ode to a Grecian Urn,* and which has stuck in my memory, from the time I was about ten or eleven to this day. *Beauty is truth, truth beauty, that is all ye know on earth and all ye need to know.* As I mentioned in the first chapter of this book, these lines were the spur for me to try to make sense of my conflicting worlds. The first two lines from a section of Césaire's Cahier struck me just as forcibly.

> And a voice declares that for centuries Europe
> has stuffed us with lies and crammed us with plague,
> for it is not true that:
> the work of man is finished
> we have nothing to do in the world
> we are the parasites of the world
> our job is to keep in step with the world.
> The work of man is only just beginning
> It remains for him to conquer
> at the four corners of his fervour
> every rigid prohibition.
> No race holds a monopoly of beauty, intelligence and strength
> there is room for all at the meeting-place of conquest
> we know now that the sun revolves round our earth illuminating the plot which
> we alone have selected
> that every star falls at our command from the sky to
> the earth without limit or cease."

It seemed to me that somehow Europe had got it wrong. We all belong, we all participate in the long journey of getting to know ourselves; to grapple with the mystery of life. I yearned as Césaire did *"to answer the universal hunger, the universal thirst.................*

> *Look! the tree of our hands is for all."*

To me this last sentence conjured up the powerful image of a black man, with out stretched arms, symbolizing a tree with its roots firmly rooted in the soil of Africa. The tree is a symbol of wholeness with branches reaching upwards, its roots firmly rooted in mother earth.

Negritude & Animism

Aimé Césaire of Martinique and Leopold Senghor of Senegal were poets, who, In Paris, in the 1930's, expressed their anguish in a universal cry for wholeness. Negritude was a revolt against colonial values – glorifying the African past and praising the traditional communal values of harmony based on intuition, caring and emotion – the 'dark senses' in other words, that seem more real than Western values based purely on reason and logic. It was a *'state of total belonging',* beyond division and separation from Mother Earth – a feeling I had on so many occasions when I had visited Africa; driving along the Rift Valley in Kenya, later to spend a night at the Tree Top Hotel, not even contemplating retiring to bed, the primeval pull of the wild beats snorting and jostling around the water hole. Time had stopped still – we were all, animals and humans caught up in a single moment of existence.

And that moment in the devout atmosphere of an ancient Coptic Church in the heart of Addis Ababa, [far removed from the hunger, fear and suspicion outside], down into the hushed depths of the Crypt where entombed Emperors lay shrouded in aeons of time…. meeting the eyes of a young acolyte, clear, like those of a young baby gazing up at you without judgment.

Or the early light of dawn on my seventieth birthday, by the Victoria Falls in Zimbabwe; the moon still gazing down reluctant to bid the night goodbye; the bird song, the rising sun weaving a miraculous rainbow on the vaporous screen of mists and spray wafting above the rumbling water fall. Then time had again stood still as I paid homage to the moment in a slow *tai chi* meditation.

I recalled sailing down the great Zambezi river, the swirling dark waters, pregnant with life beneath the surface and along the shores, knowing that soon the river will plunge down over the precipice of the waterfall. The power of it all. I recalled D.H. Lawrence's lines, *"The sense of greatness, vastness, and newness, in the air. And the strange, dusky, grey eucalyptus-smelling sense of depth, strange depth in the air, as of a great deep well of potency, which life had not yet tapped...As if life still held great wells of reserve vitality, strange unknown wells of secret life-source, dusky, of a strange, dim, aromatic sap which had never stirred in the veins of man, to consciousness and effect."* [*The Boy in the Bush*]

Moments that tied me to Africa. And I thought of negritude, my mind conjuring up the dark waters of another African river, the Niger, her sprawling labyrinth of tributaries, veins linking ancient African kingdoms – Mali and Timbuktu, Benin and Senegal, in a seamless animistic whole.

Years later I would sail down the greatest river of all, the Nile linking Upper and Lower Egypt, the cool recesses of the King's Chamber in the dead centre of the great Pyramid at Giza, one of the great wonders of our world, standing by the great sarcophagus and intoning the sacred vowel OM – the reverberations filling the chamber. And on to Karnak, the towering columns and obelisks, mysterious symbols of a lost civilization, whilst Europe slumbered on.

Negritude was a sense of being, of understanding; a call for the emergence of a new man. Just as 'Black is Beautiful' was echoed by the modern feminist movement, so this call for new values can now be seen to have echoed the poets of Europe – the descent into hell in order to come into the light. A synthesis of alchemical knowledge and traditional values, it is a universal concept, a universal plea for wholeness.

Césaire spoke for the colonized in body and in mind. Although in those West Indian Islands which were part of the French Empire a black man might achieve some doubtful dignity through the French system of assimilation, that process was unacceptable to Césaire. After studying in Paris, Césaire resigned from the Communist Party of France because he had come to recognize that *"the peculiarity of our place in the world.. isn't to be confused with anybody else's. The peculiarity of our problems aren't to be reduced to subordinate forms of any other problem. The peculiarity of our history, laced with terrible misfortunes belong to no other history. The peculiarity of our culture.. we intend to live and to make live in an ever more real manner."* As Franz Fannon put it: *"The colonised is elevated above jungle status in proportion to his adoption of the Mother Country's cultural standards."*

The educated blacks had discovered that they were rejected by a civilisation which they had assimilated. Educated in France, Senghor was a man of two worlds, Africa and Europe. His rhapsodic poems to negritude spring from his strong feelings of belonging to his native land, and that African culture and sensibility existed before the imposition of European culture. At the same time, he was a French intellectual. He was the first African member of the *Académie Française*, widely regarded as the most distinguished French intellectual association. But he never lost sight of the limitations of Western culture, its divorce from nature, its fragmentation. For Senghor it was his identification with his "blackness" without reference to culture, language, or geography, embracing all people within the Africa Diaspora.

"Negritude is the whole complex of civilized values – cultural, economic, social and political – which characterize the black peoples or, more precisely, the Negro-African world. All these values are essentially informed by intuitive reason...The sense of communion, the gift of myth-making, the gift of rhythm..." [Negritude & African Socialism in St.Anthony's papers on African Affairs No.2, ed. K.Kirkwood, Chatto & Windus p11]. It was to become the basis for Afro-centrism as opposed to the Euro-centrism which has sought to define our modern world.

As I performed his Cahier in the 1970's, Césaire's vision seemed to conjure up an image of a new world not based on enterprise and dominion but one of living in harmony with our world. It seemed to *"symbolise and sum up what is probably the 20th Century's most important phenomenon: the powerful surge next to the old and the new world, of a third world both very new and very old."* [Eshleman & Smith, The Collected Poetry of Césaire: University of California Press, 1983]

Today the concept of negritude has lost its appeal as no longer historically relevant. Negritude, as Senghor conceived it, is largely discredited, and not just by the West. It has been seen as limited in its ideological, and political significance. But from my reading of the *Cahier* by Césaire, I began to see it in a completely different and ultimately significant light. It was not just an oppositional concept of one system against another, however limited or justifiable that may be, but in fact, a universal concept that goes beyond secular academic theorizing with its specialized and fragmented tradition. It was a concept applicable to our divorce from nature and so for all peoples.

Language in particular, has created dualism, as has the entrenched Western Cartesian view of reality, themes I have been attempting to address in this book. At best *negritude* cannot be defined. It can only be hinted at: as that deep African nilotic concept of total belonging; an animism or panpsychism of an interior awareness, of an infinite root that sees that there is a force *vitale* that links all of creation, thus capable of giving meaning to existence.

My own dream adventure with the Cahier has been so powerful, so formative, that it led to many of the convictions that I now have. As I have described, by 1973 I had become an increasingly frustrated and angry man. I had known a measure of success, but had come to feel it a borrowed success, or on lease from an alien world. Enoch Powell had made it quite respectable for people to express openly their racism. At the same time black actors were being told that they were not sufficiently experienced. Yet, when in 1974, I set up with John Mapondera the Drum Arts Centre in London in order to provide just that experience, I had been accused of being separatist and divisive. I see now that when, all those years ago, I performed Césaire's poem as a one man show I had come to the piece in a kind of half-sleep. The person who grasped it was the person of my anger. It would allow me to walk their stage and to bring down their curtain:

> Wait... Everything's in order. My good angel
> grazes in neon lights. I swallow sticks. My
> dignity wallows in vomit. What madness to dream
> of the marvellous dancer leaping beyond all
> that is contemptible.

But I remember that as I spoke those words, I was coming alive to something deeper than my anger. I was moving beyond rage. Slowly I realized that behind the rage I was experiencing something melting... It registered as a kind of grief. At first my anger had merely disconcerted; it did not want to know. But slowly, and beyond my volition, a change was working. I began to see through the backdrop of pain and grief a kind of end-of-the-tunnel light where, under the spell of the words, all my senses seemed to come alive. I tried to cling to the anger, but found it slipping from me.

> But at the execution let my heart preserve me from all hate
> do not make of me that man of hate
> for whom I have only hate.

When the tour was finished, I turned my back on the Return, or so I thought! That was 1978. What happened to me in the next 3 years led me to set up Concord. Now I see that the Return had merely moved underground. A few years later I had come upon the Tao Te Ching by Lao Tzu. From that time the philosophy of both these books, in their different ways, underlay all I have tried to do. It formed the basis of my identification with a major shift in consciousness which I believe is taking place all over the world today.

What in 1978 I plunged into thinking was a vehicle for black assertiveness, black power, black consciousness was, I now see, the inspiration not of the force of division, but of the force of reconciliation. Césaire's poem, is no more a rallying cry to some utopian Black Citadel, than Blake's Jerusalem is an anthem of British chauvinism. Both speak of that true home, every soul's birthright, the holy city of the liberated Self.

In this extraordinary light one begins to see the world history of the last 1000 years or so as the story of the world coming to know itself; the imperialism of the white;. the encounter of white and black, the repression, the breakdown, the breakout, the gradual agony of integration. Where, if successful, does this individuation lead if not to My Native Land. Our Native Land. What does this suggest for the future of society? Out of what this poem has worked on me comes the conviction that, however it currently registers in anger and pain, an integration has to take place in our world. Not the integration which presupposes the primacy of Western values. The Black Goddess, currently the prime agency of healing is moving through the house, through our feelings, through our dreams. The white world must open to the black, and when it does it will find new life and new possibility.

It seems to me that we are in danger of talking about culture as if it is something separate from life itself. Somewhere I once read: "*Fish living in sea and lake do not have to think about water.*" Now I see the Return as a return to the natural state of being whole – a return to values we have somehow lost. These values once existed in traditional cultures of the world. If we think we can prescribe the future of human development we are being naive. To prescribe is like trying to script our dreams. The imagination, which is the shared property of black and white, will unfold according to its own dreaming. But the individual, black or white, if he or she is to be useful to the imagination, now has no choice but to be open to the energies of integration and by striving for wholeness in his personal life help the dreaming process.

Perhaps because of our language, with its definitions of blackness, the true relationship between blackness and the dreaming soul has never been realized – as it is in, for instance, the Chinese symbol for wholeness – the yin and the yang. The dream is the way nature informs the conscious mind. The language of dreams is not words but images; like the Tao dreams speak to you but it is difficult to express them in words; they are a way of achieving balance between the conscious and the unconscious and so are therapeutic – the reconciliation of opposites.

The black goddess, it seems to me, is everywhere but still she is invisible. Instead of clinging to false myths like the white man's burden we should see that the gold of the Incas led to naked lust, the sweat and the labour of the exploited the real jewels in a tarnished crown. We need both the dark and the light, the blackness of the night for the soul to dream; the light of day to see the wonders of all creation. By cultivating the dark, instead of denying it, we can rediscover our connectedness with Nature. By being close to Nature we may learn more about our true natures.

By integrating the two aspects, the masculine and the feminine we can become whole. Without the feminine we would not be able to recreate ourselves; without the dark earth we would not be able to draw sustenance; without the dark night we would not sleep deep and replenish ourselves, or know ecstasy; without the spirit as well as the body we will not be whole. From the black we can learn spontaneity and joy. It is not by accident that black music is the pulse of popular culture world wide. We dance to it, make love to it, are healed by it. When we unwittingly empathize with it we are fleetingly in the realm of the goddess, the realm of being. Black people recognize each other as soul brothers and soul sisters and soul food partakes of the spirit of communion as well as feeding the body. What would our hospitals be without our black nurses? And black mothers have been nurse-maids to white children as they are to black.

According to the Jungian analyst, Anne Baring, *"The West desperately needs to confront the shadow side of its nature which it has projected onto other races, looking down on them as inferior and kept as far as possible under control because of the feared unknown, the unseen, the split between the conscious aspect and the unconscious, instinctive aspect. It is part of the general unconsciousness of the western psyche."* [letter to author]

By projecting our 'darkness' onto a fictitious 'other' we destroy ourselves and our environment. To quote Laurens Van Der Post again. *"But we have come dangerously late to this new awareness. We do not understand that we cannot do to others what we do not do to ourselves. We cannot murder and kill outside without murdering and killing within. We turn our hate on to the native, the dark people of the world, from Tokyo to Terra del Fuego, because we have trampled on our own dark natures. We have added to our unreality, made ourselves less than human, so that that dark side of ourselves, our shadowy twin, has to murder or be murdered."* [*Venture to the Interior*]

Césaire's poem is a plea for wholeness, a recognition of that blackness which transcends race. It was not as limited in its meaning as the term negritude has come to mean. Césaire identified with that state of total belonging that can only be found with an integration of mind and spirit, man and nature, ancient African animism and spirituality.

> *my negritude is not a stone*
> *nor deafness flung out against the clamour of the day*
> *my negritude is not a white speck of dead water*
> *on the dead eye of the earth*

He was in search of his spiritual roots in Mother Africa, an odyssey beyond the dark places of the mind colonialism had imposed on his world, in order to rediscover his true identity. It was a journey that I also had to make; and has led me to this point in my life when I can speculate on our common human roots and how recent research in genetics and linguistics is leading to a new understanding of our relationship to each other, to our planet and to all living species. Such an awareness, of the Unity of all Life, will have psychological implications not only for those who have the power to control and dominate, but also for those who are at the receiving end of political and economic domination. Such an awareness will hopefully transform our limited view of reality; to an understanding that diversity is the very imprint of Nature, that everything is connected. It may well lead to a more just and caring world with concern for the ecology and for each other; a world free from warfare and domination.

If we return to our native land, "knowing the place for the first time", we can stop worrying about the future. Every true return is a new departure. And that is what Césaire's poem is about.

> To leave. My heart was throbbing with an insistent
> desire to give. To leave... I would arrive sleek
> and young in that country, my country,
> and I would say to that country
> whose clay is part of my flesh;
> 'I have wandered far
> and I am coming back to the lonely ugliness
> of your wounds. I would come to that country,
> my country, and I would say to it:
> Kiss me without fear
> and if I do not know what to say
> it is still for you that I speak'.
> And I would say to it
> My mouth shall be the mouth of misfortunes
> which have no mouth
> my voice the freedom of those freedoms
> which break down in the prison-cell of despair.
> And, coming, I would say to myself:
> 'Beware, my body and my soul,
> beware above all of crossing your arms
> and assuming the sterile attitude of the spectator,
>
> because life is not a spectacle,
> because a sea of sorrows is not a proscenium,
> because a man who cries out is not a dancing bear'.

References

The Dancing Wu Li Masters; Zukav,Gary: Rider, 1991

The Black Goddess & the Sixth Sense; Peter Redgrove: Bloomsbury Books, l987

Black Athena Vol.1 The Fabrication of Ancient Greece; Martin Bernal: Free Association Press, l987

Africa: History of a Continent; Basil Davidson: Weidenfeld & Nicholson, l966

The African Origins of Civilization – Myth or Reality; Chiekh Anta Diop: Lawrence Hill & Co., l974

Cult of the Black Virgin; Ean Begg: Resurgence No.ll7 Malcolm Miles, 1986

Testament to the Bushmen; Lawrence Van Der Post: Penguin, 1984

Mysteries of the Dreamtime; James Cowan: Prism Press, 1990

Jung and the Story of our Time; Lawrence Van Der Post, Penguin, 1976

Jung the Wisdom of the Dream; Segaller/Berger: Channel 4 Books, 1989

Ancient Philosophy, Mystery & Magic; Peter Kingsley: Channel 4 Books, 1989

Life into Art, Keith Sagar, Penguin 1985

Epilogue – The Return

I belong, therefore I am

John Mbiti

We shall not cease from exploration and the end of all our exploring will be to arrive where we started and know the place for the first time

T.S. Eliot

When I set out on my personal journey all those decades ago, I never realized that it would lead to the momentous discovery that I had been on a cyclical journey back to my *native land* and that I would know the place for the first time. Nor did I realise that we all have to make that journey; for it is only by honouring our individual journeys that we become whole; empowered to speak our truth.

What I also learned is that we are all members of one human family and our *native land* is mother earth herself: a reality borne out by those remarkable pictures from space when the first astronauts, on their historic journey, landed on the moon. Looking back from its barren surface, they caught sight of the earth, a blue planet cradled in cloud sailing and miraculously suspended in the vastness of interstellar space. On our Television screens we were simultaneously seeing for the very first time our home, our Planet – a beautiful living eco-system and part of a vast and mysterious Universe. And we were deeply touched by the indescribable beauty and wonder and sense of awe of a reality of which we are not ordinarily aware.

Without a sense of awe at the miracle of life and of creation we are not complete and our lives seem mundane and meaningless. We fail to see that we are part of one human family, that everything is connected; that our differences are what make us unique and part of the great paradox that underlies all of creation – unity in diversity. Integrating our individual uniqueness and our belonging to a larger human family is what makes us truly human. We are part of a whole and that whole is within us. This is the knowledge that has been lost along the way – that we are fractals of the crystal of creation and not just facets of that crystal.

Once we thought our world was flat, now we can go to the moon and back. Our science has done away with the superstitions of early man only to replace them with super-scientism. Why is it we want to go to the moon and explore the reaches of outer space? It is none other than our desire to connect with what is vastly greater than we think ourselves to be. Our quest is a spiritual quest and science is only one way of trying to comprehend the mystery. Because society has turned its back on religion or the possibility of any spiritual dimension to life, we are stuck in a paradigm that has eroded human values and has threatened our very survival. Because we dare not go against the received wisdom of the primacy of scientific knowledge, we have nowhere to turn. But deep down we know that science is itself probing the mystery of life and creation. The new Quantum physics is stating that the old materialistic model is outdated, that there is more to it than empirical proof. Whilst Science has replaced religion, conflicting Religions have also created confusion by claiming that they each have all the answers to the mystery of life; that their God, or vision of a Supreme Intelligence is the only one, thus creating more confusion and division.

One of the greatest scientists of all time was Albert Einstein who wrote that *"The most beautiful and most profound emotion we can experience is the sensation of the mystical… It is the sower of all true science. He to whom this emotion is a stranger, who can no longer stand rapt in awe, is as good as dead. That deeply emotional conviction of the presence of a superior reasoning power, which is revealed in the comprehensible universe, is my idea of God."*

As Brian Swimme and Thomas Berry have suggested in their book, *The Universe Story, "The capacity of Einstein to transform the Newtonian science of his day through his teaching of relativity required a shamanic quality of imagination as well as exceptional intellectual subtlety. So we might say that the next phase of scientific development will require above all the insight of shamanic powers, for only with these powers can the story of the universe be told in the true depth of its meaning."* As we have seen, most indigenous cultures knew of these powers, that underlying everything, animate and inanimate, there exists a 'vital essence' – a 'modimo' which allowed them to live in total harmony with nature.

As a perpetual outsider in Britain, I have been made to address questions of race, identity and language as part of my quest. Along the way I came up against the prevailing Western worldview incorporating dualism and the fragmentation of knowledge into constituent parts – the privileging of one part over another. I found that racism is but one manifestation of a culture based on division and domination and is directly implicated in the deracination of man and nature. My path has been the endeavour to bring all the strands of my experience into something that transcends specialist categories; to create a reality that makes sense to me. In the process I have learned that we all create our realities by what we believe but that we all have the power to change our perception of almost everything we have been led to believe.

As a qualified barrister, I have endeavoured to assemble my evidence from a wide variety of sources to illustrate how Western thinking is compartmentalized; how specialist faculties are created for all disciplines. This ethos of division is at the very heart of the human tragedy facing us today. The Western cultural props of Eurocentricism, materialism and secularism tend to rely on empirical science as the only method of inquiry into the nature of the Universe, thus creating division between religion, philosophy and science. They are also responsible for the psychological rift between man and nature, the cause of our present ecological crisis. Humanity itself has been divided into different races through the study of anthropology and *eugenics*, both justifying policies of divide-and-rule, and exacerbating racial and tribal tensions, warfare and genocide. The world itself has been divided into the haves and the have-nots; the developed and the non-developed; the powerful nations assuming that their culture, or *civilization* is best and should be adopted by the rest of the world, if not imposed on it; and so they manipulate the world's economy solely for their benefit.

Most of the problems facing us today are very difficult to deal with in a predominantly secular context, and it will be necessary for us to reassess our current ideas of spirituality, which is beyond Religion. The latter is historically fraught with conflict and only serves to protect one group or nation from another. People shun the S-word because we have lost our connection with our true natures and with Nature. Spirituality is an individual experience of something bigger than us, something that brings out the best in us, something that paradoxically unifies the human tribe. I believe that we have lost that sense of community in which all things are connected; man and nature, earth and cosmos; a notion curiously confirmed by recent scientific discoveries that human beings, animals and plants all share the same DNA code.

An awareness of the unity of all life will bring about <u>radical</u> change for It goes to the very <u>root</u> causes of the disease that afflicts the world community – unlimited materialism, greed and militarism. In other words, we may be able to bring peace and hope to our fragmented and tortured world. I believe that such change is implicit in the knowledge that an evolution of consciousness is taking place and that only then will we begin to take responsibility for our actions, as well as being empowered to influence the course of events around us.

What I find quite synchronistic, is that the words *radical* and *root*, both come from the Latin *radix,* as do the words *radial* and *radiant,* as Christian de Quincey, a professor of Consciousness Studies has pointed out (*Radical Nature*). Radial, as we all know, means branching out. The human race has branched out into its distinct races but all from a common root – that Mitochondrial Eve, with whom we share the same maternal genes. It is only when the various branches, or races, see themselves as intrinsically different from each other that they become divorced from the tree of life itself, losing their connectedness with each other and with Nature. In other words, they lose their *radiance* – their Spirit. As we have seen, in ancient African culture, *"there existed a close relationship between man, Muntu, and nature, a Nilotic concept of force which unifies the whole of creation."*

This force is positive; it unifies the relationships between the external and the spiritual worlds – the human, as well as the animal, the animate as well as the inanimate. All things radiate 'seriti' or modimo, which, like God himself, is everywhere. This animism or *panpsychism* may be suggesting that there is an interior source of universal attraction, *"the infinite root that moves us towards deeper meaning"*, a *radial* energy (as the French Jesuit paleontologist, Teilhard de Chardin, has put it), connecting all elements of the Cosmos – that *"the stuff of the Universe is spirit-matter. No other substance than this could produce the human molecule"*. In other words, Spirit pervades all of nature; matter is not composed of dead stuff.

My work with Concord in the 1980's was to celebrate this connectedness –the cultural diversity of modern Britain. At the time there was still some resistance to the concept of a multicultural Britain but as a young man in the Caribbean I had been part of multicultural society and experienced the riches of its diverse cultures. I was later to write about one aspect of Caribbean culture in *Ring of Steel* (Macmillan, 1999) – the alchemical story of the birth of the Trinidad steelpan; a transmutation of industrial waste material into the twentieth century's only acoustic musical invention. Initially despised in its homeland, the instrument had to travel before taking its place in West Indian culture. Pan, as the instrument is known, is a prime symbol of unity in diversity, a subjectivity that transcends individuality and mere belonging to one racial or national group. It is also an allegory of what is perhaps desperately needed as we confront the global crisis facing mankind at this time – survival through global truth and reconciliation.

Today it is still necessary for us to redefine what we mean by multiculturalism and what it is to be British. Multiculturalism is part of an expanding culture flowering out of a chequered history and providing a unique and relevant opportunity to show that it is not merely a political expedient of an umbrella of peoples, co-existing by limited cultural exchange, but a true cross-cultural model based on a spiritual understanding of the Universe. We need to cut across all conventional categories and realise the potential for unity in diversity not only in Britain, but throughout the 'civilized' world.

Historically, Britain has been conservative, resistant to change. But we live in a rapidly changing world. In the last two decades we have seen political barriers – such as the Berlin wall – and systems – the Communist world – crumble. There is certainly no danger of anything so drastic taking place in Britain and there is no threat of cultural breakdown. Britain has shown that it can accommodate people from its old Commonwealth. According to Arnold Toynbee, an essential element in cultural breakdown if it were to happen, would be a loss of flexibility. When social structures and behaviour patterns become so rigid that society cannot adapt to changing situations, it will be unable to carry on the creative process of cultural evolution. Although a cultural mainstream may become petrified by clinging to fixed ideas and rigid patterns of behaviour, 'creative minorities' will bring about a pattern of interaction leading to growth. "*The dominant social institutions will refuse to hand over their leading roles to these new cultural forces, but they will inevitably go on to decline and disintegrate, and the creative minorities may be able to transform some of the old elements into a new configuration. The process of cultural evolution will then continue, but in new circumstances and with new protagonists.*" [*A Study of History*]

And that is what I believe could take place in Britain and so influence the rest of the world. Britain as head of a commonwealth of nations could still exert a moral force in the world despite its past. In fact this is the only role open to it. Change is desperately needed: a new awareness, a new consciousness, a new way in which we view ourselves and our world. That such change is necessary is hardly in dispute. The survival of our planet, of our credibility as intelligent beings and our dignity and self respect depend upon it. We need a new manifesto for reclaiming our lost Soul, the transmutation of the shadow of the industrial West.

The general unconsciousness of the western psyche projects the shadow side of its nature because of fear of the unknown, the unseen, its divorce from Nature – the split in our own nature between the conscious aspect and the largely unconscious, instinctive aspect, in order to dominate and control. The way of the West has invaded our dreams, polluted our rivers and seas, clogged our minds and lungs, the very breath we breathe, the crops we consume and has corroded our consciousness. Our world is in a state of crisis yet it is business as usual.

Today our very survival is threatened. The 'global' think-tank, the Club of Rome, has argued that we need to urgently re-evaluate our priorities, that we are well on the way to an environmental catastrophe that can obliterate all life on earth. The recently formed Club of Budapest recognising the urgency of the global crisis, has concluded that nothing less than a planetary shift in consciousness is needed if mankind is to survive the pressures of over-population and un-sustainability – that it would entail the most radical change from the bottom up and that we must all, as individuals, take responsibility for its implementation.

Change as we have seen implies personal transformation at a very deep level, leading to compassion for others who are not just those closest to us, to all peoples. Yet can we really expect an entire materialist culture of dominance to transform itself? The threatened environmental catastrophe will have to be imminent before attitudes change. Despite its technological prowess, its science and its philosophical treatises, the West refuses to address issues that go to the very heart of the global crisis. It fails to ratify international agreements on any issue that goes against its self-interest. Twenty percent of the population consume 86 percent of its goods and services, over half its energy and nearly half its meat and fish. While the majority of the people in the world scrape an existence, those in the West slumber on, believing that science will somehow come to their rescue.

The Clubs of Rome and Budapest have highlighted the crisis. As an individual trapped within the western paradigm I have become aware that my experiences are part and parcel of the depressing global malaise. Because of the inherent difficulty of going against one's family and culture, it perhaps takes an outsider/insider to see beyond the culture trap to seek a wider constituency of truth and meaning. I have been both – part of the culture by birth and education, I have also been an outsider, sometimes for my views but often only because of my race. Psychologically, it is very difficult to go against the generally accepted beliefs of the culture into which one is born or lives. We inherit from our peers their beliefs, their taboos, their attitudes towards other religions, and ethnic groups. As Carolyn Myss states, *"Our tribes 'activate' our thinking processes. It is extremely difficult to be at variance with one's tribe. Being part of a culture is extraordinarily empowering. As long as we make choices consonant with the culture of which we are part, we are protected. It is very painful to hold views that others reject outright. An individual who questions the status quo, becomes an outsider and can be shunned or ridiculed by society. He may even be considered insane, a heretic or rebel. In extreme cases, he may be even be imprisoned."* [*Anatomy of The Spirit*]

The prevailing dominant world culture has imposed its values on the rest of the world to such an extent that it has created a blanket *consensus reality* on a large section of humanity. The West determines our view of reality, the way things are or should be and this in turn has led to economic control, not only of the resources but of people in the rest of the world. This cultural and economic imperialism is at the root of almost all the problems facing the world today. In order to counter this dominance, we will need a new kind of revolution. We do have a choice individually to influence change. We are all linked and connected to all life in the Universe: we are the same stuff as the stars above us; part of the consciousness of the planet and responsible for the world we inhabit: every thought impacts for good or for bad on that collective consciousness.

Responsibility for change is not only that of the white establishment. Black people must also change. They must not want to integrate into a purely materialistic value system and cherish only the toys of the technological West. They will have to influence the changes that society will have to make in order to make it more humane. By their very presence in British society, black people are engaging Britain in a soul-searching reappraisal of its moral, ethical and political position. In 1998/99 the BBC had the courage to broadcast three significant documentary series, *Windrush, Into Africa,* and the *Race Card.* Channel 4 followed with *Britain's Slave Trade.* This was a significant breakthrough but it is just as important that black people rediscover the values and traditions of the cultures from which they are descended. Martin Luther King in America and Nelson Mandela in South Africa have shown what is possible.

The answer for the peoples of the "Third" world is to see that the 'development' the West talks about is a euphemism for dependency on Western values. They must rediscover their own traditional values, which will empower them to seek solutions to their problems in their own way.

Change is the responsibility of all. For white people, confronting the shadow of racial superiority might not be a traumatic experience. They may find that the black they so fear and reject may heal and remake the nation into a more caring, just and more powerful one. Britain is now a microcosm of the world; She may have lost an Empire, but that Empire now has given her the gift of itself, of allowing her to know herself, and in the knowing, perhaps, redefine what are acceptable standards for a civilized nation at the start of a new century. Viewed from the distance of the moon, the astonishing thing about the earth is that it is <u>alive</u> and part of an infinite Universe which is ordered and interconnected; and knowing this we will know who we are, and see ourselves in each other, that we are all part of a unique and beautiful Planet if we would let it be; otherwise we perish with it. Knowing this we will tread lightly on it and learn to live with, if not love, each other.

ooo0ooo

The events of September 11 2001, have made it quite clear that the major challenge we face today is rooted in outdated Western concepts of domination and control. But I also believe that they have acted as a catalyst beyond a superficial polarization of East and West; beyond the insular worldviews of conflicting systems. We are all part of the whole process. We are moving beyond a worldview of separation from other races and species and from nature: Evolution can no longer be understood in purely materialistic terms – as a narrow interpretation of natural selection or the survival of the fittest.

We cannot observe the world outside without seeing that we are part of that world. Our inner landscape is just as important as the landscape we perceive by our five senses alone. This awareness unfortunately is not as yet common knowledge and so has not altered global consciousness, or there would be more compassion towards our fellow human beings in the co-called third world; ecological issues would now be high on the agenda of all nations, as would an imperative for economic justice and reverence for the unity of all life and the holistic nature of the Universe.

I believe that most of us go through life frustrated that we cannot understand the meaning of life and consequently feel lost, bewildered and unfulfilled. For me, life is a university of getting to know oneself and to grapple with the extraordinary mystery. Although we have learned a great deal about our bodies and the physical universe, we still cannot comprehend what makes them function, nor the Intelligence that created the Cosmos. Neither our scientists, nor our philosophers, our religious leaders or politicians can provide the answers. There seems to be no coherent system linking all knowledge. And if there were wise men, no one would take any notice.

I was soon to realise that it was *how* I responded to all the fragmentation and inequities that was important. In a sense, I considered myself to be very fortunate. Most of us never have the opportunity to plumb so deeply feelings of alienation and separation. This may be because we never question the established orthodoxy of received wisdom. At the most basic level we all need to belong. Belonging means caring for one another and being loyal to one's country and to its institutions.

In 1986, long before the changes that have taken place in South Africa, Gabriel Setiloane had written, "It is important… that, in the bitterness of the struggle, they (black people) should not lose sight of the real goals and values they are struggling for... affording the youth an opportunity at self-understanding, sociologically (why they resent separation and Balkanization – because it is in their interest to 'belong' and be in 'vital participation'), and psychologically (refusing to be treated and treat others as things to be manipulated for selfish ends)..." [*African Theology*]

Black people will have to revert to their African roots, that is, a grounding in the concept of Modimo and of total participation As the black South African John Mbiti has said *"I belong, therefore I am";* just the opposite of Descartes' dictum; the awareness that as a human being he is part of that whole which is Universe; his blackness rooted in traditional values of humanity and that the Soul is the source of Being permeating all of Nature. In other words he must seek to liberate the Soul of Africa from the image projected on to it by the West's own loss of Soul.

In Britain we will also have to acknowledge the contribution made by black people throughout history for they possess vast potential to help revitalize this country's fortunes. Despite the involuntary nature of their past contribution (e.g. slavery) they can still contribute, voluntarily, to present society if made to feel part of it. Black people fought in both world wars. My service in the Royal Air Force in the second war may not have been prompted by any sense of patriotism (merely an escape from a colonial situation) but many black services men looked to Britain as their mother country. They will continue to contribute despite the fact that racism is endemic in Europe and in Britain. A National Opinion Poll in 1992 suggested that 67% of white people thought that Britain was racist. Things have not changed much since that Poll was taken. In the wake of events like the Stephen Lawrence affair we have come to acknowledge that racism exists at the institutional level.

Racism, as we have discussed, is only one manifestation of a culture grounded in dualism. It is symptomatic of the fragmentation of knowledge and issues into categories which have no connection with each other. Ecological problems, like racism, go back a long way but as they are directly linked to the psychological rift between man and nature, they cannot be seen as unrelated to each other – making it impossible to express a concern for ecology and be racist at the same time. The 2002 Earth Summit held in Johannesburg, attempted to address some of the major ecological problems facing humanity, but in the absence of an American delegation, its effect was limited to mere paternalistic rhetoric. What chance had it to succeed when the most powerful nation on earth, one which lays claim to be the champion of civilization, democracy, justice and fair play, boycotted it.

Facing up to the prejudices of our societies and the changes that are necessary in order to keep pace with a rapidly changing world is as difficult as facing up to one's own shortcomings. According to Jung:

> the dread and resistance which every natural human being experiences when it comes to delving too deeply into himself is, at bottom, the fear of the journey to Hades

[Psychology and Alchemy CW 12/439]

This becomes the case when an individual realises that his own personal growth dictates that he separate himself from the beliefs of the prevailing paradigm. Yet, this may be exactly what is needed on our journey of self-discovery. It is also necessary if we are to bring about social transformation and the evolution of planetary consciousness which I see as taking place.

This dilemma is even more disturbing if one is non-white and living in a Western dominated society. As an outsider you may be forced to question the authority and values of society and this may well lead to your becoming a freedom fighter (or 'terrorist' in the vocabulary of much of America) as was the case with Nelson Mandela. Even if such a person did not resort to extreme measures he may pursue his own ideas by non-violent means (Ghandi, Martin Luther King) or seeing himself as belonging to a wider constituency – as a member of the human family. He either has to accept that European values are sacrosanct and cannot be questioned or take a stand. I do not accept, for instance, that science alone is capable of defining reality. Neither do I accept that the West knows best and that every other culture must learn form it; nor that at some level European racism can ever be justified. Racism, as Nelson Mandela has pointed out devalues the oppressor as much as it does the oppressed. With this innate understanding I began my search for meaning.

This book bears testimony to the pain and frustration I have felt in my life and the dualism that has dogged me along the way. It is only now on the latter stages of my journey of Self discovery, that I have become rudely aware of my own dilemma – wanting to be accepted but on my own terms, wanting all the material comforts of the culture in which I live whilst knowing that I already have enough and wanting to change society without daring to change myself.

Radical change requires a certain degree of courage and history is littered with examples of people who have had the courage to challenge the status quo – Rosa Parks who refused to go to the back of the bus in the racist Deep South in America, thus starting the Civil Rights movement in America in the 1960's; the feminist movement of the 1970's (incidentally, modelled on the successful Civil Rights struggle of black Americans in the 1960's); Mahatma Ghandi's stance against British rule in India in the last century, and his example being followed by Martin Luther King in America. King addressed the whole question of racism by advocating a new consciousness of non violence, and love. His mission was a catalyst for the sweeping changes that took place in the 60's and 70's in that country. He himself said that *"To become the instrument of a great idea is a privilege that history gives only occasionally"* [*Let the Trumpet Sound*] and he went on to quote Toynbee[43] *"It may be the black man who will give the new spiritual dynamic to Western civilization that it so desperately needs to survive .....the spiritual power .....that comes from love, understanding, good will and non-violence".*

Two decades later we witnessed that remarkable change in awareness brought about when Nelson Mandela became President of South Africa, a country of apartheid and racism of the most blatant kind. Who would have imagined that such change would take place? Mandela was responsible for the most dramatic shift in racial consciousness. The world's consciousness has been effectively changed forever.

It was during those long and lonely years that my hunger for the freedom of my people became a hunger for all people, white and black. I knew as well as I knew anything that the oppressor must be liberated just as surely as the oppressed. A man who takes away another man's freedom is a prisoner of hatred, he is locked behind the bars of prejudice and narrow-mindedness. I am not truly free if I am taking away someone else's freedom, just as surely as I am not free when my freedom is taken from me. The oppressed and the oppressor alike are robbed of their humanity……. When I walked out of prison, that was my mission, to liberate the oppressed and the oppressor both

[Long Walk to Freedom]

But it was Aimé Césaire's long and passionate poem deconstructing colonialism and the slave mentality that had gripped my imagination for it pointed to a new dawn, a new man, rooted in nature and calling for the freedom of all men:

I was born of this unique race
yet knowing my tyrannical love you know
it is not by hatred of other races that I prosecute for mine.
All that I would wish is
to answer the universal hunger,
the universal thirst
to prescribe at last this unique race free
to produce from its tight intimacies the succulence of fruit
Look! The tree of our hands is for all.

[Cahier d'un retour au Pays natal]

If I learned anything from the *Cahier* of Aimé Césaire, it is that we have to deal with our own anger if one can ever hope to affect change in society. Despite the obvious dualism that underpins the Western way, we have first to acknowledge that same dualism within ourselves. Having done so we become empowered to reject the premise that we have no choice. We have no choice if we ourselves are caught in the trap of judgmental or conspiracy theories. To break out is extremely difficult, yet *we* have to change if we are to create change. Others cannot do it for us. This is the crunch.

Although I have always considered myself to be extremely lucky and have been grateful that I've had such a privileged life – good health and a certain degree of success in whatever I have set myself to do – it has been quite another matter for me to confront my tendency to judge and to project my own shortcomings on to others; to acknowledge my fears and insecurities, my lack of empathy with why things or other people are the way they are, my lack of compassion, but most of all my anger towards society.

At the psychological level, we are mostly unaware that all the trauma we have felt in our lives leave deep scars that are difficult to heal and which dictate how we react to situations that repeat themselves. Eventually it dawns on us that what we do not like out there is what we do not like about ourselves. Facing up to this requires a deep commitment to *psychological* change and it has taken me a very long time indeed to understand that anger can be transmuted into a constructive tool that can set one free. It has taken me almost an entire lifetime to discover that it is only through coming to terms with the pain, anger and frustration one has experienced that one can move beyond these and realize that an evolution of consciousness is indeed taking place – something beyond mere survival of our species. This evolution is the transformation we see in all living things about us, the shoot reaching up to the sunlight, a bud opening into an iridescent flower, a caterpillar into a butterfly – an instinctual striving to go beyond competition and mere physical survival; beyond self-interest, aggressiveness, greed and the need to dominate and control nature.

The theoretical physicist, David Bohm considers that we live in a holographic universe, in which he sees the totality of experience as an unbroken whole. It is a theory of the magnitude of Einstein's space-time continuum and as significant as Max Planck's statement that the *'term matter implied a bundle of energy which is given form by an intelligent spirit'*. Planck, as we have noted, worked out his quantum theory on the basis of the overtone series of natural harmonics (also supposedly discovered by Pythagoras).

It seems that orthodox scientific thinking, locked in fragmentation (or, in the 'explicate' order), still finds it difficult to come to terms with the change in thinking brought about by the holistic implications of Atomic Physics. We have seen that the neurophysiologist, Karl Pribram made the discovery that memory was non-localized in the brain – that the brain was holographic – just as every part of our body is a reflection of the whole. The physical body is only the end product of subtle information fields, or holograms, which change in time and are outside the reach of our normal senses.

We also looked at the fractal universe of Benoit Mandelbrot beyond Euclidean geometry, a *principle of invariance,* or *self-similarity* in which things are in the small as they are in the large – each part of a structure is similar to the whole, merely fractions or 'fractals' of each other. Mandelbrot showed that patterns in nature repeat themselves in different scales and that the earth is modelled according to these principles. In fact, we can now envisage a universe in which everything is enfolded in everything else, just as in the ancient *tai chi* Chinese symbol of the yin/yang (the supreme ultimate) is contained within the *wu chi* void or primordial state of the Universe. The opposites comprise the ultimate Reality, not the polarization of the cognitive system of the West.

What all this implies is the ultimate connectedness of the inner and the outer. It is also what the DNA sequence is teaching us. The DNA of our chromosomes contain the information to build extra copies of our bodies. Just as each point on a hologram reflects the whole image, so does the DNA of a single living cell retain the imprint of the whole person. This also parallels the smallest atom as a microcosm of the Cosmos. Being aware of all this can impart a tremendous feeling of freedom, a glimpse of Reality beyond a Science which precludes meaning in the Universe and so allow us to re-envisage our true place in the Universe: *the heart as well as the mind will have to inform us,* as John L Hitchcock has put it in his book, *At Home in the Universe.*

Perhaps it is also our language and the word *black* with its connotations of evil and unworthiness that ensnares us; or the subject/object structure of European languages that separate us from each other, them and us, black and white, good and evil, the observer and the observed (scientific empiricism). Psychologically, this attitude has had profound implications for the state of the world today. The well documented holotropic healing mode of the psychotherapist, Stanislav Grof, led him to believe that consciousness encompasses the totality of life – humanity as well as all the fauna and flora, from viruses and unicellular organisms to the most highly differentiated species – a deep understanding of the cosmic and natural laws, that would lead to greater ecological awareness and sensitivity to problems created by technology and industrialization. He believed that *"the only hope for a political, social and economic solution of the current global crisis can come from a transpersonal perspective that transcends the hopeless us-versus-them psychology, which produces at best occasional pendulum-like shifts in which the protagonists exchange the roles of oppressors and oppresses."*

An awareness of the ultimate connectedness of all things could provide a *raison d'etre* for the West in re-envisioning its role in the wider scheme of things – its relationship to the environment and to all other peoples and cultures – why we have polluted the earth, the sky and the seas; why we slaughter each other for personal gain or political power. Our knowledge, our epistemology, has somehow let us down.

Knowledge, like consciousness is an evolutionary process. We become stuck in the old paradigm if we hold on to ideas which are no longer valid or applicable; when we hold on to one version of history, usually our own; when we believe we are more civilized than, and superior to, other peoples; when we do not acknowledge the existence of civilizations that existed long before in prehistory – those, for instance, of Mesopotamia (Iraq), Sumer, Egypt, Phoenicia, Minoa and China; or that we owe most of our scientific knowledge and inventions to these ancient cultures and that they may well have been just as advanced as we are today.

Maybe it is the hubris of civilizations that has led to their demise. With supremacy has always come conquest, and conquest always breed dissent. The pendulum swings from one extreme to its opposite. Once Egypt dominated the Mediterranean world, including Greece, the Greece we have been taught to venerate as the source of our culture and Rome, the fountain of our jurisprudence. We are only now beginning to learn that Greece acknowledged the primacy of Egyptian civilization and of the connection between Pythagoras and that country.

We live in a multicultural word and we all belong to one human family. The earth is our home. No one is excluded and no one has the right to control and dominate others for their own advantage. If we do not respect others we cannot respect ourselves. We each have cultural gifts we can share with each other – different customs, cuisines, costumes, music, landscapes, art forms and medicines, from the practices of the shamans of the rain forest to Chinese acupuncture. We have a duty to care for those less fortunate than we are. There is no one version of the truth and we can learn from each other. The current belief in 'scientific truth' is self-serving for those who proclaim it and the seventh pillar of the prevailing Western paradigm, that we have no choice, is unfounded. The imbalance of the West will have to give way to a new vision of reality if we are to survive the current global crises.

According to the Tao, opposites are but aspects of each other. Where would we be without the dark night and our dreams that connect us to the universal soul? Martin Luther King's dream was none other than the rehabilitation of blackness, the black goddess and the recovery of our spirit. The prevailing Western paradigm is based on a patriarchal outlook, on radical separation. As my friend John Moat put it *"The constant underlying all this seems to be that when the innate insecurity of the masculine expresses itself in a division from the feminine, then it becomes guarded, territorial, harnesses its logos (as opposed to Eros) dynamic of its defensive need to dominate, to regulate, to rationalise, to exclude... and so attempting to extend its control against the natural and inclusive order falls back ever more paranoid into its crumbling bunker. Meanwhile 'Blackness and the Dreaming Soul' are abroad, are on the move, and the shoots of the one thousand flowers are beginning to show all across the concrete courtyard. The Tao sleeps, the Tao breathes, the Tao is awake."*

In sum, it seems that there has to be radical change in our thinking and that we do have choice, but first we have to go back to our very roots as human beings. We are all part of one human race with our roots in Africa. That continent is in our genes, our language, our history, and our culture. Africa produced one of the greatest civilizations whilst Europe was still in its dark ages and this knowledge has been withheld from us as part of the same racist theory that was used for the enslavement of peoples and for political and economic domination. African *animism* is within us all, our root drive towards oneness. In other words we are, at our very roots, one with the Universe. Everything is connected and there is a spiritual dimension to life. That we live in a holographic universe beyond duality and separation is a point of view a few Western thinkers and scientists are now recognizing. The inherent contradictions as seen from a rational viewpoint or from our contrast – knowledge perspective, do not exist in the field of quantum mechanics. By resolving the opposites, we *can* find meaning in a meaningful universe which embraces everything: dark-light, East-West, spirit-matter, matter-energy, mind-body, left-right (hemispheres), male-female, positive-negative, unity-diversity. The Tao, that universal primordial field, accommodates all. It is what gives us choice, creativity and meaning; a radical departure from the purely scientific world view which has divided man from himself and from nature and has led to the dualism that underpins the prevailing Western paradigm.

What this tells us is that we do have a capacity for consciousness and spirituality; that we can live more deeply if we understand that determinism can never give us certainty. We have to resolve what we see as contradictions by embracing the inherent *duality* that exists in Nature. It is the only freedom, the only way to bring about wholeness and healing to our world. But first we must seek the truth about our origins, not only with our science but with our hearts. We must look back to our roots in Africa, to its places of wisdom, as Pythagoras did, and make the radical change to our world view so desperately needed, and so re-envision our place in the Cosmos. This is the Cosmic reality. Unity in diversity is the ultimate truth – all is contained in an over-arching mystical embrace.

This has been the story of my own journey of Self-Discovery. It is a journey I believe we all have to make if we are to avoid self-destruction. We do not have to look for God or our understanding of our Universe, by looking out there into space, except to wonder. We are fractals, holograms of the Universe, part of all life on a very small planet, which is part of just one galaxy in an infinite number of galaxies that make up the Universe. That same Universe is within us, the millions of cells, atoms, molecules, neural and other networks that constitute our physical bodies, our hearts and minds. We all belong. It's an inner knowing, a divination that we are part of the mystery, not separate from it; and knowing this we will know ourselves, that we are part of a whole that includes everything; that an energy flows between the stones and the trees, the same energy that flows between ourselves and the stars.

Unfortunately, even an intellectual understanding that we are all made of the same stuff, entrained to the same fixed codes, is still not enough. We have to go beyond the codes, beyond intellect, beyond ordinary consciousness, beyond the Pythagorean and synaptic gaps to rediscover a consciousness we lost a long time ago for whatever reasons; a consciousness necessary for our survival.

Pythagoras' music of the spheres was not a romantic concept. Goethe's statement that Architecture is frozen music recognizes that the ratio known as the Golden Mean, is encoded in geometry, as it is in our genes and throughout nature. According to Tom Kenyon, head of the Acoustic Brain Research Centre in America, this ratio is even encoded in our hearts. The heart has seven layers of muscle, which, nested into each other in harmonic ratios, expand when we experience love.

And this surely brings us to the heart of the matter. An awareness of the ratio of unconditional love is the new consciousness – we are not separate, and when we know that we are not separate a new era will be born. *"A human being is part of a whole, called by us Universe."*

> *Thank God our time is now when wrong*
> *Comes up to face us everywhere,*
> *Never to leave us till we take*
> *The longest stride of soul men ever took.*
> *Affairs are now soul size.*
> *The enterprise*
> *Is exploration into God.*

Where are you making for? It takes
So many thousand years to wake.
But will you wake for pity's sake?

[Christopher Fry: A Sleep of prisoners]

References

The Universe Story; Brian Swimme & Thomas Berry: Harper San Francisco, 1994
Radical Nature; Christian de Quincey: Invisible Cities Press Vermont, 2002
At Home in the Universe; John L Hitchcock: Chrysalis Books, 2001
A Study of History; Arnold Toynbee: Oxford University Press, 1987
Psychology & Alchemy; C.G Jung: Bollingen, 1980
The Adventure of Self Discovery; Stanislav Grof: State University of New York Press, 1988
Anatomy of the Spirit; Carolyn Myss: Bantom Books, 1997
The Cosmic Serpent; Jeremy Narby: Phoenix, 1999
Long Walk to Freedom; Nelson Mandela: Abacus, 1995

Endnotes

[1] This movement had led to the formation in Czechoslovakia of the "Unity of the Brethren", the official name for the Moravian Church which had its origin in Moravia and Bohemia.

[2] In 1780 the Dutch colony was captured by the British who were in turn expelled by the French in 1783. A year later it was back in the hands of the Dutch. In 1795 a Republic was declared but this did not last long as the territory was again captured by the British in 1796. In 1802 it was returned to the Dutch by the Treaty of Amiens. A year later the British were back in power and in 1814 the territory now known as Guyana was officially ceded to Britain. In 1831, the three colonies of Essequibo, Demerara and Berbice were united to form British Guyana. Immediately to the East lay Dutch Guyana(Surinam) and beyond that French Guyana(Cayenne). During the past one hundred and fifty years, Venezuela to the West (originally Spanish Guyana), has been claiming about two thirds of the Country, the area comprising the whole of the county of Essequibo.

[3] Internal Air Ministry correspondence and memoranda dating from 1945, cited in Roger Lambo, *Achtung! The Black Prince: West Africans in the Royal Air Force, 1939 – 46*. See also David Killingray, ed, *Africans in Britain* (Frank Cass and Company Ltd., 1994).

Letter from Roger Lambo to the author : "The published notes Nos. 44 and 45 include the most damning quotes – PRO AIR 2/13437, entitled "Enlistment in the Post-War Air Force: Nationality Rules, 1944-51". My comment here was that this evidence "serves as a disturbing testimony of bigotry and deceit. In this regard, the memorandum of 16 August 1945, written by Air Chief Marshal Sir John C. Slessor, then the Member for Personnel on the Air Council takes the prize. His comments on the unsuitability of the gentleman with a name like "U-ba or Ah Wong", or who "looks as though he had just dropped out of a tree" are shocking, coming as they did, from a man of such stature." In note No.45 I refer to a memo of 23 August 1945, held in PRO AIR 2/13437, in which the Air Ministry agrees to drop the colour bar but to allow a process of national selection to run its course. As such "on paper coloured troops (would) be eligible for entry to the service, but the process of selection (would) eliminate them".

"The papers were a real eye-opener for me and clearly indicated the extent of racial bigotry amongst high ranking service chiefs. As reported in my article, these comments, which were made towards the end of the Second World War ran counter to evidence of the general harmony that existed between aircraft crew members, irrespective of their individual race and to the excellent contribution made by West Indians and West Africans in the RAF.

[4] Marika Sherwood, *The Colour Bar in the British Military Services 1939-45, Many Struggles*, (London, Karia, 1985)

[5] The *Banana Boat Song* is a Jamaican folk song recorded by the great Trinidadian singer, Edric Connor, extremely successful in the 1950s. It was also recorded of course by the wonderful Louise Bennett, *Mis' Lou*, as she was known in her native Jamaica: the first black person to join RADA. She and I became very friendly and she taught me a great many Jamaican folk songs. A Jamaican mento, *Day Dah Light,* meaning dawn is breaking, was about the plight of bananas loaders on ships for transportation abroad. see Evan Jones' poem *Song of the Banana Man*

[6] *A Social History*, Roy Porter [Harmondsworth; Penguin 1996, p 354]

[7] Naseem Khan's report, itself published by the Arts Council in 197... was an important step in the process.

[8] French for 'fat Tuesday'- from the French custom of using up all the fats in the house before Lent.

[9] Mandate for a National Theatre

[10] Camboulay from the French *cannes brulles*, the yearly burning off of the chaff in the cane fields, also a re-enactment to celebrate their freedom: during slavery when fire broke out on am estate the slaves were forced to put it out.

[11] Prisoners of conscience are people who: 1. have not used, or encouraged the use of, violence; 2. have not openly supported or recommended hatred for racial, religious or similar reasons to provoke people to discriminate, or to be hostile or violent and 3. are detained or imprisoned because of their political, religious or other beliefs, or their ethnic origin, sex, colour or similar reasons.

[12] The first candle had been lit on Human Rights Day, 10 December at St-Martins.

[13] The Cenobites or Pythagorikoi (Pythagoreans)

[14] Christopher Bamford in *Homage to Pythagoras*

[15] The Black Mummy Mystery, Channel 5, May 2 2003

[16] Cambridge Dictionary of Philosophy, Cambridge University Press, 1995

[17] Kirpatrick Sale p177.

[18] *ceiba pentandra*, the silk cotton, sacred tree of many Amerindian cultures.

[19] Bacon was certainly an extraordinary man – philosopher, statesman and essayist. For some he was an unparalleled genius who was the author of the works of William Shakespeare. For others he was a misogynist. e.g. Fritjof Capra, author of many influential books, The Tao of Physics, The Web of Life and The Turning Point. In the last he states: *"The ancient concept of the earth as a nurturing mother was radically transformed in Bacon's writings, and it disappeared completely as the Scientific Revolution proceeded to replace the organic view of nature with the metaphor of the earth as a machine."* And again, *"Nature in his view, had to be 'hounded in her wanderings', 'bound into service', and made a 'slave'. She was to be 'put in constraint' and the aim of the scientist was to 'torture nature's secrets from her'* Capra's source was Fred Sommers (Dualism in Descartes 1978) Capra considered that 'The Baconian spirit' profoundly changed the nature and purpose of the scientific quest".

The theoretical physicist, F. David Peat also seems to subscribe to this evaluation. In a passage from his book, Blackfoot Physics, on experimental philosophy, claims that it has recently *"come under attack for its association with a certain dominant or even 'paternalistic' attitude towards nature, the sort of thing that is contained in Francis Bacon's dictum that we should put nature on the rack and force her to reveal her secrets."*

See also Richard Tarnas *The Passion of the Western Mind (Ballantine)*

Loren Eiseley in his exhilarating book *The Firmament of Time,* summed up Bacon's method as opening *the doorway to the modern world';* that his *"world to explore opens to infinity, but it is the world of the outside. Man's whole attention is shifted outward. Even if it looks within, it is largely with the eye of science, to examine what can be learned of the personality, or what excuses for its behaviour can be found in the darker, ill-lit caverns of the brain......* *"When science developed, in the hands of Bacon and his followers, the struggle for progress ceased to be an interior struggle directed towards the good life of the soul of the individual. Instead, the enormous success of the experimental method focused attention upon the power which man could exert over nature"*

This assessment matched his advocacy of warfare: "But above all, for empires and greatness, it importeth most, that a nation do profess arms as their principal honour, study and occupation". Of the True Greatness of Kingdoms (qtd. Ted Hall)

[20]The only example of a deconstructive reading of Shakespeare's play is Césaire's Une Tempête, 'which replaces the apotheosis of Caliban with a mysterious island space which no one can possess... At the end of Césaire's play both Prospero's reluctant appeal for human warmth and Caliban's agressive songs of freedom are drowned by the sounds of the island. The only character who is not in a state of 'ex-isle' is Ariel, who represents an exemplary responsiveness to the landscape. In Ariel's disponibility, the 'inarticularity' of the island finds expression. The militant discourse of the self-assertive subject is replaced by a reticent de-centred voice...The primacy of the Césairean imagination is its capacity to conceive of the deconstructed subject, the abolition of dualism... Ariel represents an ideal moment of fusion'.

J Michael Dash in *After Europe* ed. Slemon S & Tiffin H.. Dangaroo 1989 (p20)

[21] *Alas, Poor Darwin* (H&S Rose, Jonathan Cape 2000) is one of the most recent, with contributions by writers from many disciplines.

Shattering the Myths of Darwinism by Richard Milton. Inner Traditions International 2000

The Story of the Earth and Man) by J.W.Dawson, Chancellor of McGill University, 1873, just 14 years after publication of *The Origin*,

Darwinism vs. Creationism Lloyd Pye [lloydpye@home.com) "Darwin and his followers were promoting a theory based on three fallacious 'gaps' in reasoning that could not be reconciled with the knowledge of the era. What is so telling about Dawson's 3 fallacies is that they remain unchanged to this day".

In his book, *Man and Nature*, Mandala Books 1978, and before the word *ecology* became part of the political and social agenda, Sayyed Hossein Nasr, listed many scientists and thinkers opposed to the theories of evolution that are now the orthodoxy* One of these was the French geologist, Lemoine, who, after reviewing 'palaeontological proofs' of evolution for a French encyclopaedia on Living Organisms, wrote *"It follows from this account that the theory of evolution is impossible. In reality, despite appearances, no one any longer believes in it, and one speaks, without attaching any importance to it, of evolution to denote linkage – or more evolved, less evolved in the sense of more perfected, because it is the conventional language, admitted and almost obligatory in the scientific world. Evolution is a kind of dogma, in which the priests no longer believe, but which they maintain for the people."* Nasr mentioned other dissenters:

Louis Agassiz, the 19th century biologist

M Caulery "The problem of Evolution" 1931

L. Bounoure, French biologist Le Monde et la Vie 1963

Bertrant-Sternet

D. Dewar: The Transformist Illusion 1957

E.L. Grant-Watson: Nature Abounding 1941 Enigmas of Natural History (n.d.) and The Mystery of Physical Life 1964

D'Arcy Thomson, biologist.

F.R.S.Thompson Science and Common Sense

It seems that Darwin himself had his doubts (he admitted this in a letter to a friend). Yet this unproved theory has become established orthodoxy, guarded jealously by the members of the scientific club, who among themselves decide what the paradigm should be. Such procedures only show up the limitations of science.

In The Giraffe's Neck by Sir Francis Hitching, Jay Gould, a recognised pillar of Darwinism in

America, is quoted as saying: "I well remember how the synthetic theory [neo-Darwinism] beguiled me with its unifying power when I was a graduate student in the mid-1960s. Since then I have been watching it slowly unravel as a universal description of evolution... I have been reluctant to admit it, but if Ernst Mayr's characterisation of the synthetic theory is accurate, then that theory, as a general proposition, is effectively dead, despite its persistence as text-book orthodoxy...."

[Hiching stated his source as "Is a new and general theory of evolution emerging? Palaebiology, 6.1 (1980)] Ernst Mayr: "[There is] no clear evidence for any change of a species into a different genus or for the gradual origin of an evolutionary novelty" Towards a new philosophy of biology 1988

Robert Wesson; Beyond Natural Selection 1991

J Madeline Nash: When Life Exploded 1995

James Shapiro; National Review 16.9.06

Andrez Langaney: ce que l'on ne sais pas de l'evolution. La Researche 1997

Pier Luigi Luisi: 1993 Thinking about Biology

[Above 5 from Jeremy Narby; The Cosmic Serpent]

Other dissenters:

Lynn Margulis (who developed the Gaia theory with James Lovelock) Symbiogenesis theory of evolution. "Darwinism as a minor Anglo-Saxon religious sect"

Samuel Butler, 19th c. novelist and social theorist. His argument is summarised in one of the best modern critiques, by

Jacques Barzun: Darwin, Marx and Wagner--Critique of a Heritage (Garden City, NY: Doubleday, 1955).

J W Dawson: The Story of the Earth. Three fallacious gaps in the reasoning – 1.that life can spontaneously animate from organic material;2.the gap between animal & vegetable life; and 3. The gap between any species of animal or plant and any other species.

Thomas H Morgan: Nobel Prize for work on Heredity

Colin Patterson Director British Museum qd Lloyd Pye: Darwinism v Creationism, Rense.Com

Norman Macbeth, Darwin Retried--An Appeal to Reason (New York: Dell Publishing Company, 1973). Macbeth, an attorney, focused on illogical ties in Darwinism. Makes mention of Henry Adams' turn-of-the-century assessment of Darwinism: It "doesn't have a leg to stand on."

Buckminster Fuller, Operating Manual for Spaceship Earth. Regards Darwin and his kind as "science slaves" of the piratic ruling powers.

Arnold C. Brackman, A Delicate Arrangement--The Strange Case of Charles Darwin & Alfred Russel Wallace Focuses on the political background to the publication of the Origin, esp. role of certain members of the Royal Society in pushing Darwin's claim to "primacy" first published work on the matter of the origin of species by means of natural selection was by Wallace.

Petr Kropotkin, a Russian prince and naturalist/evolutionist who took issue with Darwin's presumption that evolution arises out of competition. Kropotkin published an excellent book on evolution early in the 20th century--Mutual Aid--A Factor of Evolution. Generally, he supported the idea that evolution is a product of "mutualism," i.e. mutual aid. "Mutualism" as a key to evolution is carried into our own time via the work of Dr. Lynn Margulis ("symbiosis").

H.Graham Cannon, Lamarck and Modern Genetics (Westport, CT: Greenwood Press Publishers,

1975). Lamarck, the originator of evolutionary science (1809), argued for the "inheritance of acquired characteristics" as a key to evolution. Darwinism denies that characteristics developed by generation 1 can be inherited by generation 2. Some recent work is supportive of Lamarck. The Giraffe's Neck, Sir Frances Hitching

Niles Eldredge, Reinventing Darwin--The Great Debate at the High Table of Evolutionary Theory (New York: John Wiley & Sons, 1995.) Eldredge, a palaeontologist (bone man) and Darwinist, takes issue with the "ultra-Darwinism" of Richard Dawkins (The Blind Watchmaker; The Selfish Gene,

Sir Francis Hicking; the Giraffe's Neck

Arthur Koestler The Ghost in the Machine. Koestler, a radical thinker of the last century and a brave critic of neo-Darwinism, nevertheless subscribed to its pervasive doctrine on the 'natural' condition of man. His belief in a *ghost in the machine* or fatal flaw in the evolution of the human brain was proof that the neo-Darwinian virus had distorted his view of reality For it is not Nature that has let us down, but the other way around.

A. David Berlinski, mathematician 1996; The Deniable Darwin, commentary, June 1996

Michael Behe, biochemist 1996 Darwin's Black Boy 1996

Miles "Shattering the Myths of Darwinism"

James Dwight Dana (19th C geologist)

Theodore Hall Avoiding Extinction, 1995,The Ark--Surviving the Flood of Disinformation

Bruce Lipton (Fractal Evolution.) "Biology of Consciousness" a refutation of the Primacy of DNA doctrine. "The

Science of innate Intelligence," 2-tapevideo($59.95U.S)

H Bergson 'Creative Evolution' (1911) mentioned by Rupert Sheldrake, himself, it seems, standing on the shelf

EVOLUTIONISTS SPEAK OUT AGAINST THEIR THEORY

[22] 'Seriti'... is like an aura around the human person, an invisible shadow or cloud or mist forming something like a magnetic or radar field. It gives forth into the traffic or weltering pool of life in community the uniqueness of each person and each object. While physically its seat is understood to be inside the human body, in the blood, its source is beyond and outside the human physical body."

[23] *Ring of Steel: pan sound and symbol,* Macmillan, 1999.

[24] A series of Pythagorean fifths create an infinite spiral. Mathematically, the ratio of 2.1 doubled 7times gives a frequency 128 times higher than when you started. Whilst 3.2 x 12 equals 129.75. Divide this by 128 you get 1.0136 – the Pythagoras Comma. The comma expressed in numerical terms, was 1.0136 and was none other than the *tiny gap* or sacred number of the gods of the ancient Egyptians which applied not only to music but to astrology and cosmology.

[25] Western Music theory has something called the *circle of fifths*, a purely graphic representation of keynotes with their signatures in the shape of a circle – the notes progress clockwise in ascending fifths (C_G_D etc).

[26] JUST INTONATION [Just Intonation is limited to one key. Its aim is to make the intervals as concordant as possible with both one another and with the harmonics of the key note and of closely related notes. Most of the frequency ratios can be expressed in terns of comparatively small numbers, indicating consonant harmonies – *Science & Music* Sir James Jeans]

[27] mean-tone scale an earlier attempt to solve the problem caused by the Pythagorean comma. There have been many systems of tuning throughout history of music.

[28] Chu Tsai Yu's tempered scale of twelve notes was almost mathematically perfect – by transforming the 3:2 ratio of the fifth to 750:500, his resulting cycle of fifths became 749:500, but although closer to the Pythagorean ideal, it was of not practical application.

[29] Sacred Geometry is an ancient mystic science of the relationship between human and crystalline forms of creation, a metaphor for harmony and universal order. It explores, inter alia, the *Phi* ratio (1.618) – the Golden Mean which is encoded in all forms of life. [The 3.2 ratio of the perfect fifth in music (0.666) is close to the phi ratio]. In Greece it represented the most pleasing proportions and was adopted as the basis of Classical Architecture. It can be found in the proportions of the King's Chamber in the Great Pyramid in Egypt and Leonardo da Vinci based his famous drawing of the human anatomy on it and which. Le Corbusier adapted for his "modular man" which peopled his modernist early 20th century buildings.

[30] (1,1,2,3,5,8,13,21...) found in the growth patterns of leaves and flowers in nature moving in opposite directions; straight radii and rotating circles. A ratio or pattern of unity and order in the way things grow, a unity of complementary opposites common in all forms of life. And what we term *irrational* numbers are not unreasonable, It would appear that In patterns of organic growth the *irrational* phi ratio of the golden section (1.618) reveals that there is indeed an infinite and intangible side to our world" [Gyorgy Doczi *The Power of Limits*]

[31] Axons are the usually long extension of a nerve fiber that generally conducts impulses away from the body of the nerve cell and *dendrites* are a branched protoplasmic extension of a nerve cell that conducts impulses from adjacent cells inward toward the cell body in our brains in order to transmit information of all kinds. [Tom Kenyon: *Brain States*]

[32] In *Healing Sounds,* Jonathan Goldman speculates that the fundamental may be the struck sound, whilst the harmonics which are created the unstruck. *"Perhaps they are the bridge between the physical and the metaphysical".* He quotes Pir Vilayat Khan *"The overtones can be followed with the conscious mind and used as a 'Jacobs' ladder' to climb to other planes of consciousness":* In other words, <u>listening</u> can be used as a tool for enhanced consciousness. *"There is acknowledged an understanding of the Shabda, the 'Sound Current', which can be ridden like a flying horse to other planes of existence. This is accomplished through meditation on sound"*

[33] Mandelbrot put forward a new system of geometry and mathematics to replace (or coexist with) the Euclidean whole integers system12, based on fractions (of whole integers) or *fractals* as they are called. He shows that Nature exhibits a *'different level of complexity'* not explainable by Euclidean geometry; that underlying natural phenomena there is a *family of shapes (fractals)* involving *chance* and that their *regularities and irregularities* are statistical.

[34] For the Greeks, the sound of hissing snakes – syrigmos (also the sound of pipes) represented victory over the power of darkness – a sign of entry into another world. In Indian the cobra is sacred and the Kundalini, or serpent power spiralling through the spinal chord, represented the awakening of the basic energy of creation.

The snake dance of the Hopi Indians was an interplay of man and Nature. Sometimes the serpent is represented as a circle (another symbol of wholeness) that swallows its own tail. This is an age-old symbol which can be seen in 3rd Century Greek manuscript [Man & his Symbols: C.G.Jung] and in the Benin serpent-dragon, Ouroboros. This particular image of the serpent may well be part of the collective unconscious which may surface in our dreams.

The Hindu Sesha with the twin creators, Vishnu and Lakshmi, reclining on its coils; the Ida and Pingali spirals around the chakras, or psychic centres of the body; the rainbow serpent of the

Australian aborigine; Quetzalcoatl, the Aztecs' plumed serpent; the Haitian Damballah.

35 What is not generally known is that the real work leading to this discovery was done by Rosalind Franklin who died of cancer 5 years later at the age of 27, her contribution completely unacknowledged [*Molecules of Emotion*; Candace R Pert] Franklin worked on her project independently of Maurice Wilkins at Cambridge University.. Wilkins showed a photograph taken by Franklin without her consent (the two hardly spoke to each other) to Watkins, an unscrupulous American researcher who guessed that the photo suggested a helix; and who showed it the Crick, who solved the mystery by building a model of the DNA Double Helix – the script of all life. Both Crick and Watkins won the Nobel Prize. Watkins maintains that he did what any one would have done in the circumstances. He actually said later in life that he had been accused of playing God and replied "If we didn't, who would?"

36 Eugenics was a product of Francis Galton, a relative of Charles Darwin. It was first applied on a large scale in the United States and later adopted by the Germans. Recently, the state government of Virginia in America offered a public apology for the eugenics practices of the 1920's.

37 By Lee Silver

38 In which he saw a snake dancing and biting its own tail led to his discovery of the molecular structure of benzene. He interpreted the dream to mean that the structure was a closed carbon ring and fundamental to organic chemistry. [Textbook of Organic Chemistry 1861]

39 Big Business and now Government. Blair's New Labour had completely copied President Clinton's *focus group* techniques, developed by Freudian psychologists, in order to be elected. Despite all the fine words of creating a caring society, its real aim was not to liberate people, but to control them.

40 Harmonic conscious emptiness, symbolised by zero and the infinite spiral of harmonic energy ratios (the octave and the natural fifth) transport the listener to a deep level of consciousness; The harmonic ratios model the emptiness of the Absolute void circle*, the *Wu Chi* containing the *yin/yang* of the *Tai Chi* (the Supreme Ultimate) symbol.

41 Astronomy (terms like azimuth, nadir and zenith are still in use, as are the names of many stars – Algol, Betelgeuse, Aldebaran etc.). An Arab mathematician, Al Khwarizmi (derivation of the word algorithm = rules for calculation) introduced the *arabic* numerals [0-1-2-3-], as well as *zero*, and our decimal system, all of which originated in India, to Europe; medicine- Avicenna (981-1037) was not only a physician, but a philosopher, mathematician and musician and al-Zahravi/ Albucasis (936-1013) was the pioneer of modern surgery The Father of Chemistry was Jabin Ibn Haiyan Al – Idrisi (1099-1166)

42 The yang and the yin are represented symbolically by a full line and a broken one. Combined in four different ways they form four digrams which applied to manifested forms represent the whole of existence. The four *digrams*: become eight *trigrams* (representing, heaven, earth, marsh, fire, thunder, wind, water and mountain) and in turn, combined two by two, form sixty-four hexagrams which represent all aspects of existence.

43 How very strange it is that it was Toynbee who stated: "It will be seen that when we classify mankind by colour, the only primary race that has not made a creative contribution to any civilization is the Black Race "(ibid)

Index

Lightning Source UK Ltd.
Milton Keynes UK
UKOW07f0119030117
291259UK00010B/301/P